PENNY DREADFUL

BASED ON THE SERIES CREATED BY JOHN LOGAN

SHOWTIME

TITAN
COMICS

TITAN COMICS

SENIOR COMICS EDITOR
Andrew James
TITAN COMICS EDITORIAL
Tom Williams, Jessica
Burton & Amoona Saohin
PRODUCTION ASSISTANT
Peter James
PRODUCTION
SUPERVISORS
Jackie Flook, Maria
Pearson
PRODUCTION MANAGER
Obi Onuora
ART DIRECTOR
Oz Browne
SENIOR SALES MANAGER
Steve Tothill
PRESS OFFICER
Will O'Mullane
COMICS BRAND MANAGER
Lucy Ripper
DIRECT SALES /
MARKETING MANAGER
Ricky Claydon
COMMERCIAL MANAGER
Michelle Fairlamb
PUBLISHING MANAGER
Darryl Tothill
PUBLISHING DIRECTOR
Chris Teather
OPERATIONS DIRECTOR
Leigh Baulch
EXECUTIVE DIRECTOR
Vivian Cheung
PUBLISHER
Nick Landau

Penny Dreadful Volume 1
Regular SC ISBN: 9781785853685
FP Exclusive ISBN: 9781785859755

Published by Titan Comics, a division of Titan Publishing Group,
Ltd., 144 Southwark Street, London SE1 0UP, UK.

A CIP catalogue record for this title is available from the
British Library

First edition: March 2017

10 9 8 7 6 5 4 3 2 1

Printed in China.

PENNY DREADFUL

BASED ON THE SERIES CREATED
BY JOHN LOGAN

STORY BY
**KRYSTY WILSON-CAIRNS,
ANDREW HINDERAKER
& CHRIS KING**

WRITTEN BY
**KRYSTY WILSON-CAIRNS
& CHRIS KING**

ILLUSTRATED BY
LOUIE DE MARTINIS

LETTERED BY
**SIMON BOWLAND &
ROB STEEN**

EDITOR
LIZZIE KAYE

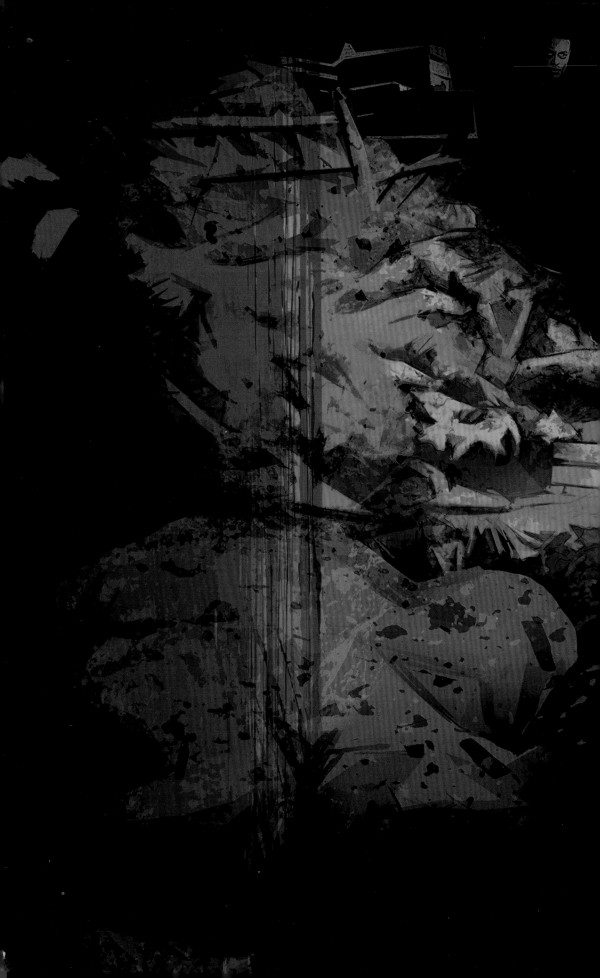

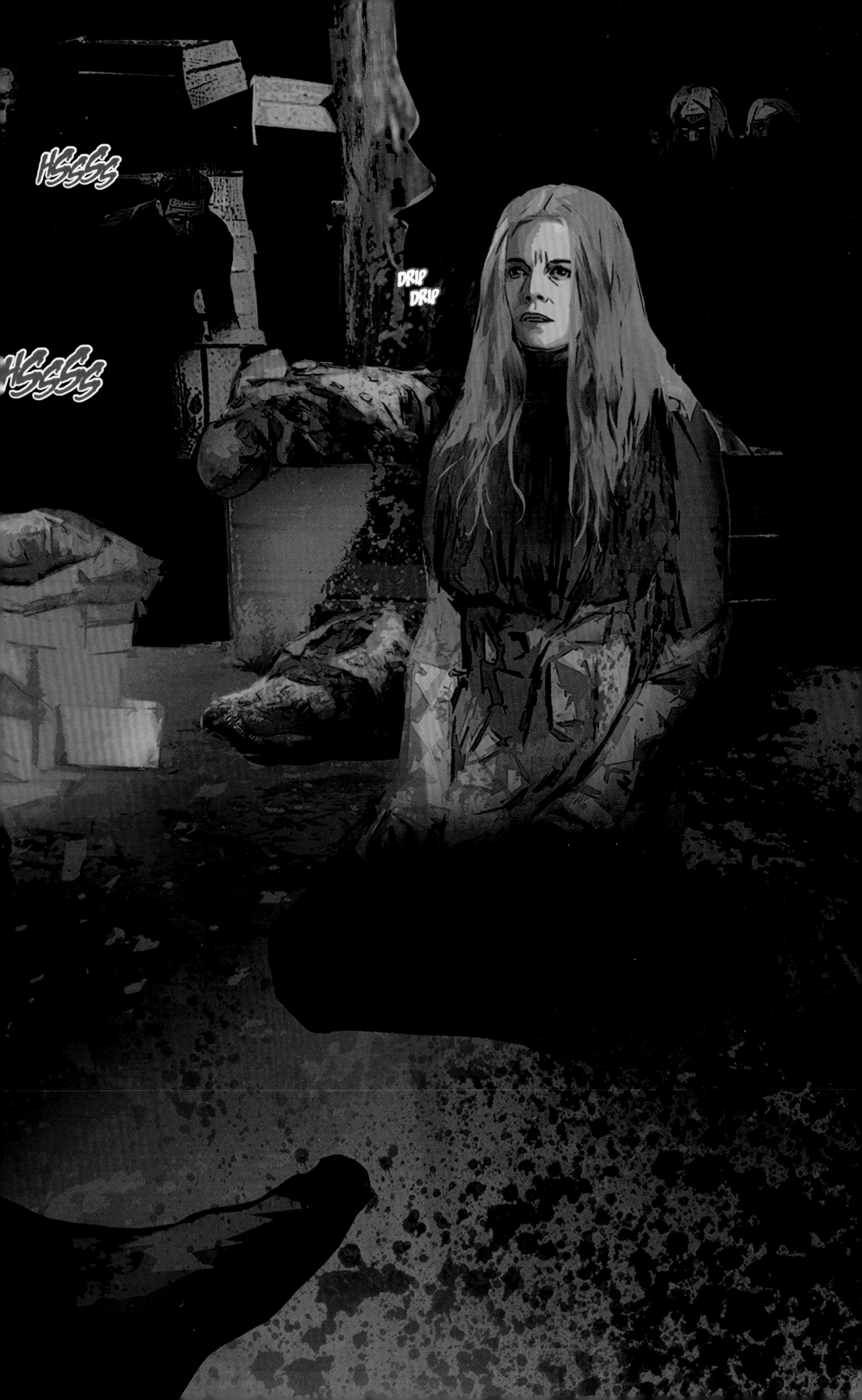
HSSSS
DRIP
DRIP
HSSSS

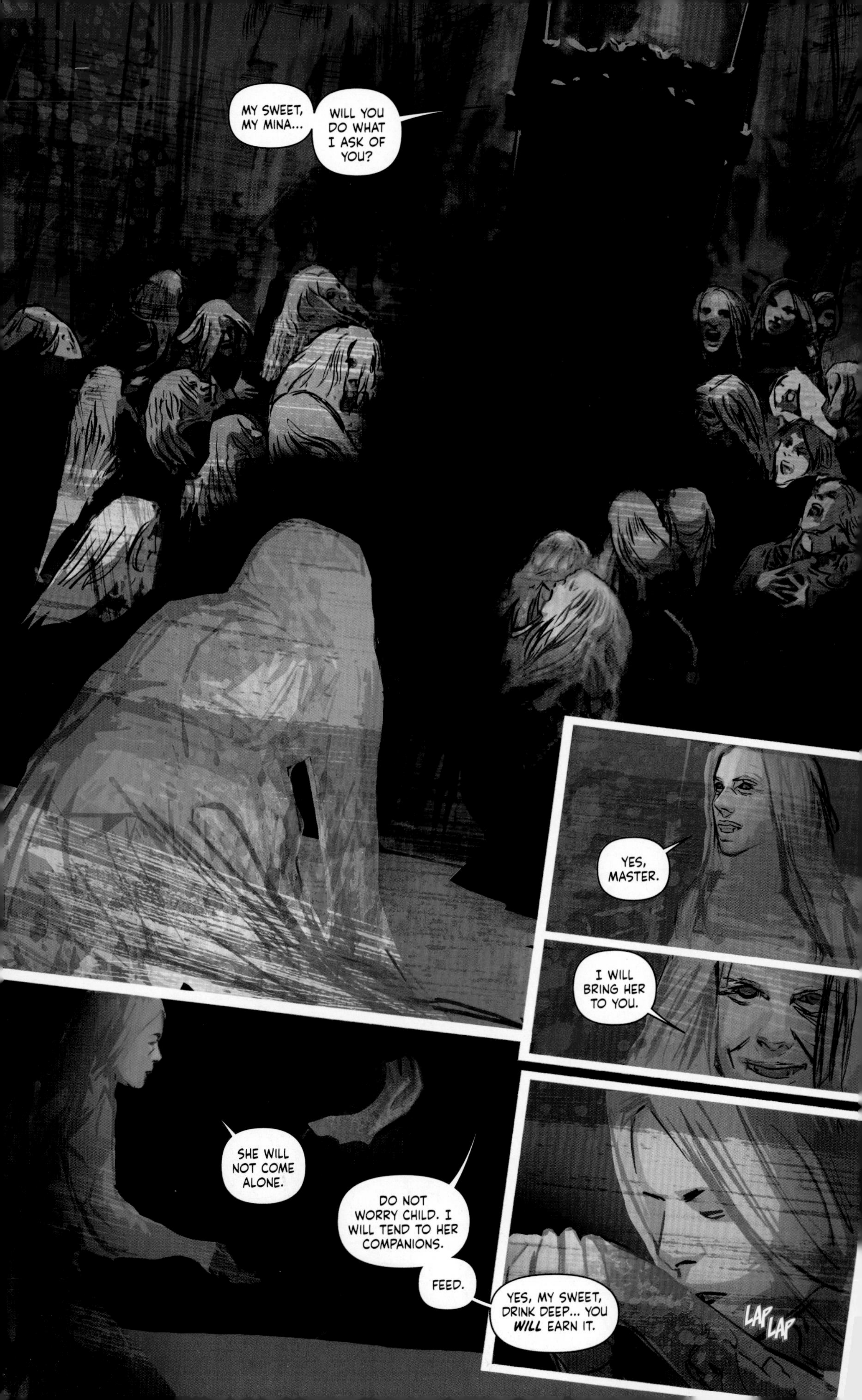
MY SWEET, MY MINA...
WILL YOU DO WHAT I ASK OF YOU?
YES, MASTER.
I WILL BRING HER TO YOU.
SHE WILL NOT COME ALONE.
DO NOT WORRY CHILD. I WILL TEND TO HER COMPANIONS.
FEED.
YES, MY SWEET, DRINK DEEP... YOU *WILL* EARN IT.
LAP LAP

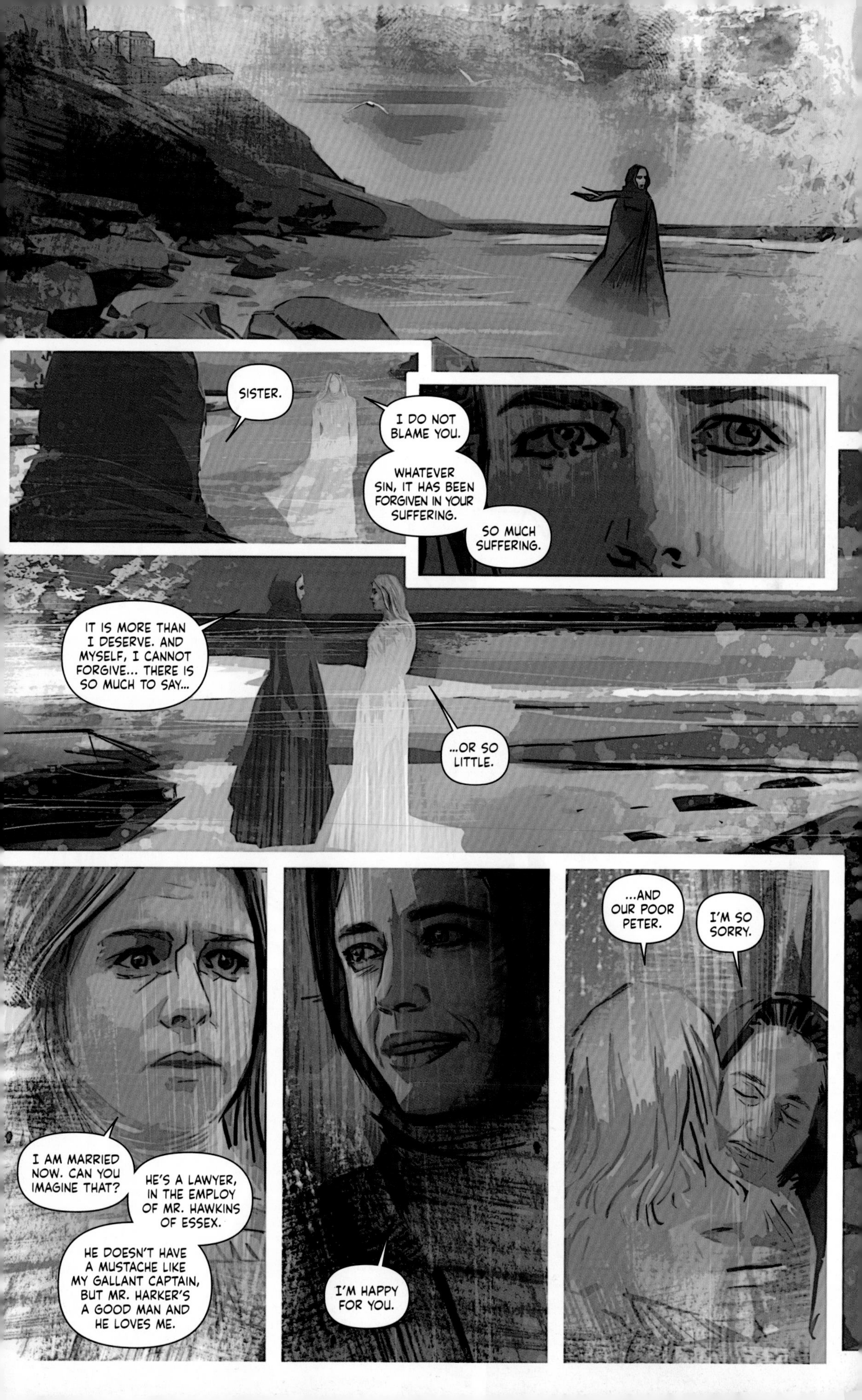
SISTER.
I DO NOT BLAME YOU.
WHATEVER SIN, IT HAS BEEN FORGIVEN IN YOUR SUFFERING.
SO MUCH SUFFERING.
IT IS MORE THAN I DESERVE. AND MYSELF, I CANNOT FORGIVE... THERE IS SO MUCH TO SAY...
...OR SO LITTLE.
I AM MARRIED NOW. CAN YOU IMAGINE THAT?
HE'S A LAWYER, IN THE EMPLOY OF MR. HAWKINS OF ESSEX.
HE DOESN'T HAVE A MUSTACHE LIKE MY GALLANT CAPTAIN, BUT MR. HARKER'S A GOOD MAN AND HE LOVES ME.
I'M HAPPY FOR YOU.
...AND OUR POOR PETER.
I'M SO SORRY.

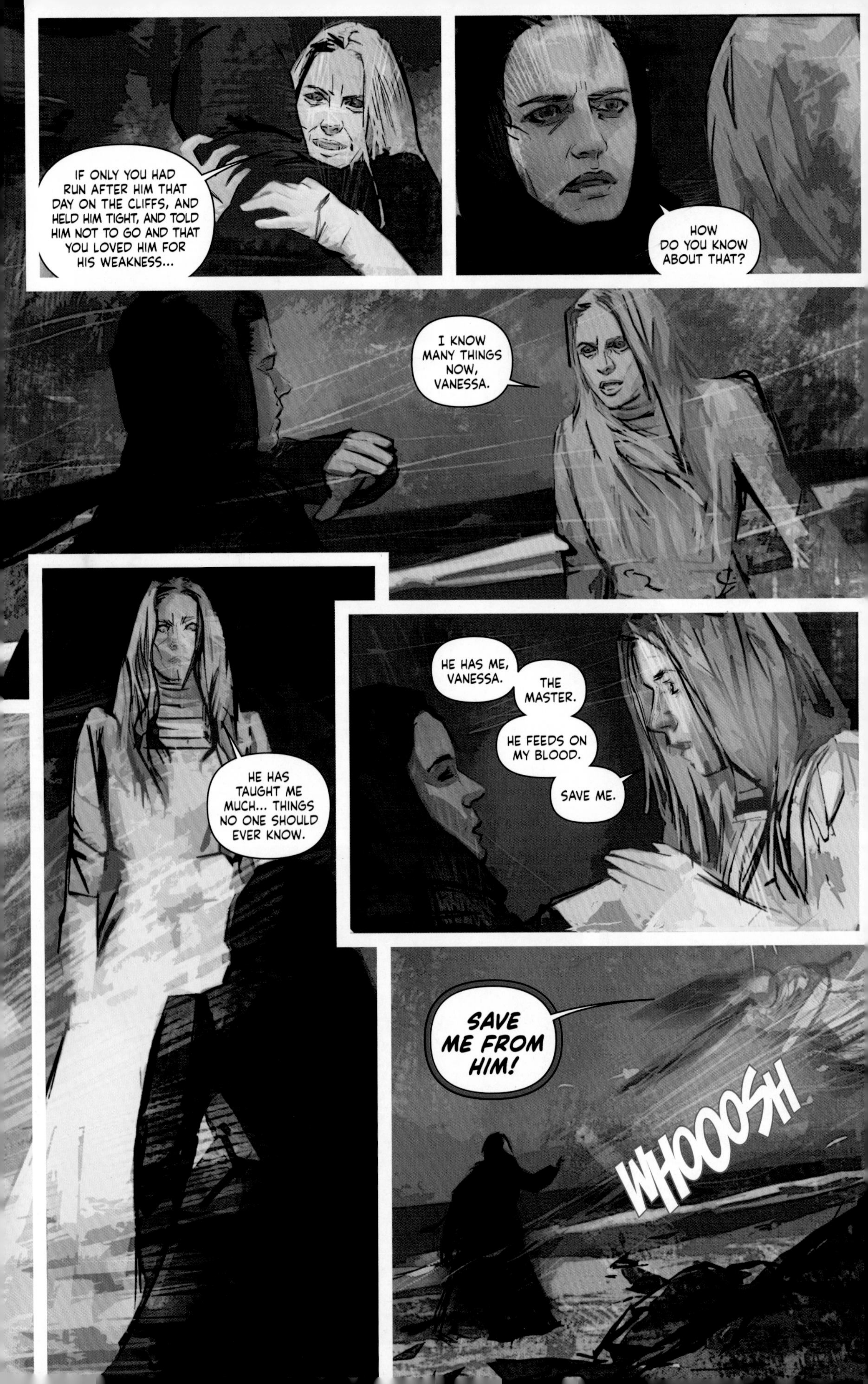
IF ONLY YOU HAD RUN AFTER HIM THAT DAY ON THE CLIFFS, AND HELD HIM TIGHT, AND TOLD HIM NOT TO GO AND THAT YOU LOVED HIM FOR HIS WEAKNESS...
HOW DO YOU KNOW ABOUT THAT?
I KNOW MANY THINGS NOW, VANESSA.
HE HAS TAUGHT ME MUCH... THINGS NO ONE SHOULD EVER KNOW.
HE HAS ME, VANESSA.
THE MASTER.
HE FEEDS ON MY BLOOD.
SAVE ME.
SAVE ME FROM HIM!
WHOOOSH

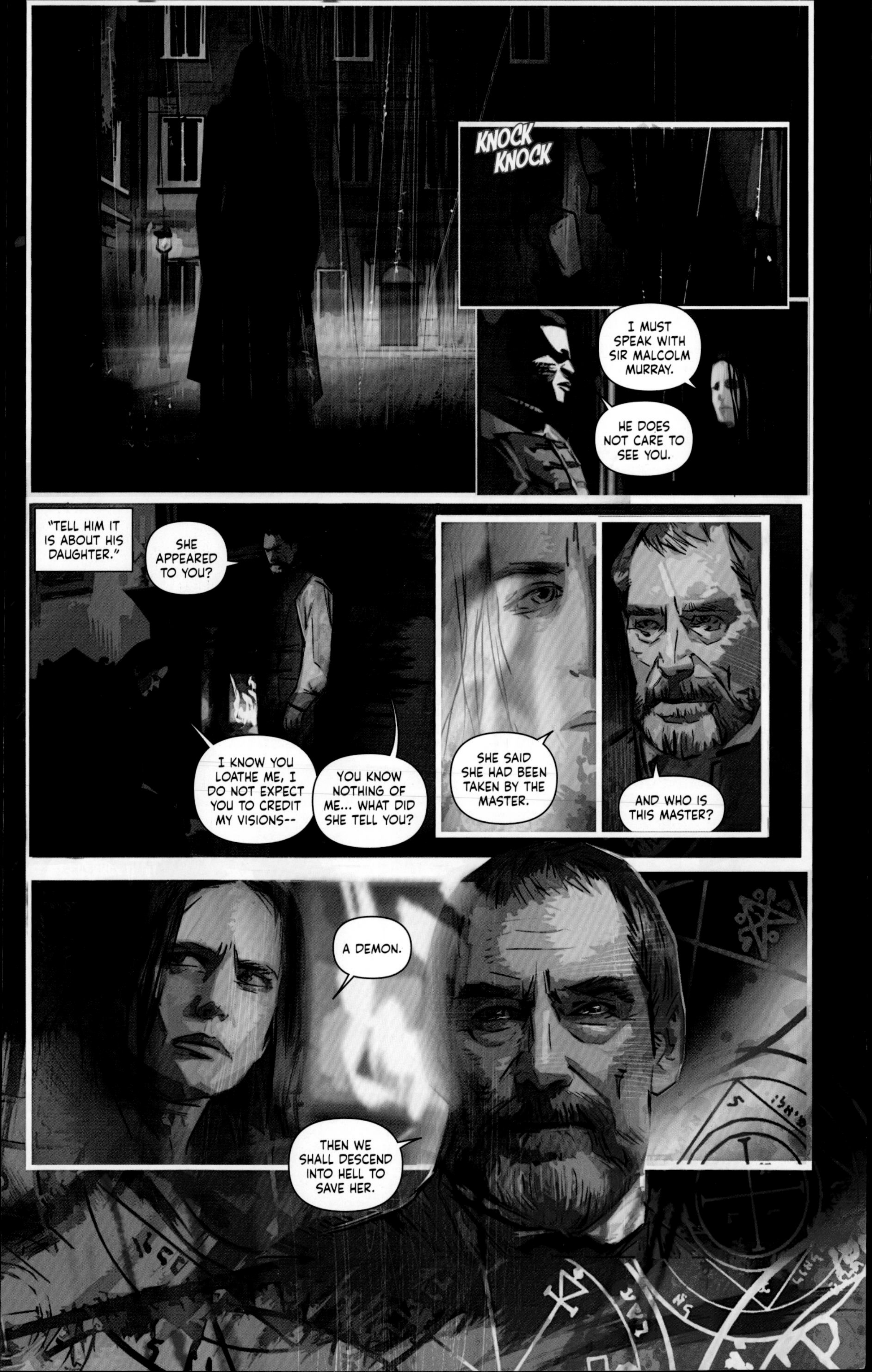
KNOCK KNOCK
I MUST SPEAK WITH SIR MALCOLM MURRAY.
HE DOES NOT CARE TO SEE YOU.
"TELL HIM IT IS ABOUT HIS DAUGHTER."
SHE APPEARED TO YOU?
I KNOW YOU LOATHE ME, I DO NOT EXPECT YOU TO CREDIT MY VISIONS--
YOU KNOW NOTHING OF ME... WHAT DID SHE TELL YOU?
SHE SAID SHE HAD BEEN TAKEN BY THE MASTER.
AND WHO IS THIS MASTER?
A DEMON.
THEN WE SHALL DESCEND INTO HELL TO SAVE HER.

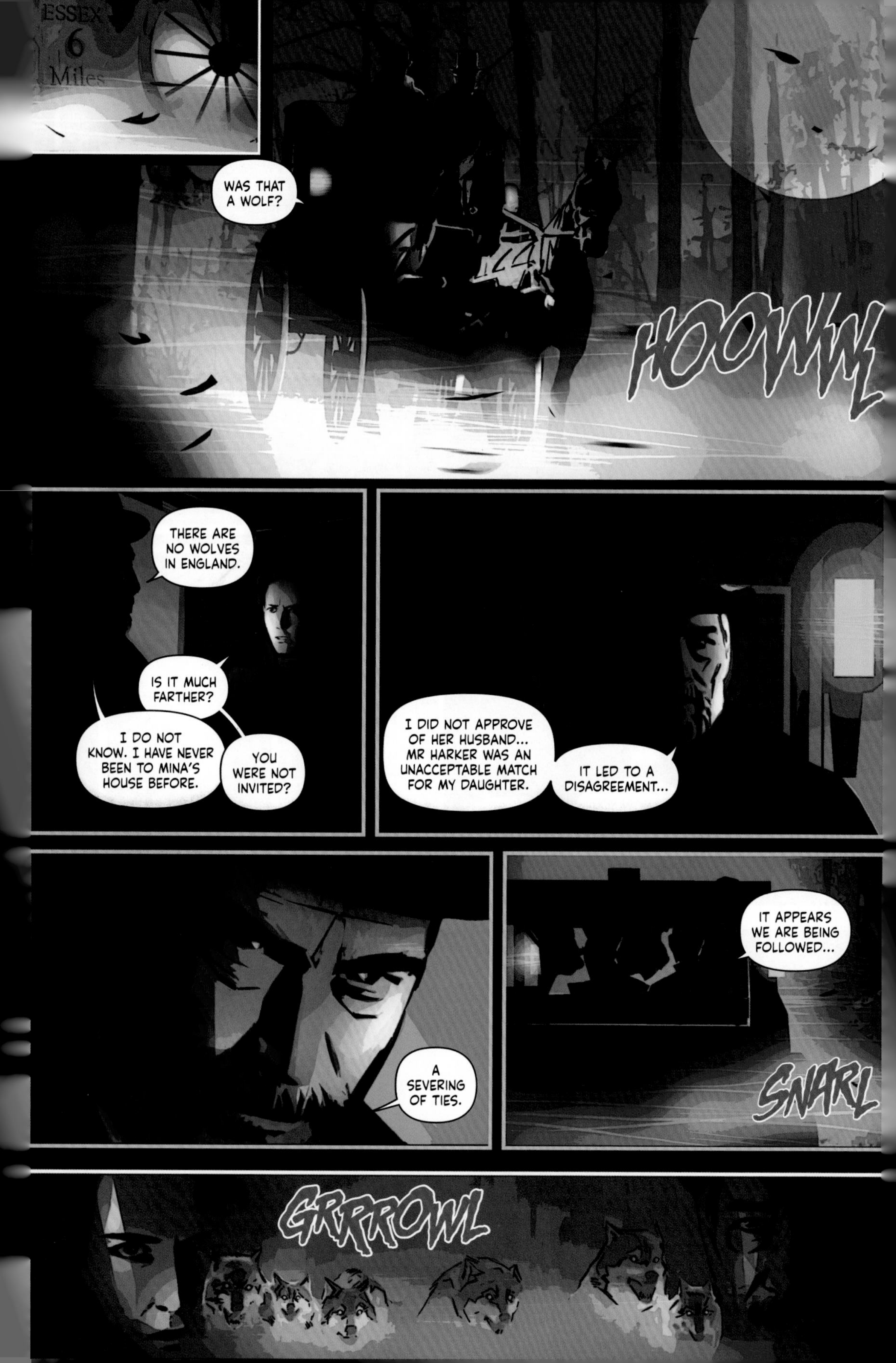
ESSEX
6
Miles
WAS THAT A WOLF?
HOOWWL
THERE ARE NO WOLVES IN ENGLAND.
IS IT MUCH FARTHER?
I DO NOT KNOW. I HAVE NEVER BEEN TO MINA'S HOUSE BEFORE.
YOU WERE NOT INVITED?
I DID NOT APPROVE OF HER HUSBAND... MR HARKER WAS AN UNACCEPTABLE MATCH FOR MY DAUGHTER.
IT LED TO A DISAGREEMENT...
A SEVERING OF TIES.
IT APPEARS WE ARE BEING FOLLOWED...
SNARL
GRRROWL

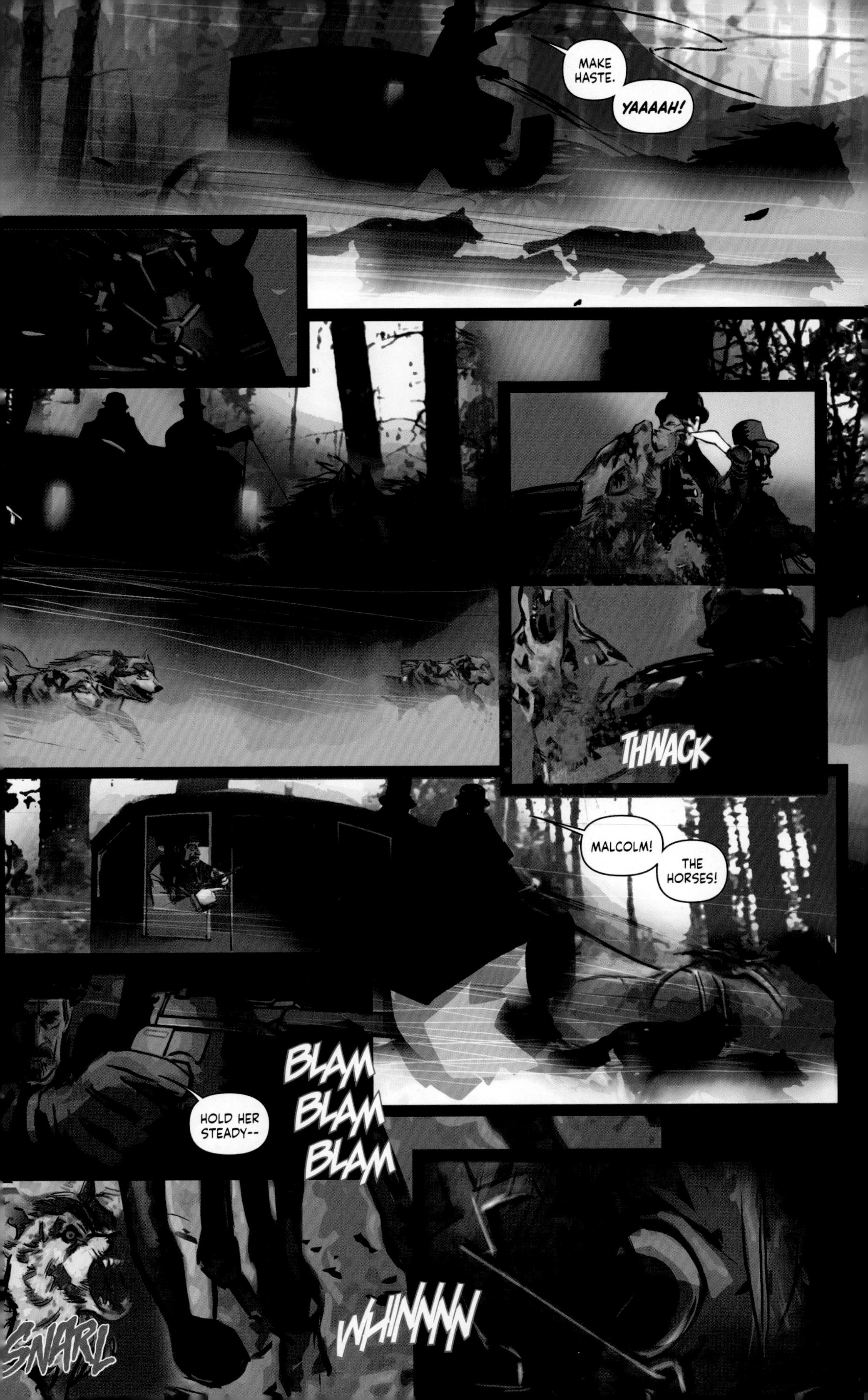
MAKE HASTE.
YAAAAH!
THWACK
MALCOLM!
THE HORSES!
BLAM
BLAM
BLAM
HOLD HER STEADY--
SNARL
WHINNNN

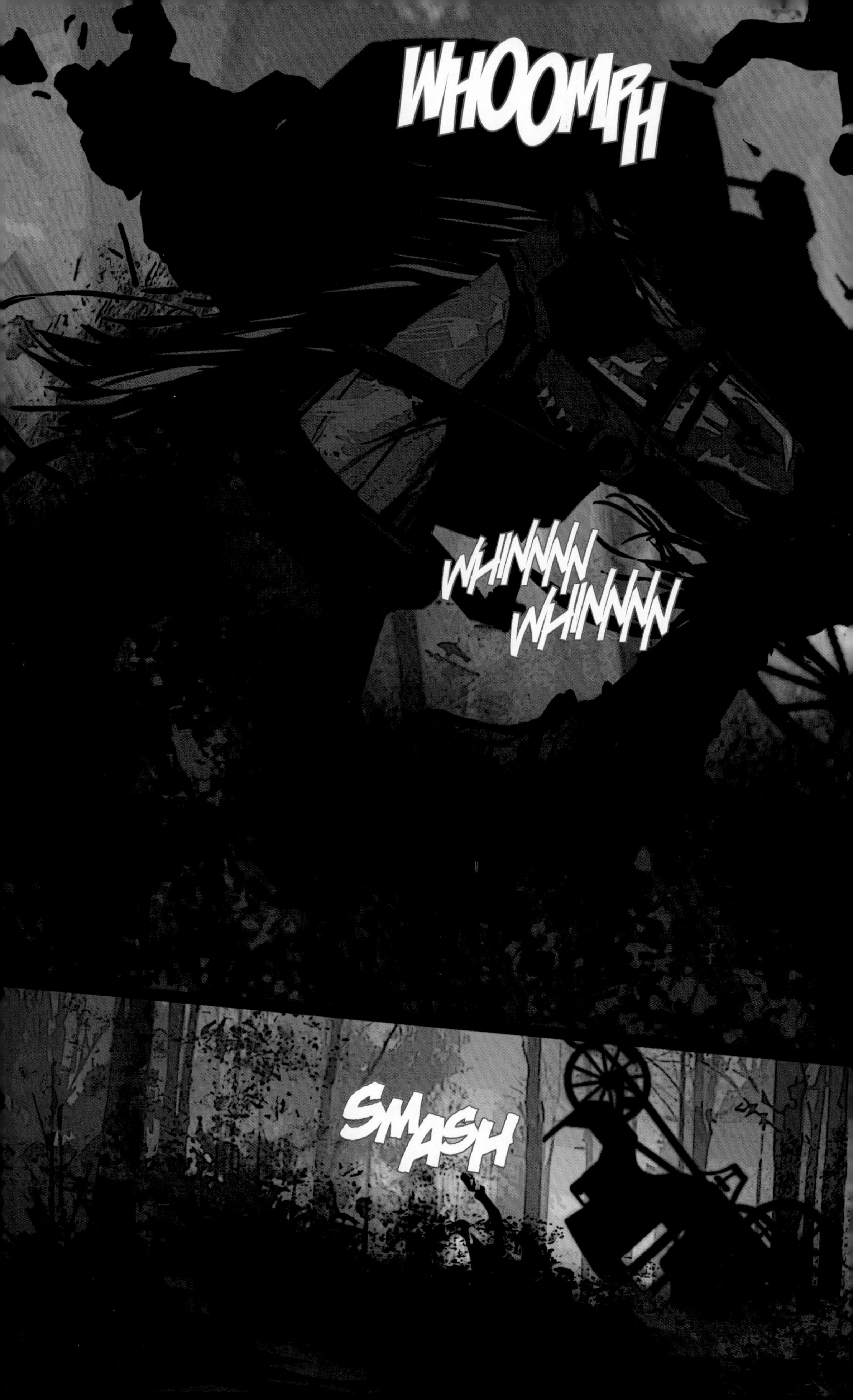
WHOOMPH
WHINNN
WHINNN
SMASH

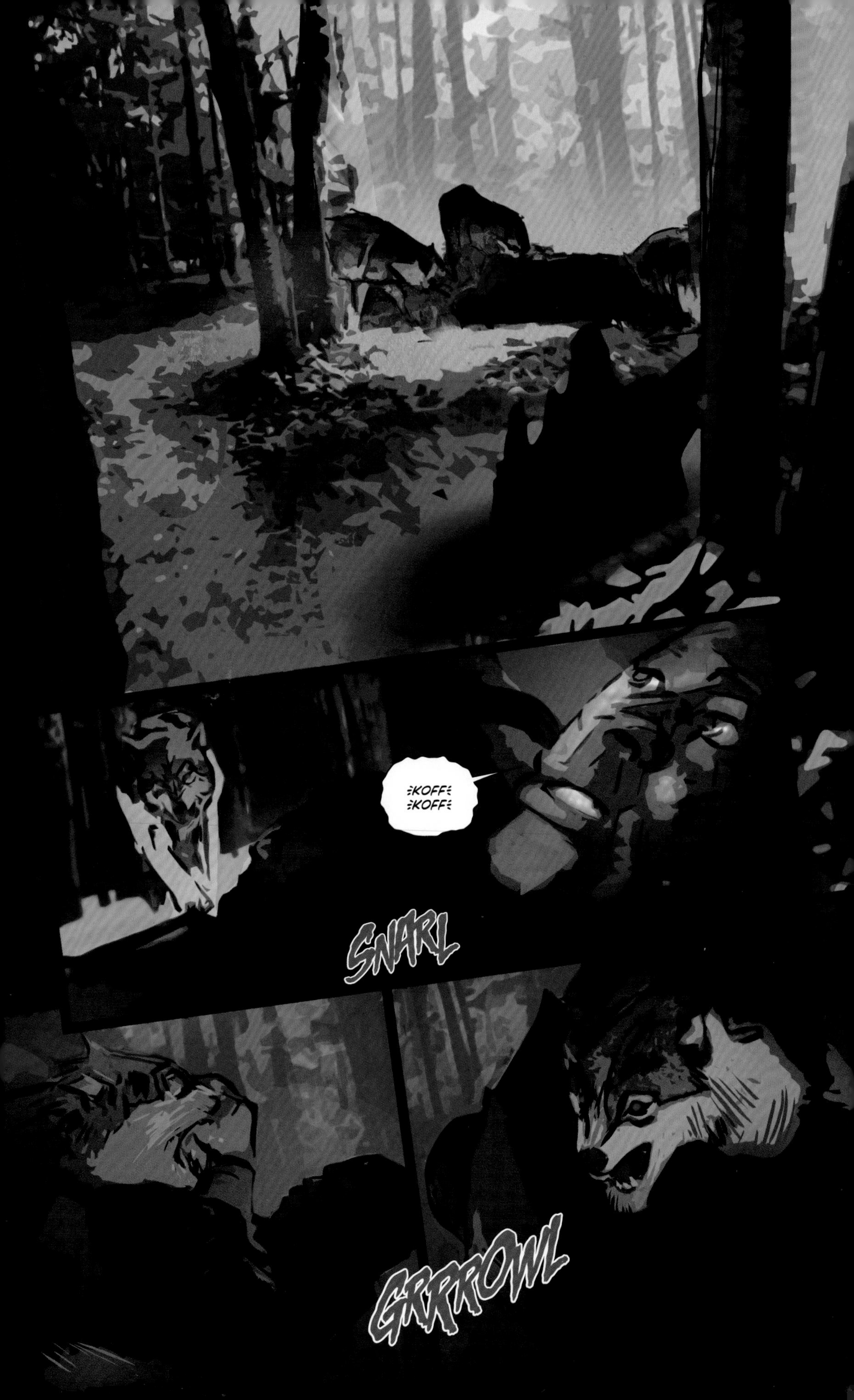
KOFF KOFF
SNARL
GRRROWL

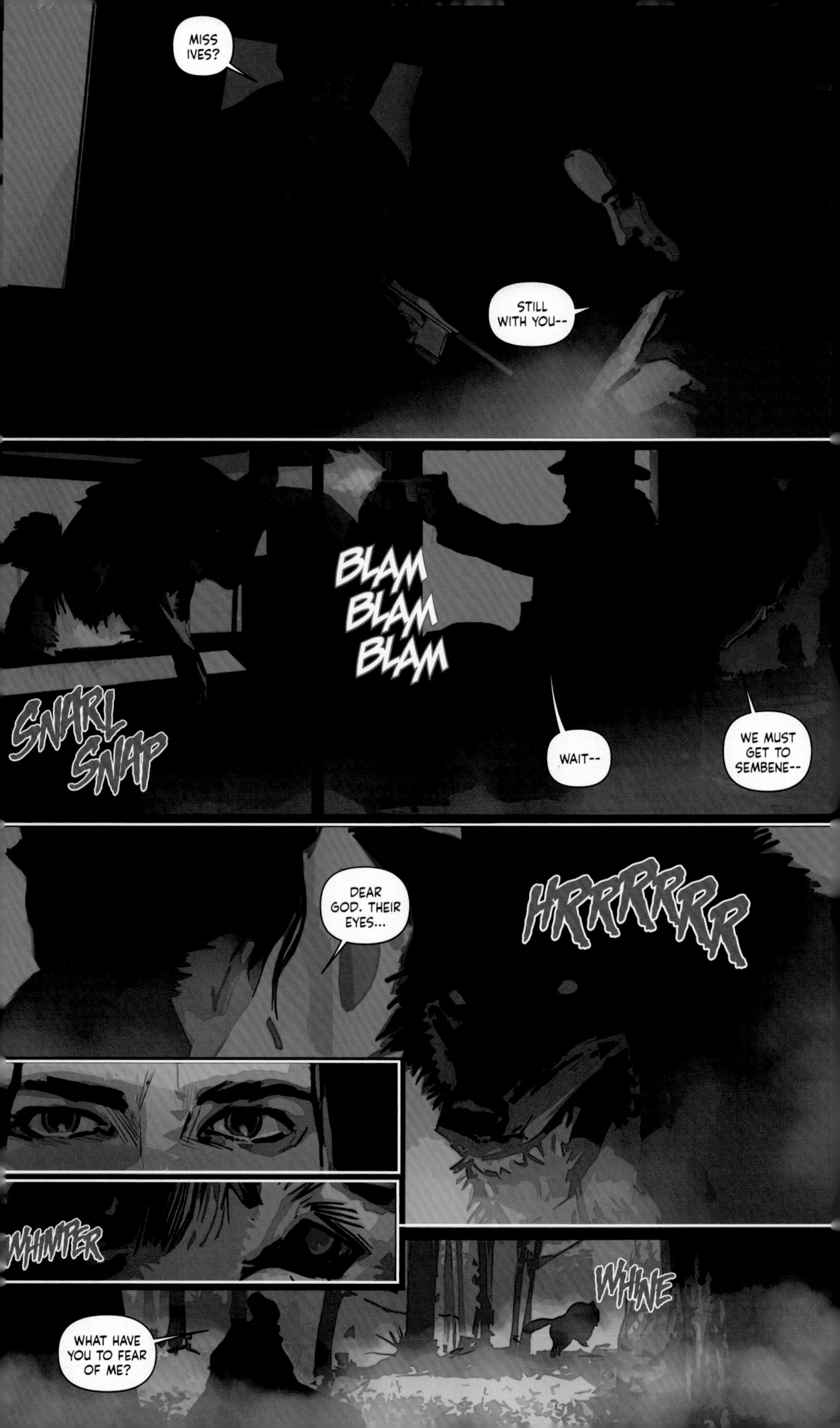
MISS IVES?
STILL WITH YOU--
BLAM BLAM BLAM
SNARL SNAP
WAIT--
WE MUST GET TO SEMBENE--
DEAR GOD. THEIR EYES...
HRRRRRRR
WHIMPER
WHINE
WHAT HAVE YOU TO FEAR OF ME?

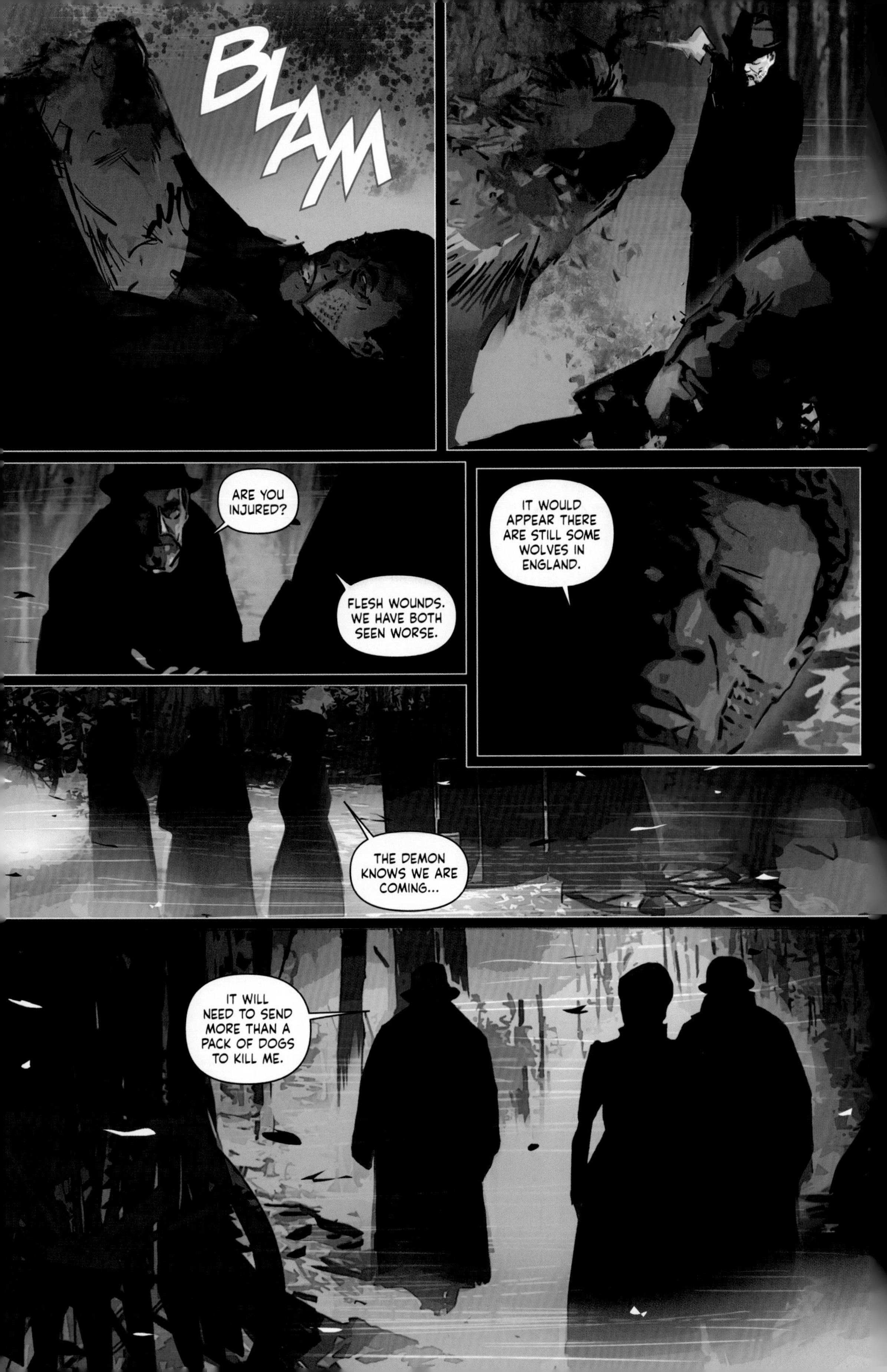
BLAM
ARE YOU INJURED?
FLESH WOUNDS. WE HAVE BOTH SEEN WORSE.
IT WOULD APPEAR THERE ARE STILL SOME WOLVES IN ENGLAND.
THE DEMON KNOWS WE ARE COMING...
IT WILL NEED TO SEND MORE THAN A PACK OF DOGS TO KILL ME.

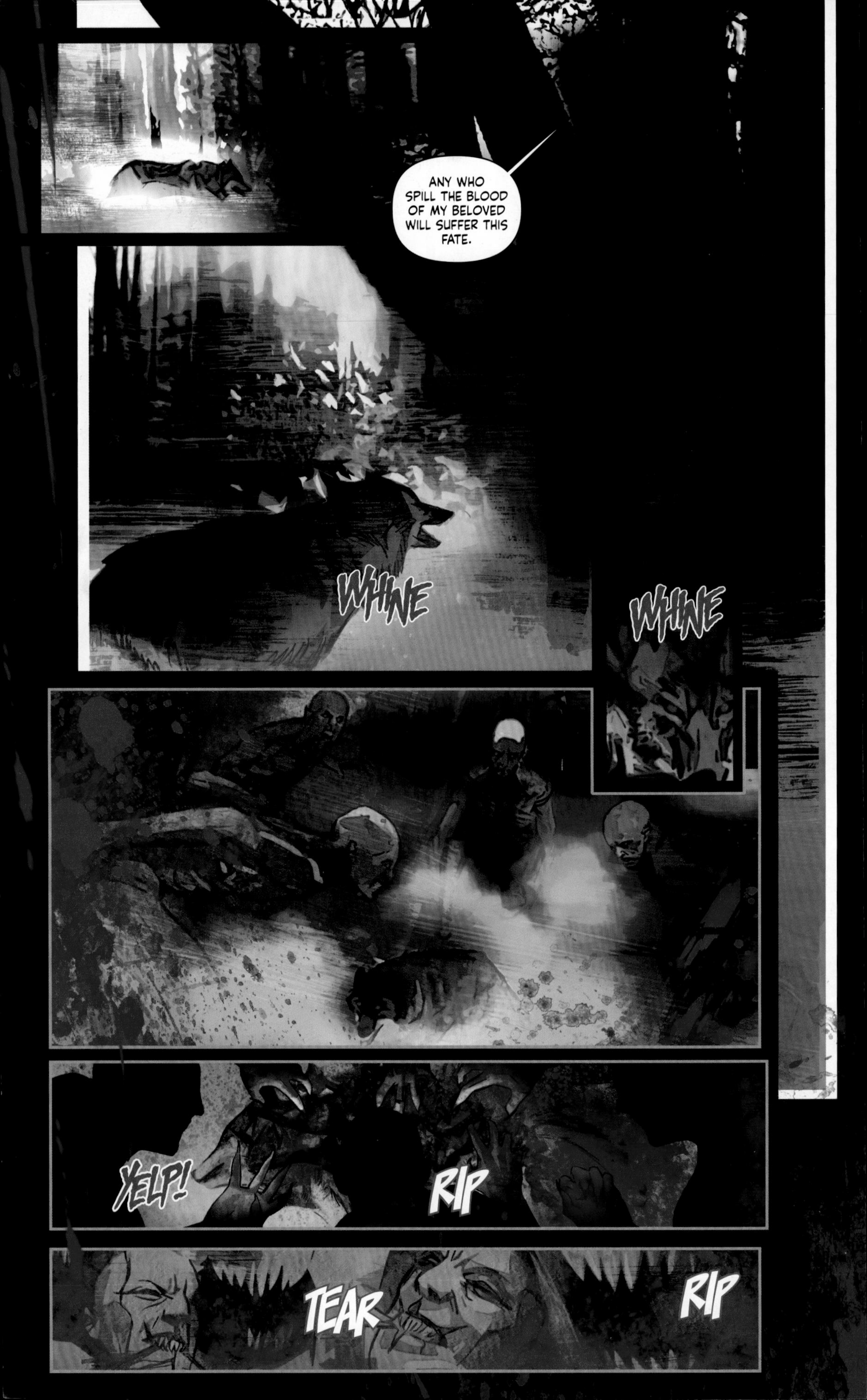
ANY WHO SPILL THE BLOOD OF MY BELOVED WILL SUFFER THIS FATE.
WHINE
WHINE
YELP!
RIP
TEAR
RIP

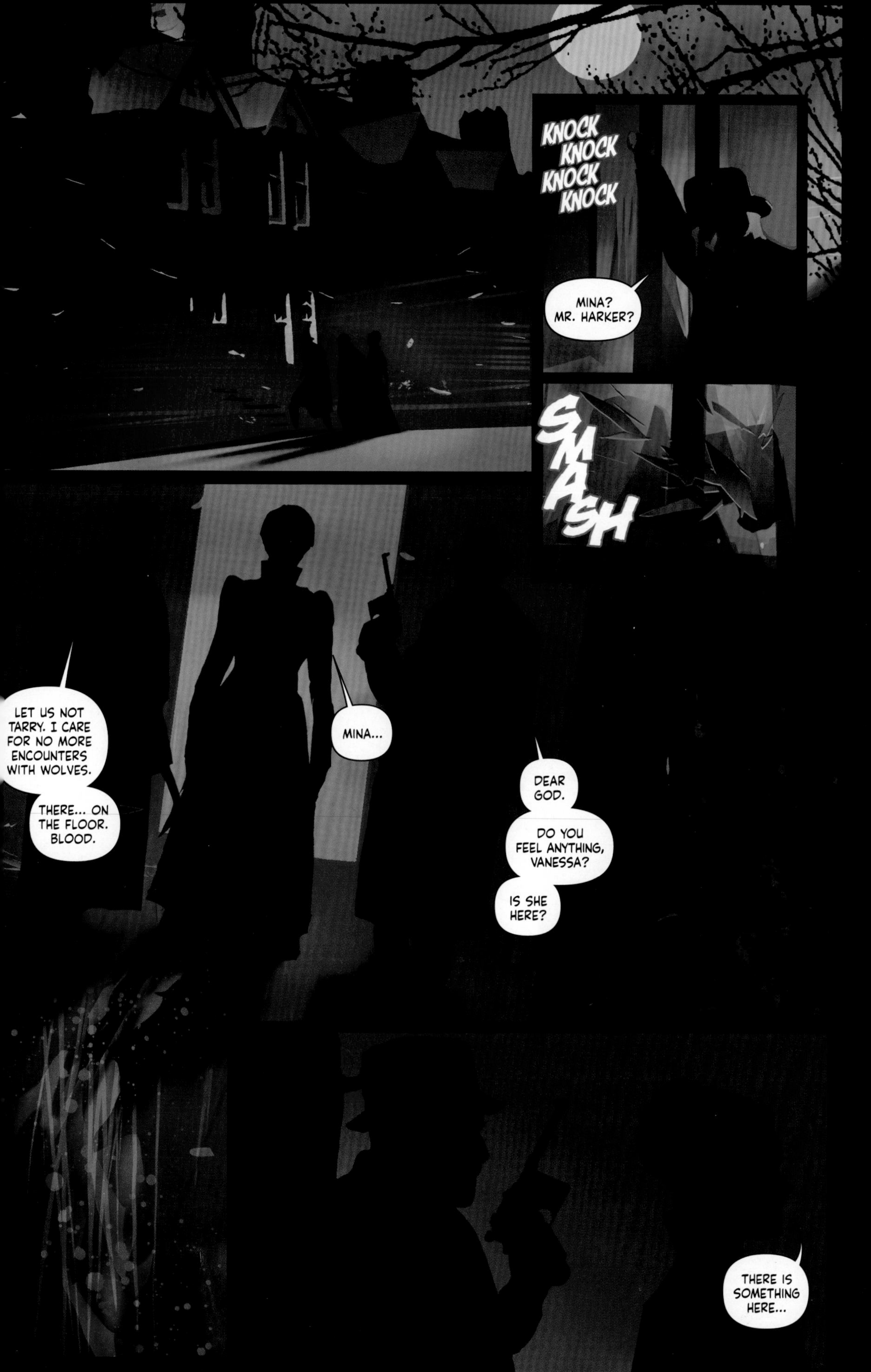
KNOCK KNOCK KNOCK KNOCK
MINA? MR. HARKER?
SMASH
LET US NOT TARRY. I CARE FOR NO MORE ENCOUNTERS WITH WOLVES.
THERE... ON THE FLOOR. BLOOD.
MINA...
DEAR GOD.
DO YOU FEEL ANYTHING, VANESSA?
IS SHE HERE?
THERE IS SOMETHING HERE...

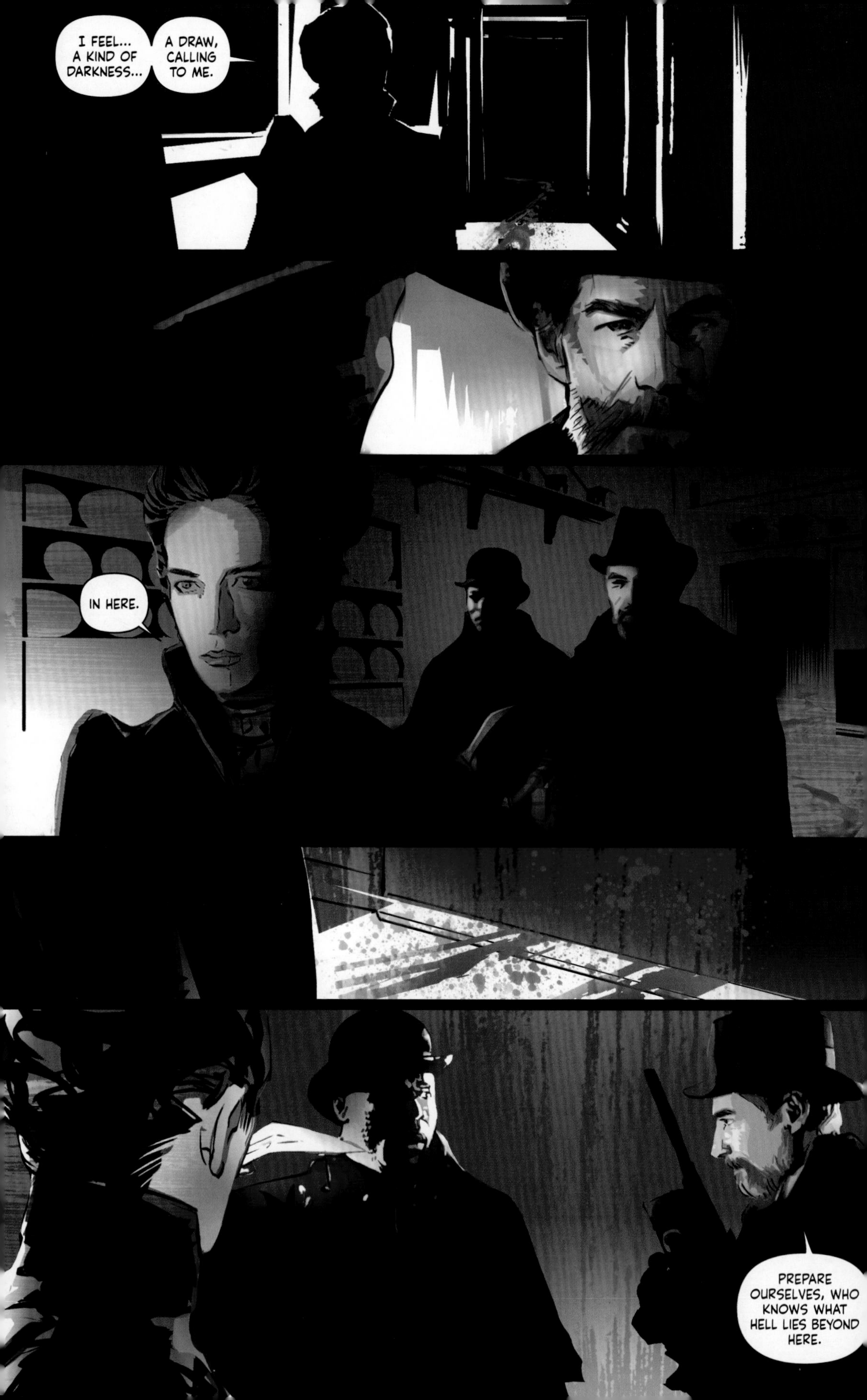
I FEEL... A KIND OF DARKNESS...
A DRAW, CALLING TO ME.
IN HERE.
PREPARE OURSELVES, WHO KNOWS WHAT HELL LIES BEYOND HERE.

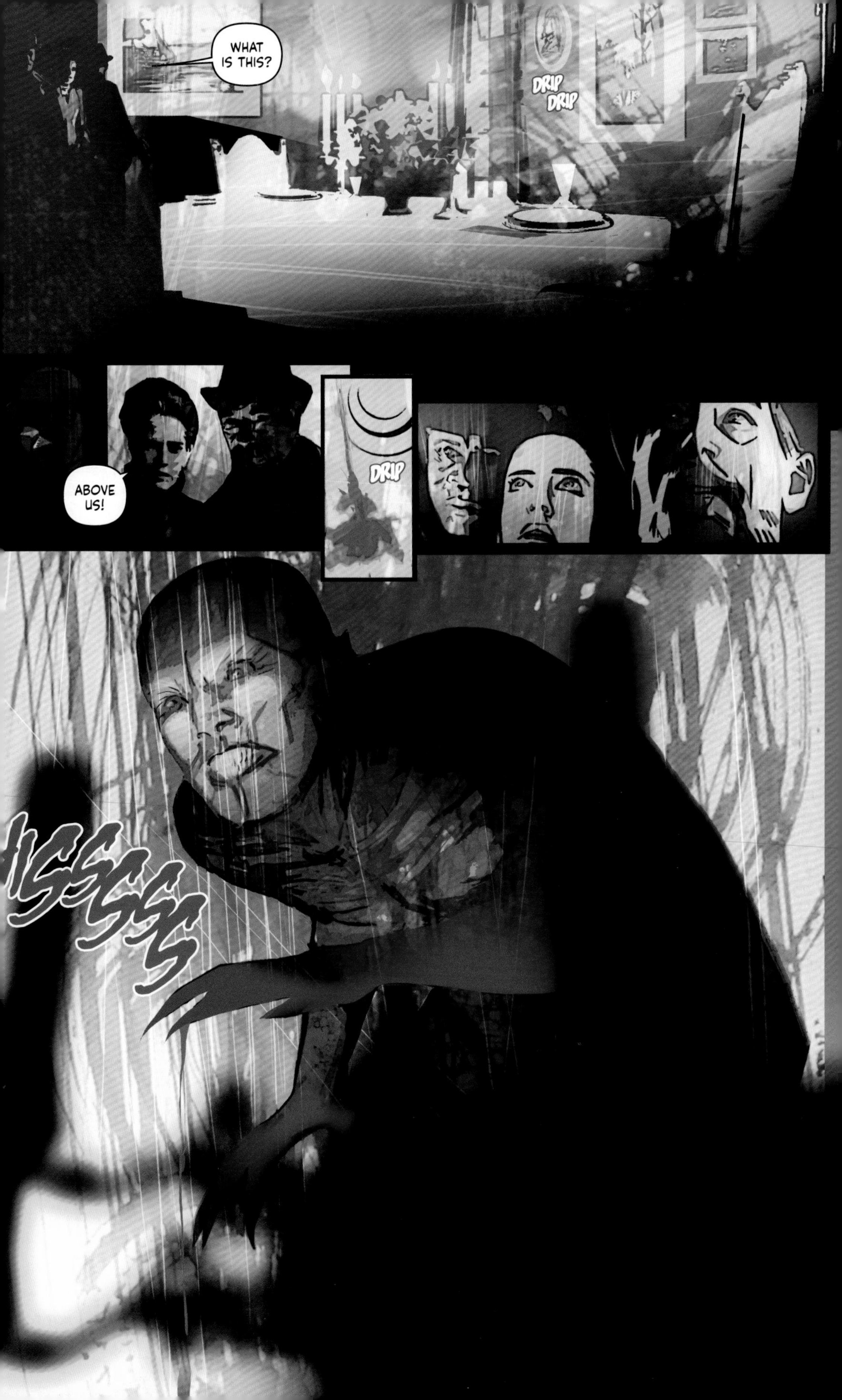
WHAT IS THIS?
DRIP
DRIP
ABOVE US!
DRIP
HISSSSS

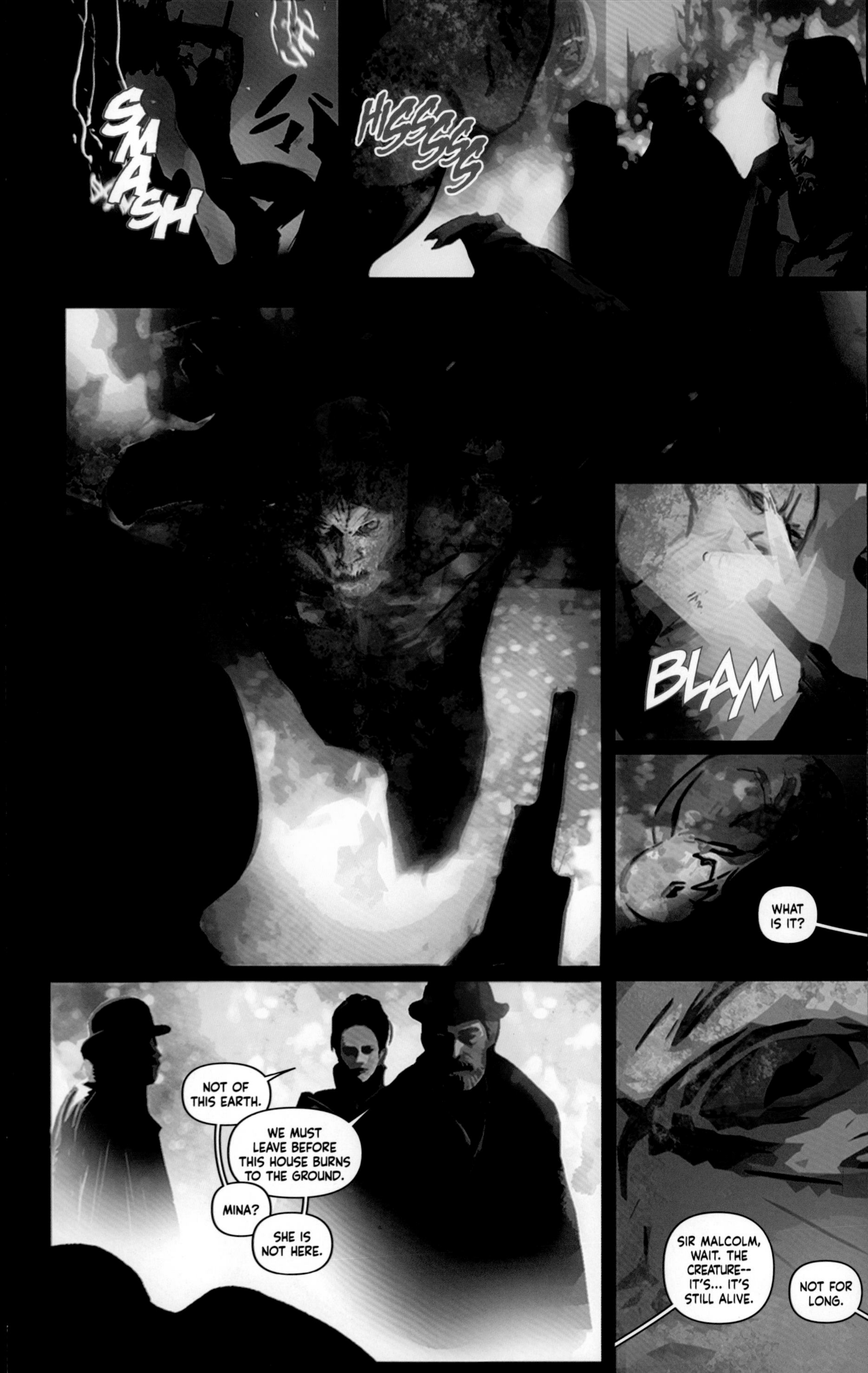
SMASH
HISSSSS
BLAM
WHAT IS IT?
NOT OF THIS EARTH.
WE MUST LEAVE BEFORE THIS HOUSE BURNS TO THE GROUND.
MINA?
SHE IS NOT HERE.
SIR MALCOLM, WAIT. THE CREATURE-- IT'S... IT'S STILL ALIVE.
NOT FOR LONG.

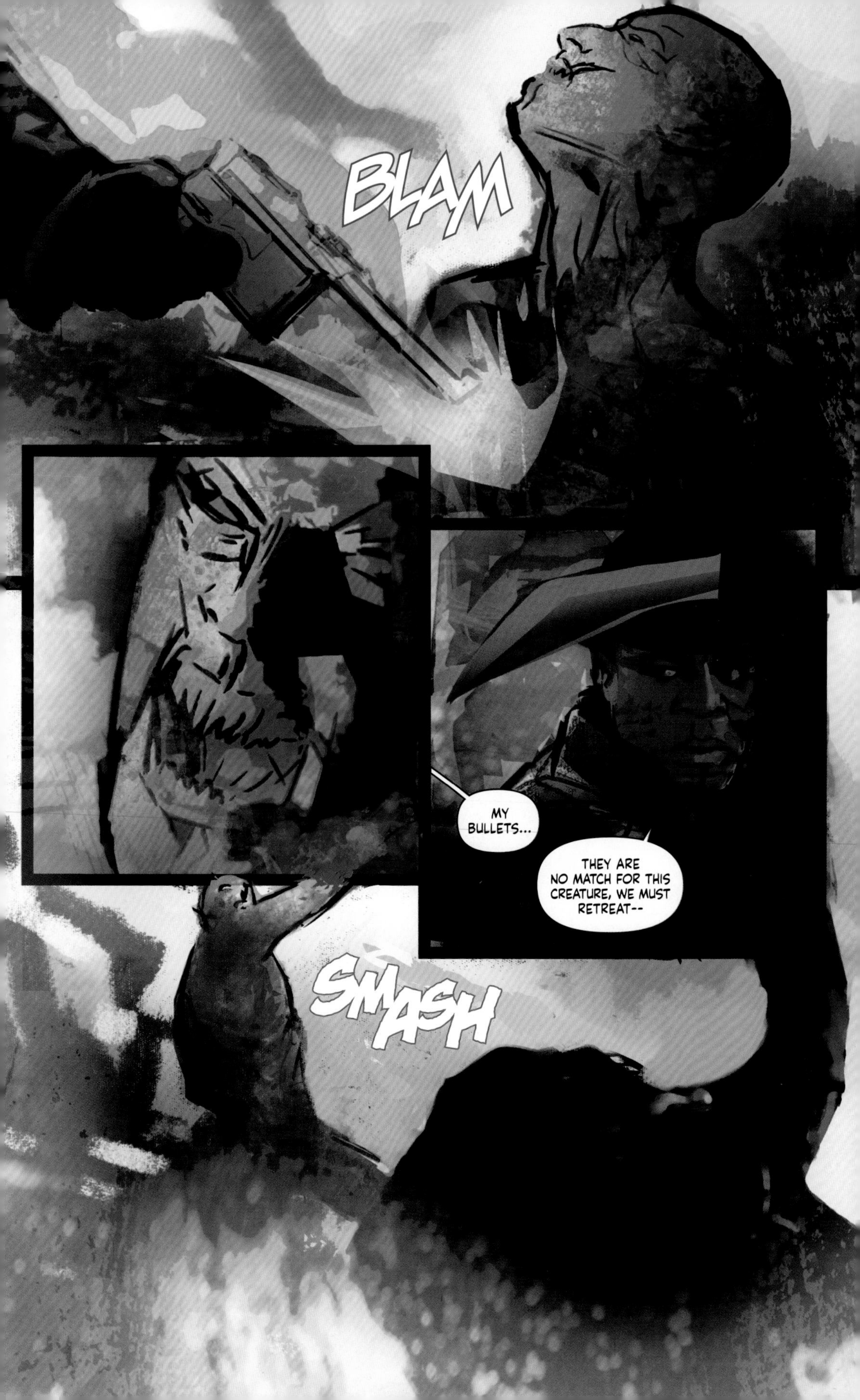
BLAM
MY BULLETS...
THEY ARE NO MATCH FOR THIS CREATURE, WE MUST RETREAT--
SMASH

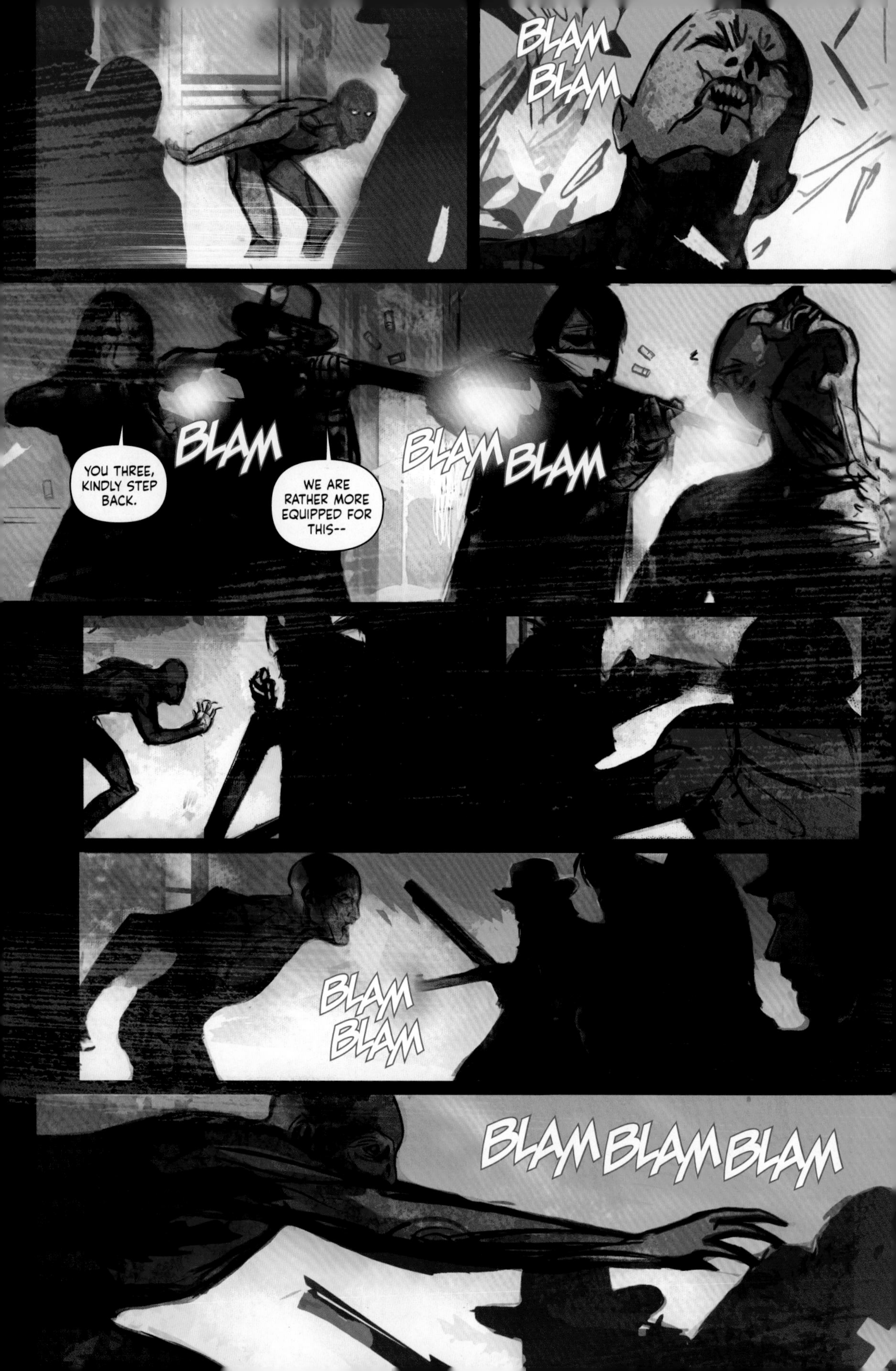
BLAM
BLAM
YOU THREE, KINDLY STEP BACK.
BLAM
WE ARE RATHER MORE EQUIPPED FOR THIS--
BLAM BLAM
BLAM
BLAM
BLAM BLAM BLAM

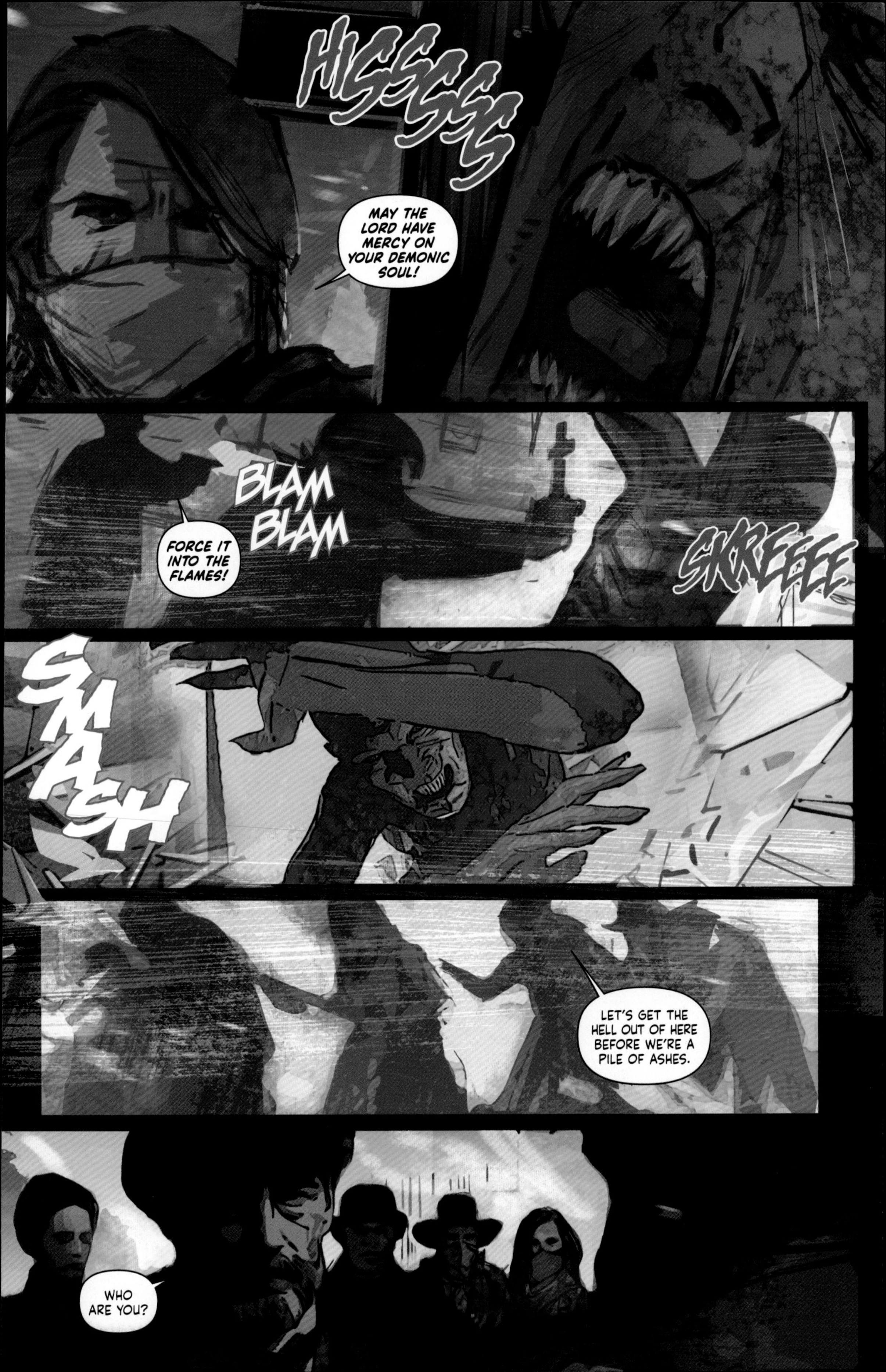
HISSSSS
MAY THE LORD HAVE MERCY ON YOUR DEMONIC SOUL!
BLAM BLAM
FORCE IT INTO THE FLAMES!
SKREEEE
SMASH
LET'S GET THE HELL OUT OF HERE BEFORE WE'RE A PILE OF ASHES.
WHO ARE YOU?

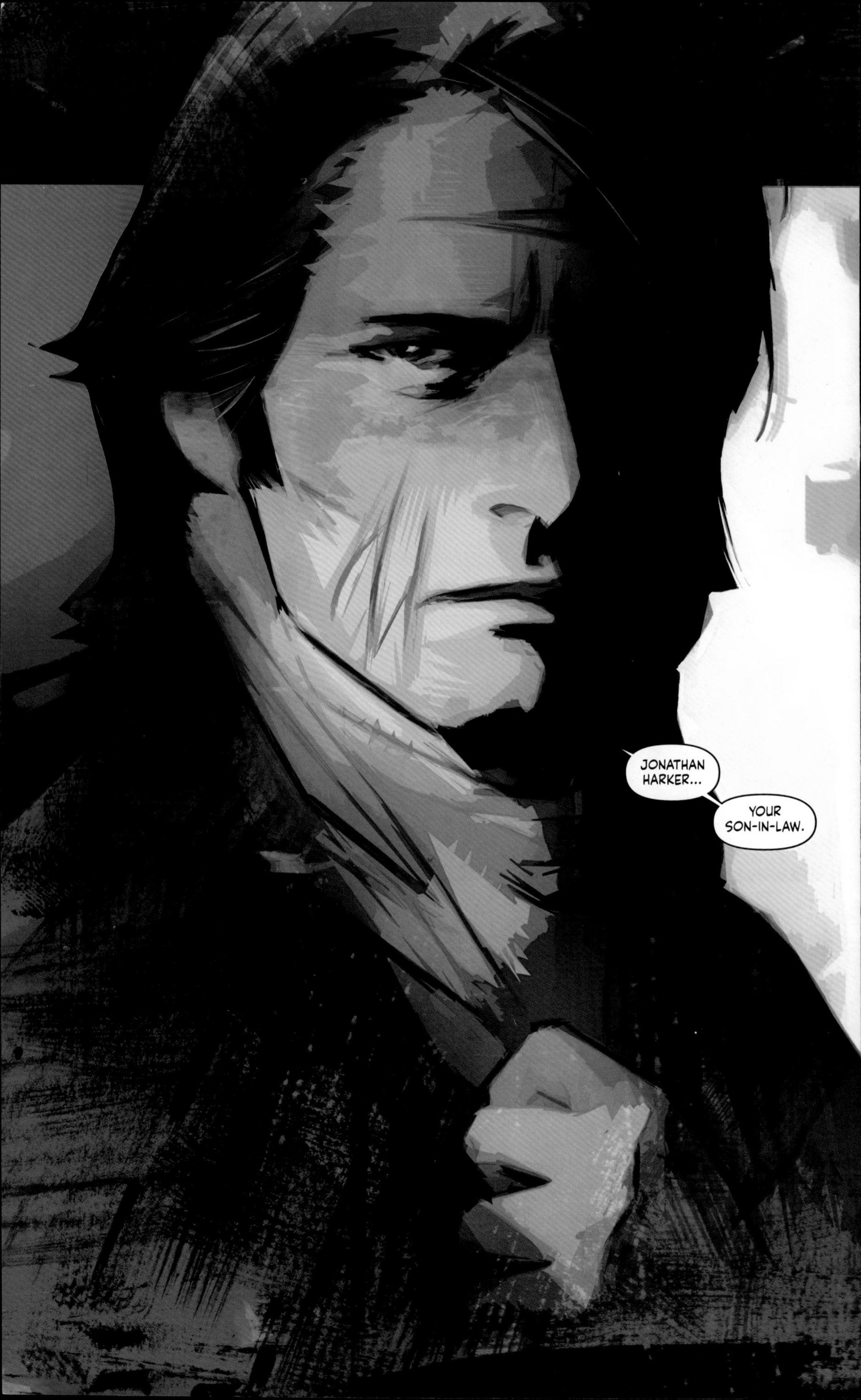
JONATHAN HARKER...
YOUR SON-IN-LAW.

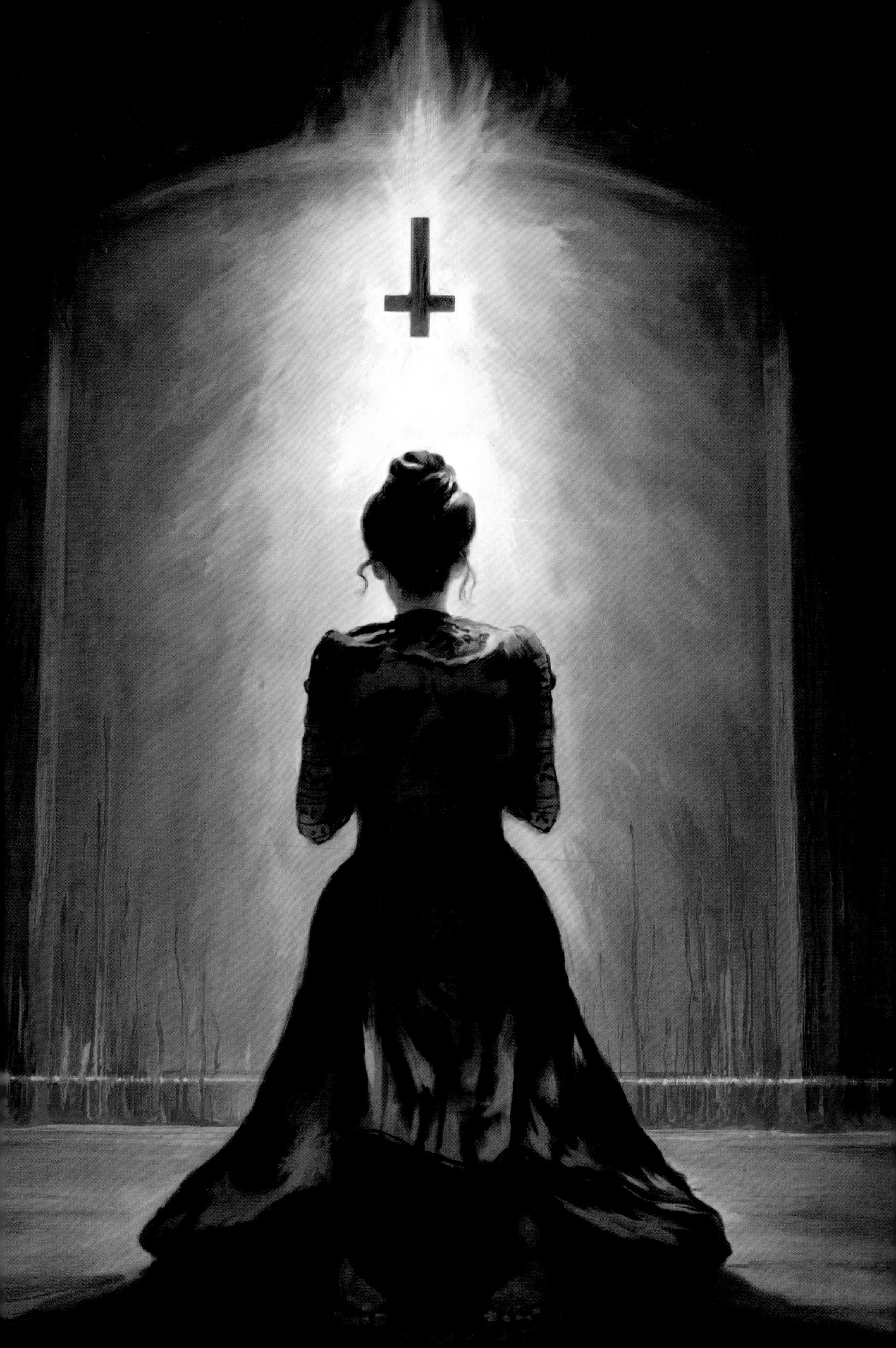

#2 COVER A - SHANE PIERCE

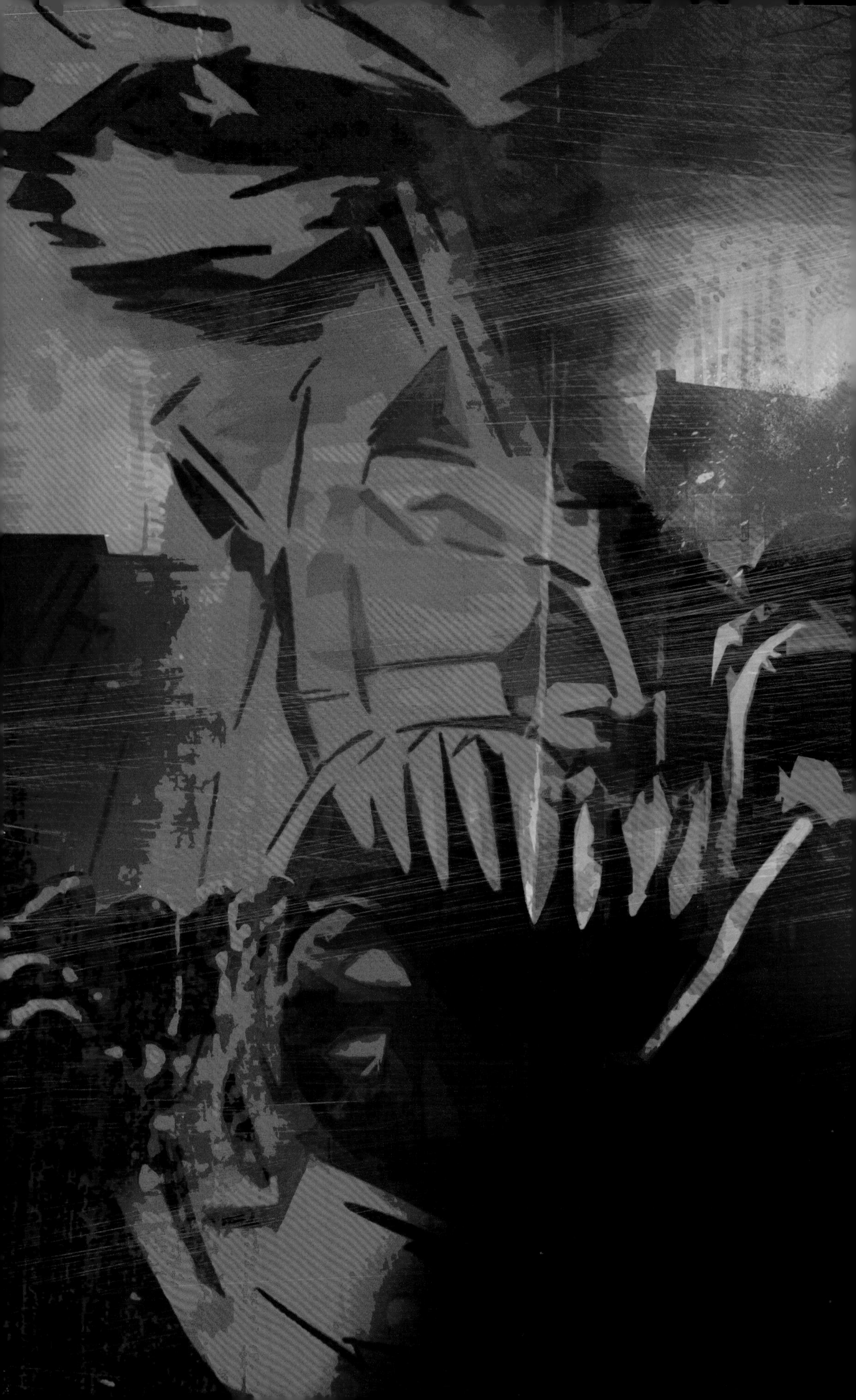

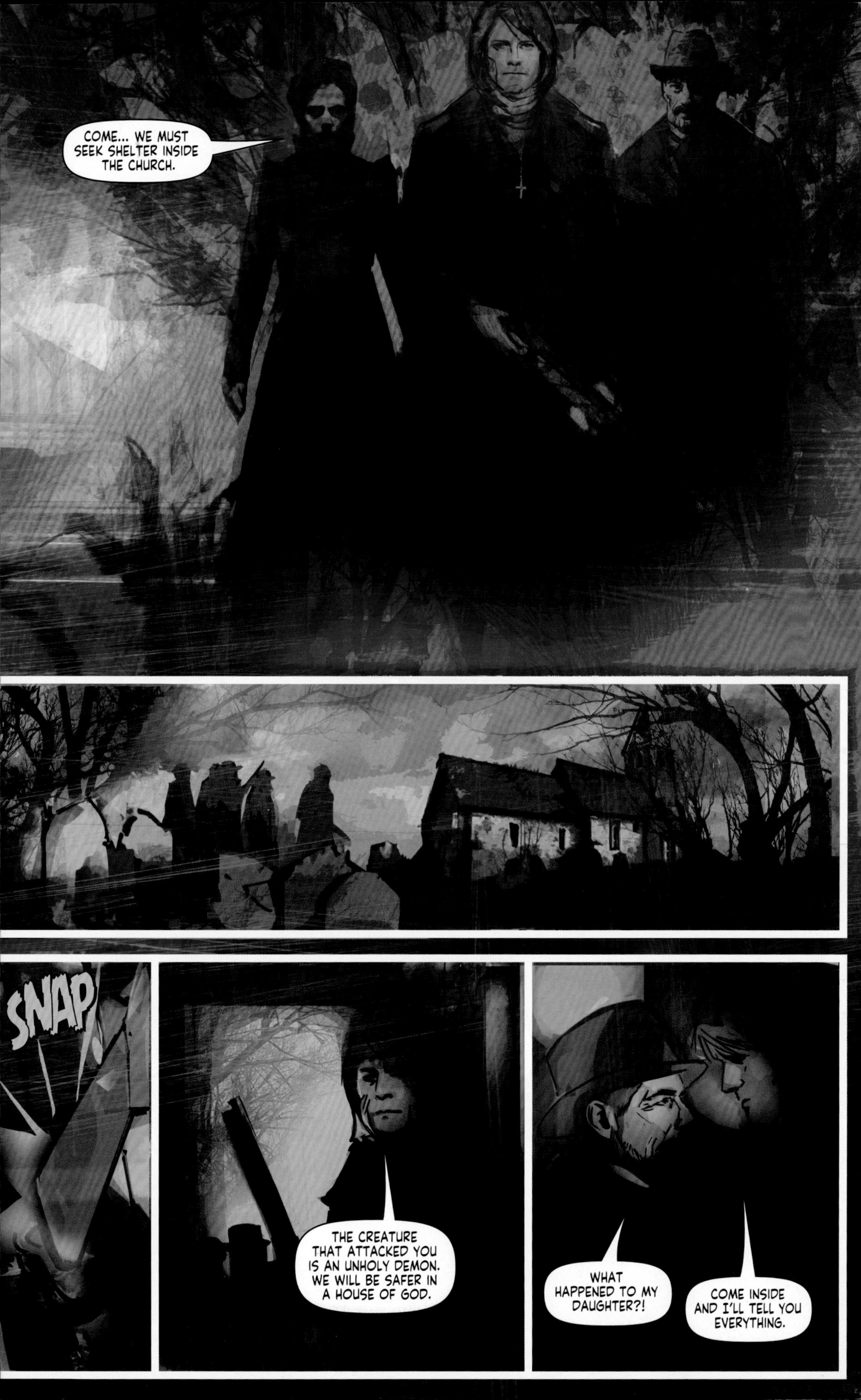
COME... WE MUST SEEK SHELTER INSIDE THE CHURCH.
SNAP
THE CREATURE THAT ATTACKED YOU IS AN UNHOLY DEMON. WE WILL BE SAFER IN A HOUSE OF GOD.
WHAT HAPPENED TO MY DAUGHTER?!
COME INSIDE AND I'LL TELL YOU EVERYTHING.

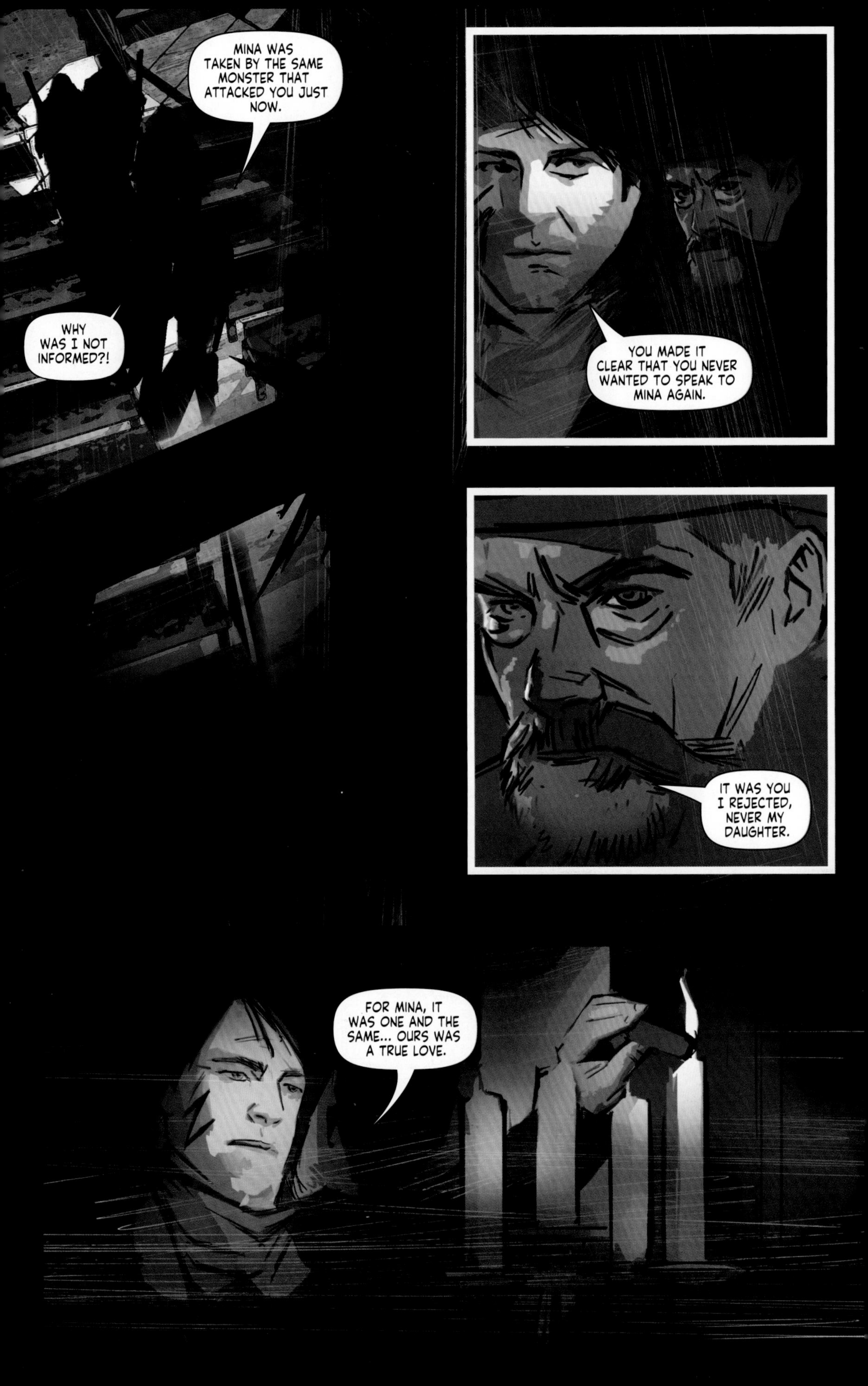
MINA WAS TAKEN BY THE SAME MONSTER THAT ATTACKED YOU JUST NOW.
WHY WAS I NOT INFORMED?!
YOU MADE IT CLEAR THAT YOU NEVER WANTED TO SPEAK TO MINA AGAIN.
IT WAS YOU I REJECTED, NEVER MY DAUGHTER.
FOR MINA, IT WAS ONE AND THE SAME... OURS WAS A TRUE LOVE.

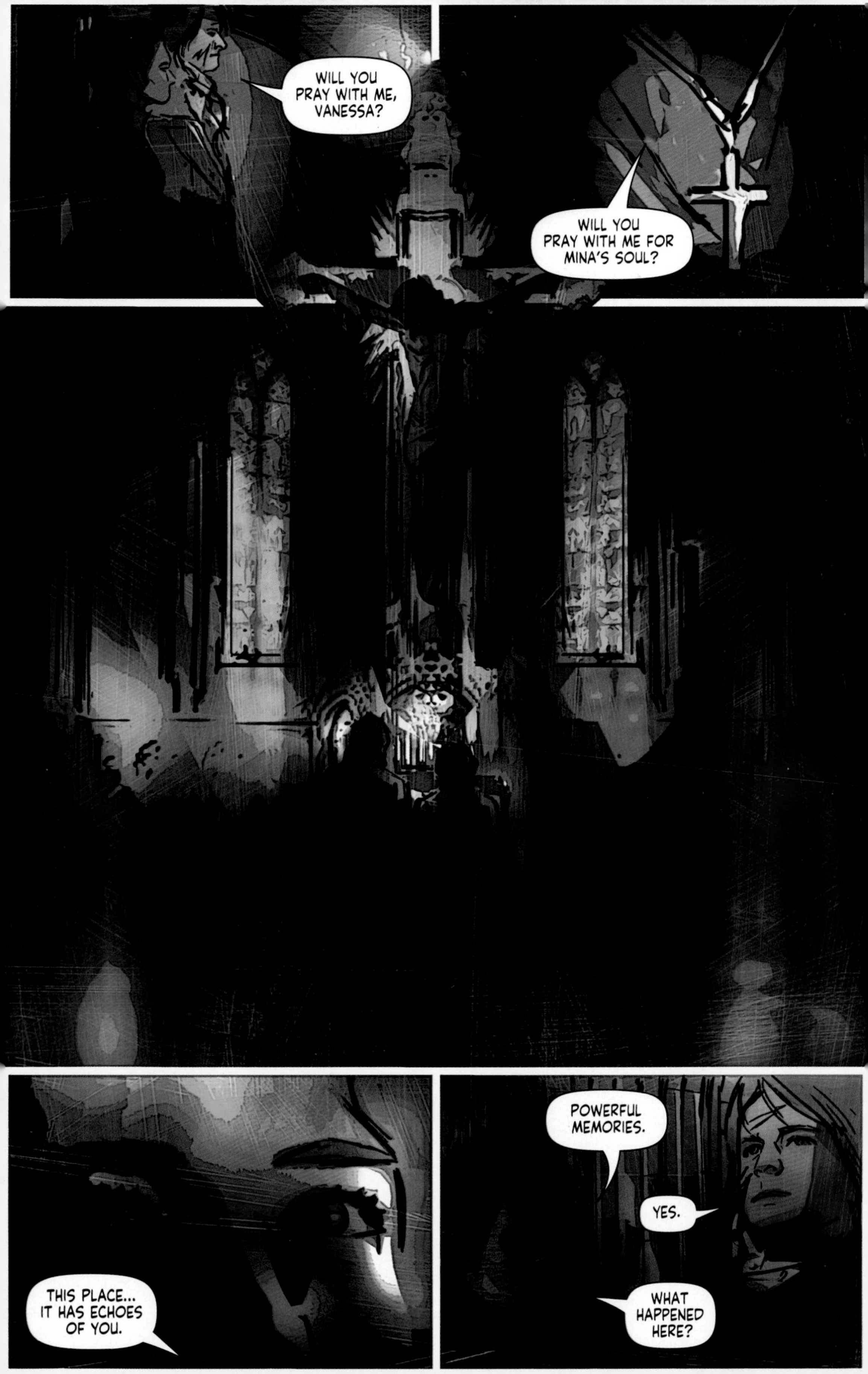
WILL YOU PRAY WITH ME, VANESSA?
WILL YOU PRAY WITH ME FOR MINA'S SOUL?
THIS PLACE... IT HAS ECHOES OF YOU.
POWERFUL MEMORIES.
YES.
WHAT HAPPENED HERE?

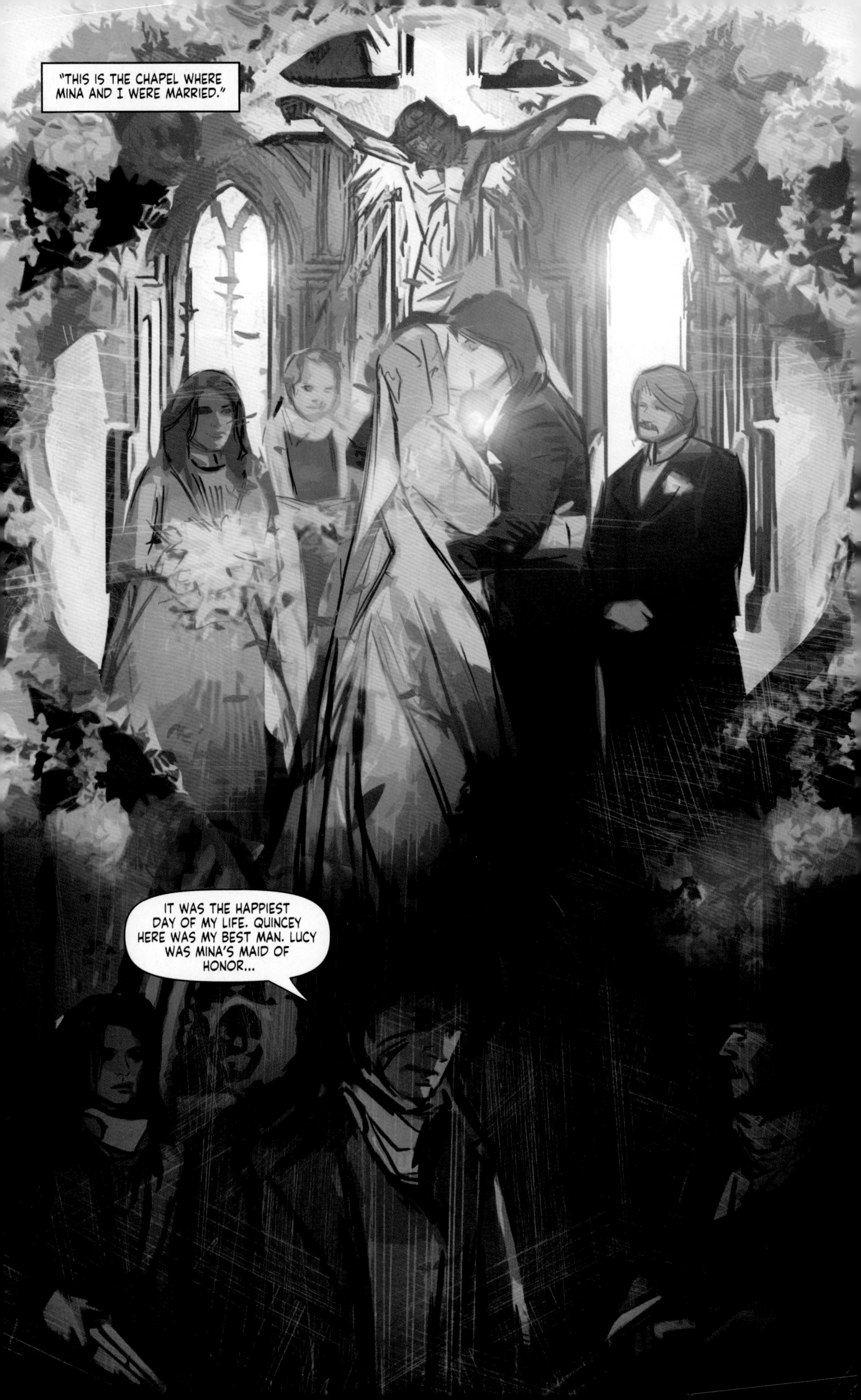
"THIS IS THE CHAPEL WHERE MINA AND I WERE MARRIED."
IT WAS THE HAPPIEST DAY OF MY LIFE. QUINCEY HERE WAS MY BEST MAN. LUCY WAS MINA'S MAID OF HONOR...

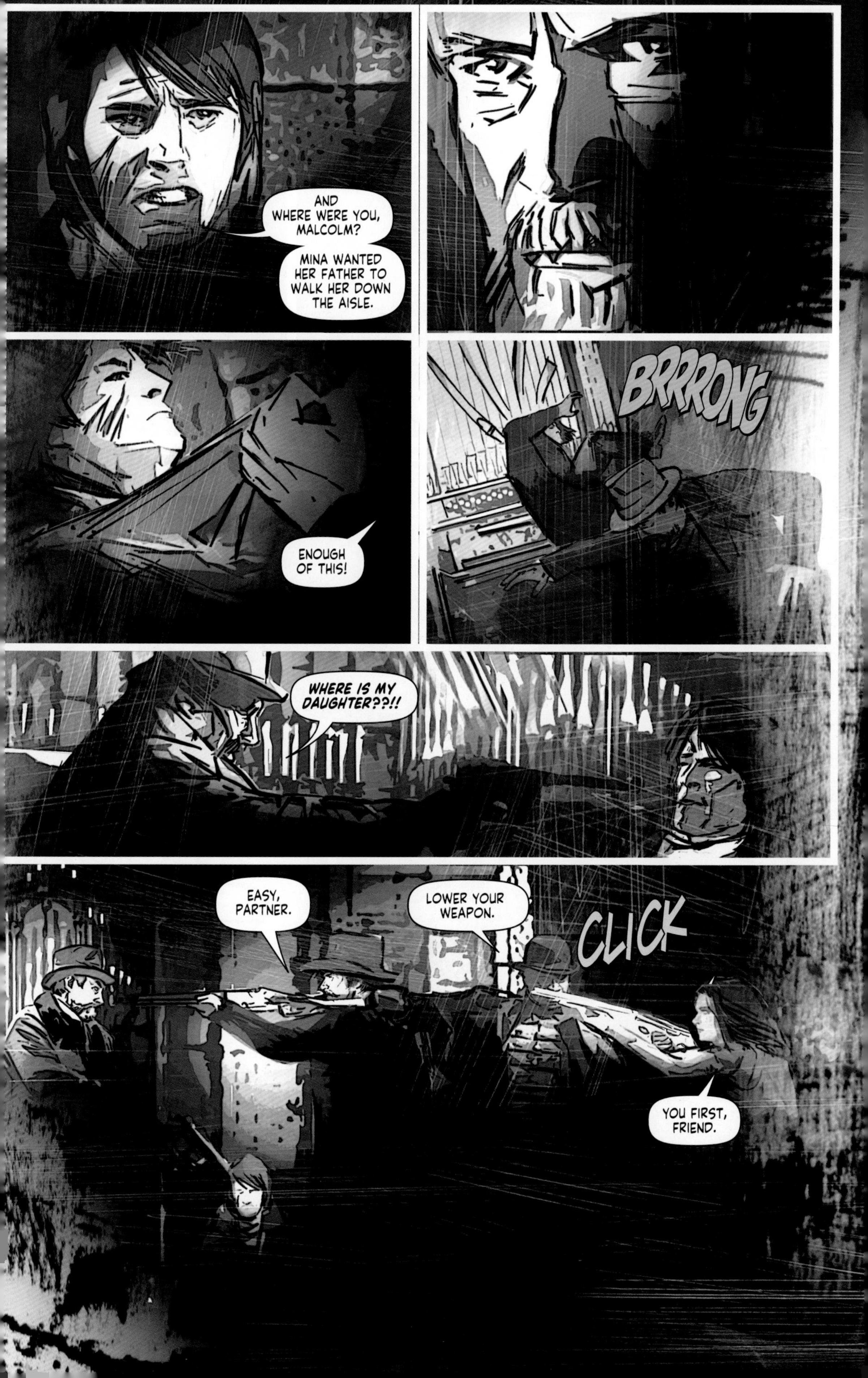
AND WHERE WERE YOU, MALCOLM?
MINA WANTED HER FATHER TO WALK HER DOWN THE AISLE.
ENOUGH OF THIS!
BRRRONG
WHERE IS MY DAUGHTER??!!
EASY, PARTNER.
LOWER YOUR WEAPON.
CLICK
YOU FIRST, FRIEND.

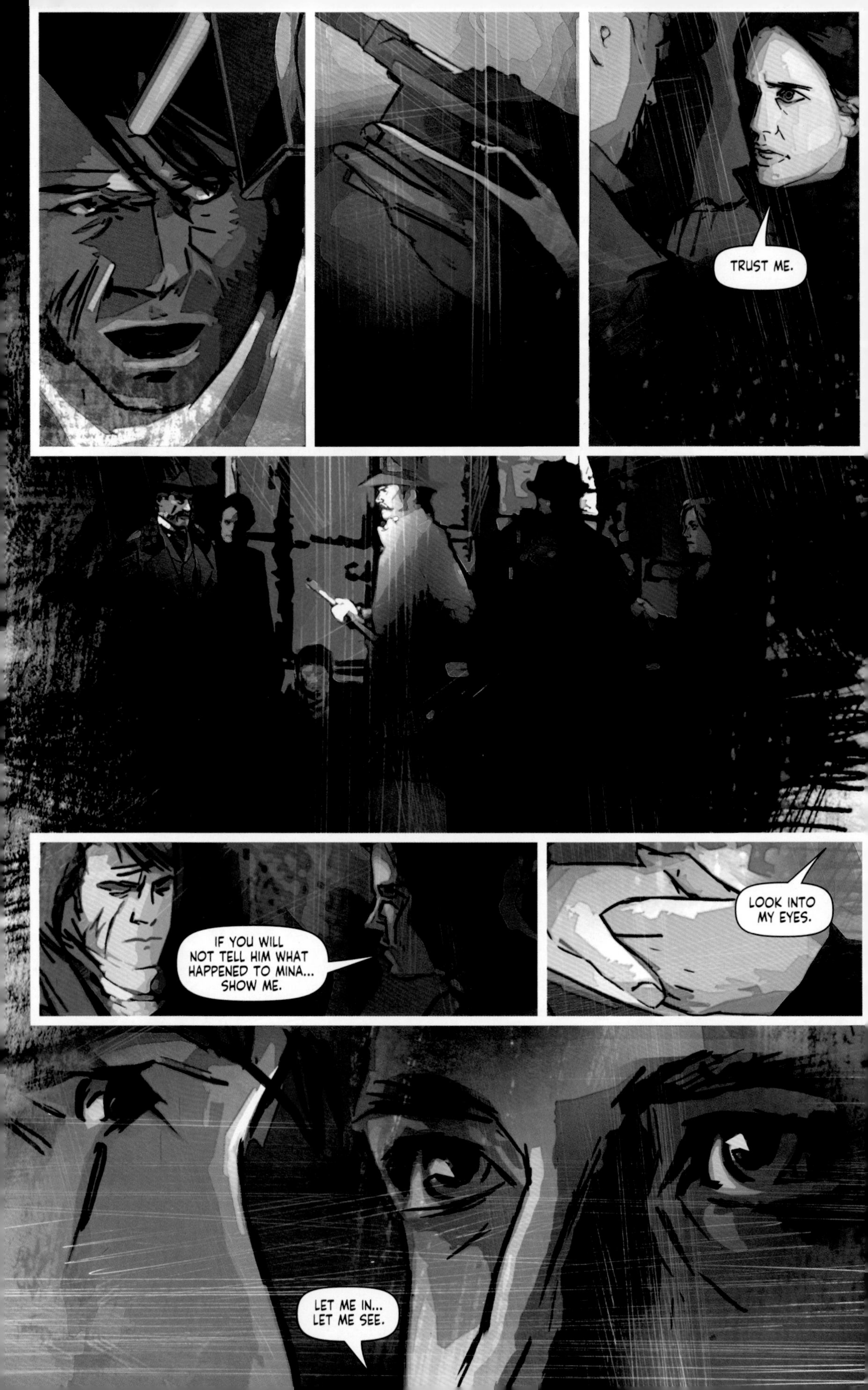
TRUST ME.
IF YOU WILL NOT TELL HIM WHAT HAPPENED TO MINA... SHOW ME.
LOOK INTO MY EYES.
LET ME IN... LET ME SEE.

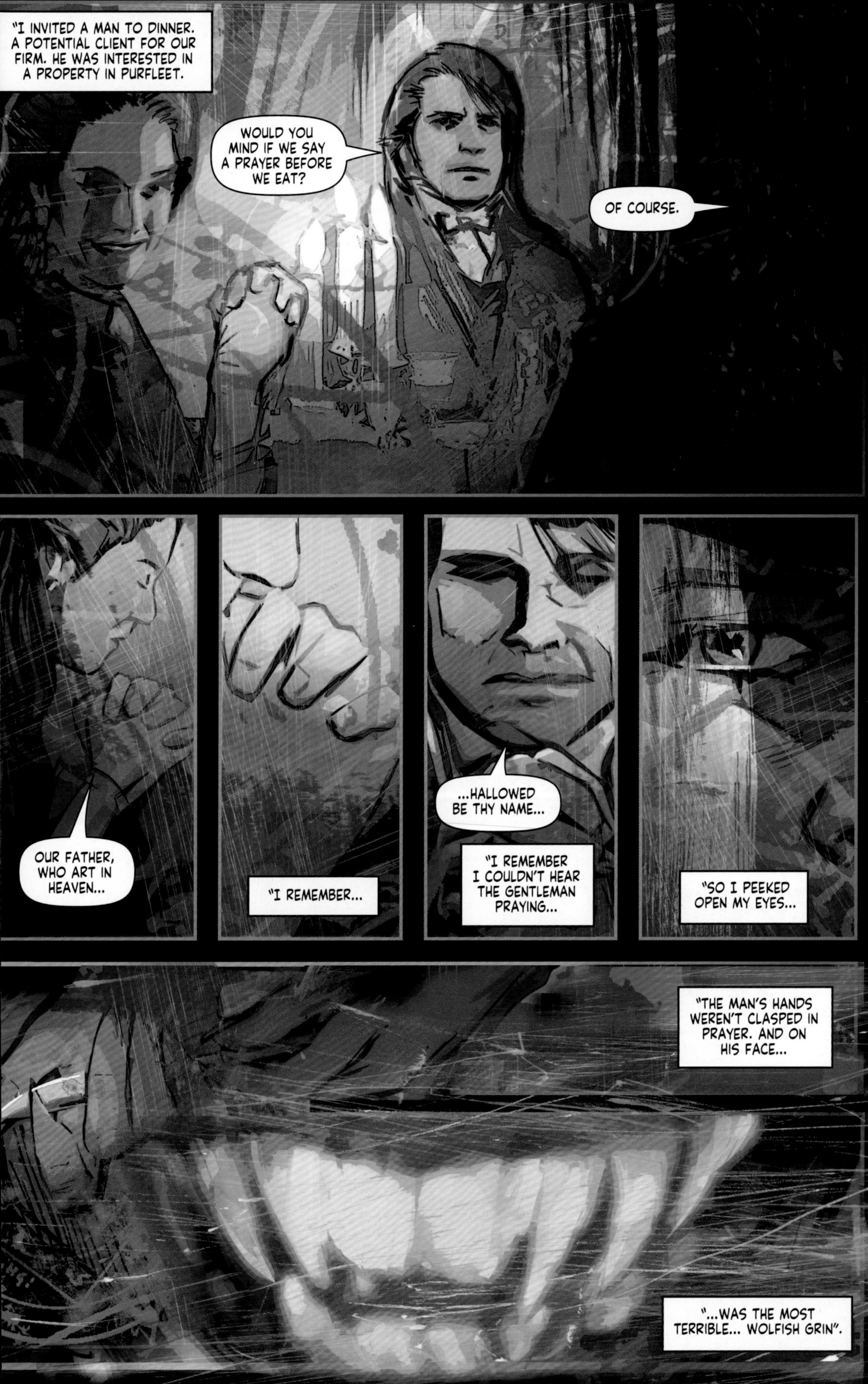
"I INVITED A MAN TO DINNER. A POTENTIAL CLIENT FOR OUR FIRM. HE WAS INTERESTED IN A PROPERTY IN PURFLEET.
WOULD YOU MIND IF WE SAY A PRAYER BEFORE WE EAT?
OF COURSE.
OUR FATHER, WHO ART IN HEAVEN...
"I REMEMBER...
...HALLOWED BE THY NAME...
"I REMEMBER I COULDN'T HEAR THE GENTLEMAN PRAYING...
"SO I PEEKED OPEN MY EYES...
"THE MAN'S HANDS WEREN'T CLASPED IN PRAYER. AND ON HIS FACE...
"...WAS THE MOST TERRIBLE... WOLFISH GRIN".

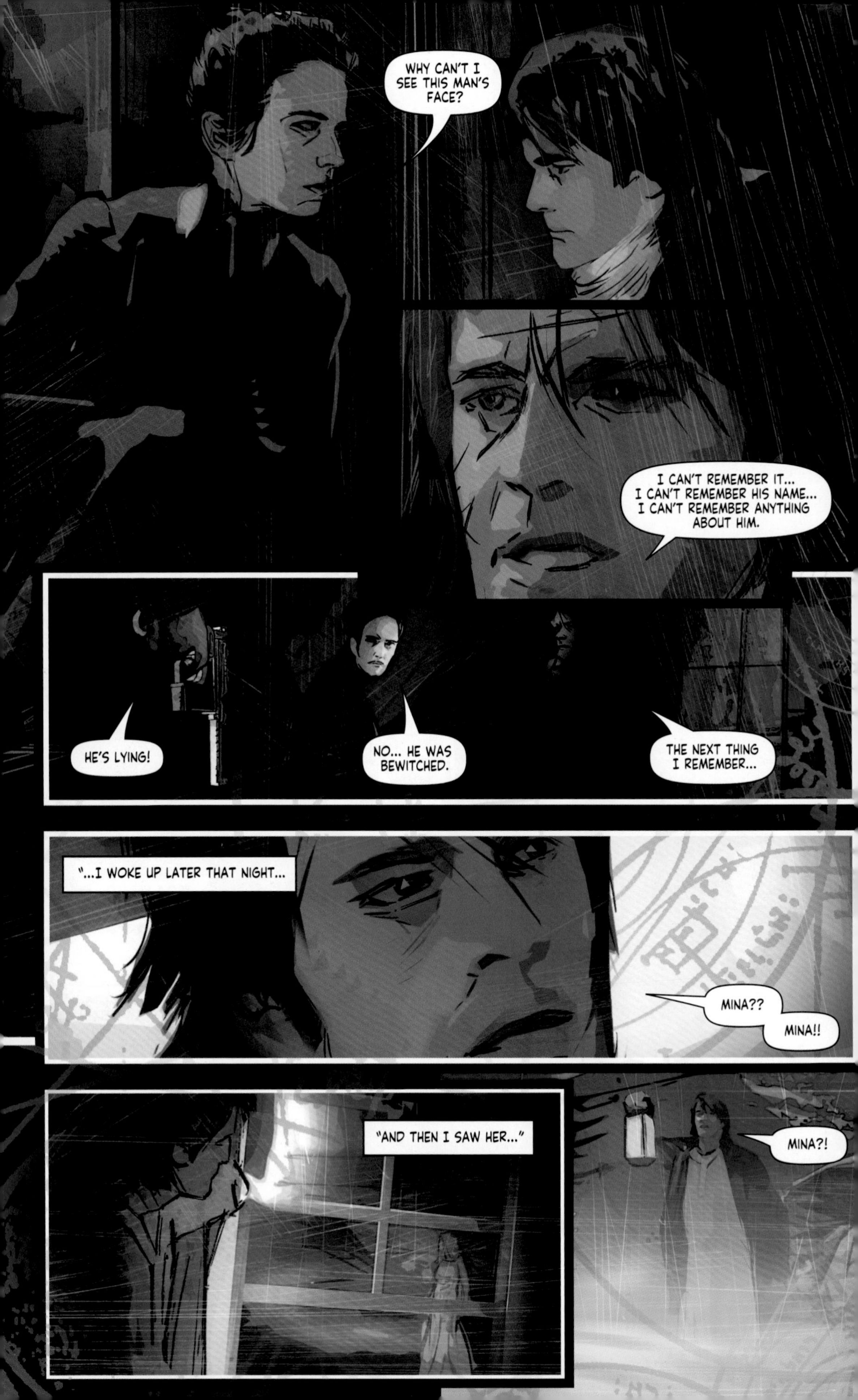
WHY CAN'T I SEE THIS MAN'S FACE?
I CAN'T REMEMBER IT... I CAN'T REMEMBER HIS NAME... I CAN'T REMEMBER ANYTHING ABOUT HIM.
HE'S LYING!
NO... HE WAS BEWITCHED.
THE NEXT THING I REMEMBER...
"...I WOKE UP LATER THAT NIGHT...
MINA??
MINA!!
"AND THEN I SAW HER..."
MINA?!

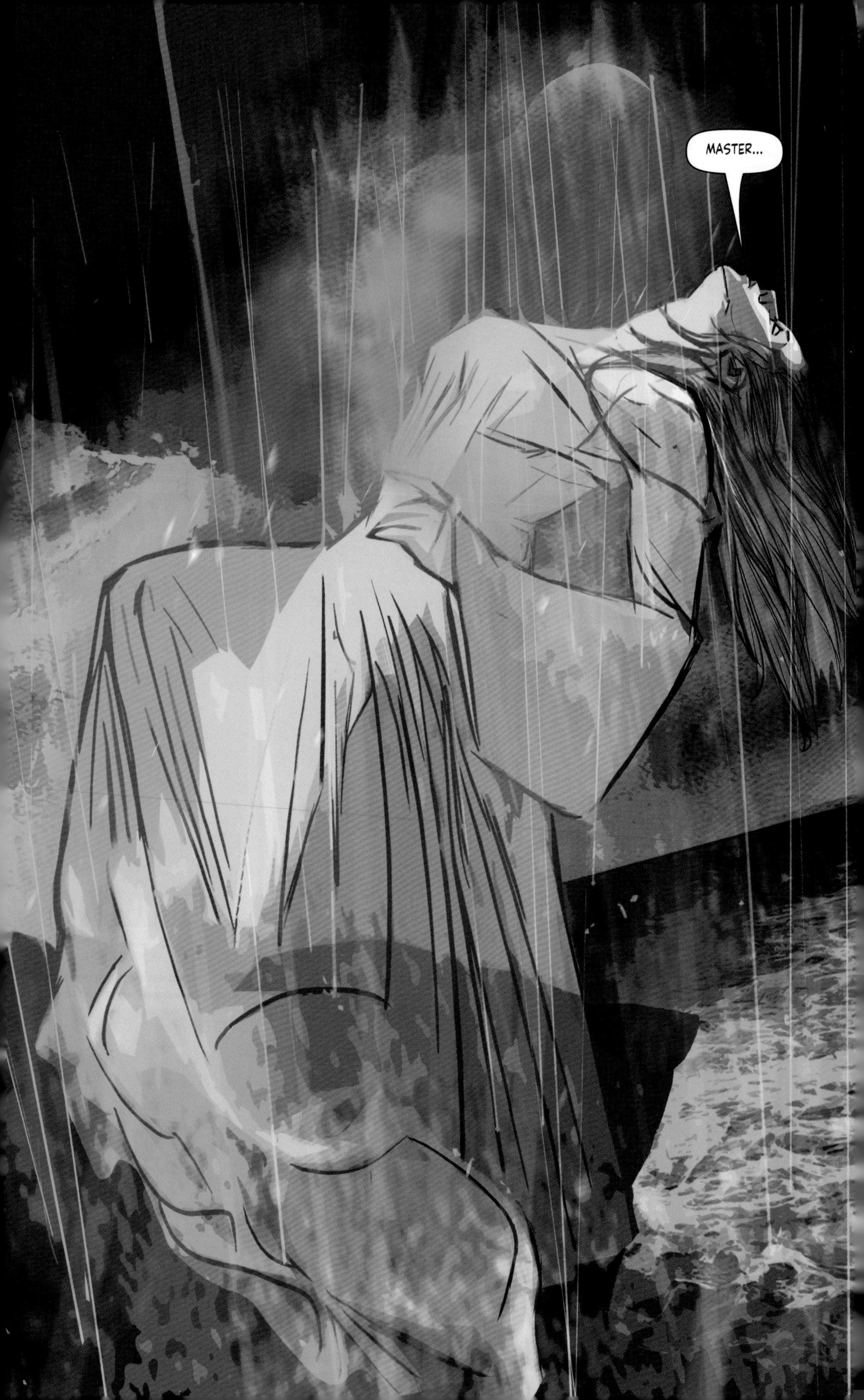
MASTER...

"THE NEXT MORNING, SHE WOKE WITH A TERRIBLE FEVER. I BELIEVED SHE HAD CAUGHT A CHILL IN THE LASHING RAIN.

...I'M SO THIRSTY.

"AND I TOLD MYSELF THAT THE PREVIOUS NIGHT SHE HAD BEE SLEEPWALKING -- NOTHING MORE

PLEASE. I'M SO THIRSTY.

"I NURSED HER AS BEST I COULD.

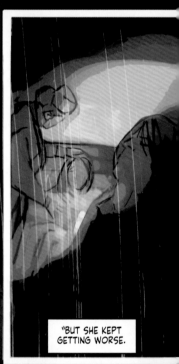

"BUT SHE KEPT GETTING WORSE.

"EVERY NIGHT SHE WOULD TRY TO SNEAK OUTSIDE...

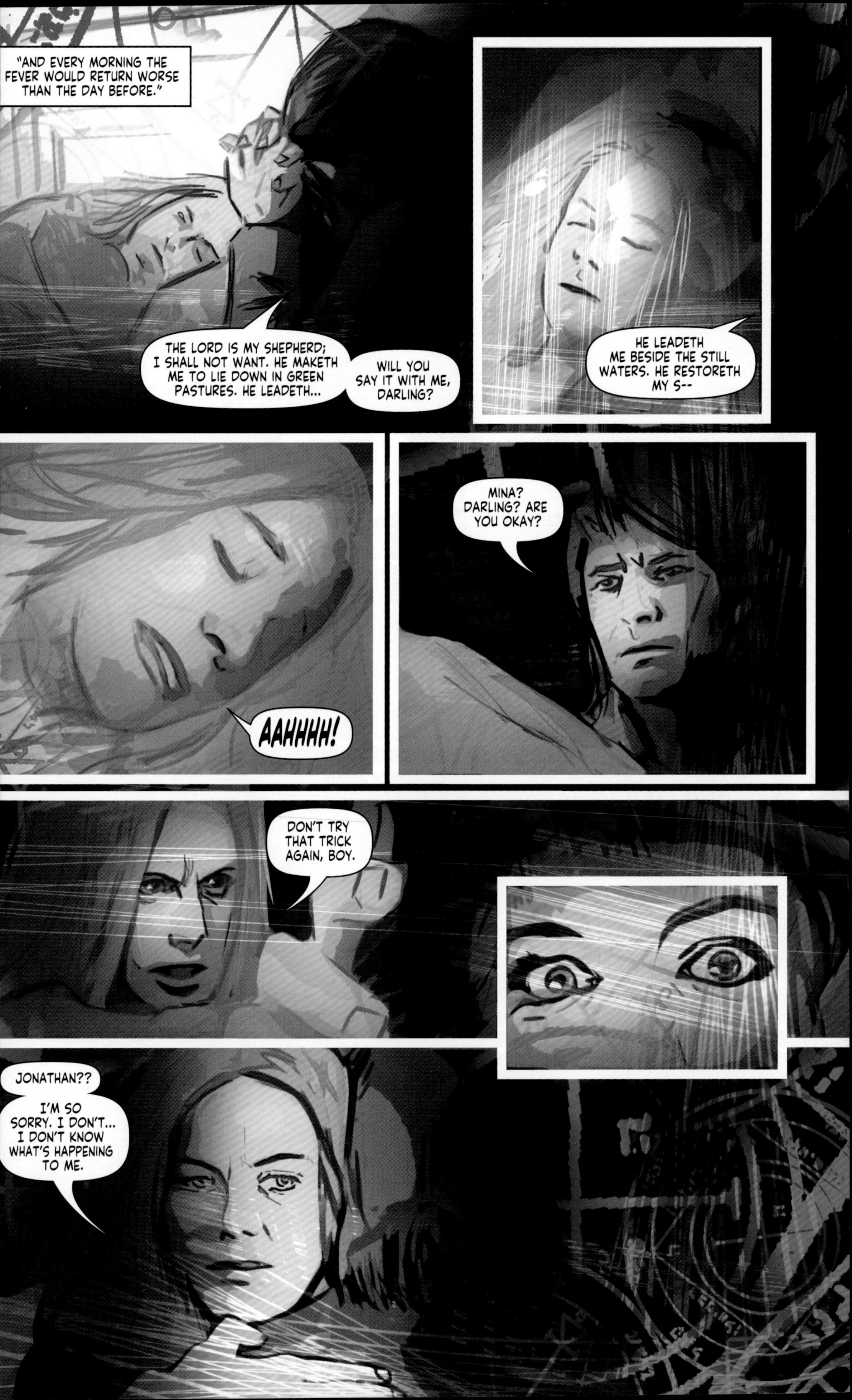
"AND EVERY MORNING THE FEVER WOULD RETURN WORSE THAN THE DAY BEFORE."
THE LORD IS MY SHEPHERD; I SHALL NOT WANT. HE MAKETH ME TO LIE DOWN IN GREEN PASTURES. HE LEADETH...
WILL YOU SAY IT WITH ME, DARLING?
HE LEADETH ME BESIDE THE STILL WATERS. HE RESTORETH MY S--
AAHHHH!
MINA? DARLING? ARE YOU OKAY?
DON'T TRY THAT TRICK AGAIN, BOY.
JONATHAN??
I'M SO SORRY. I DON'T... I DON'T KNOW WHAT'S HAPPENING TO ME.

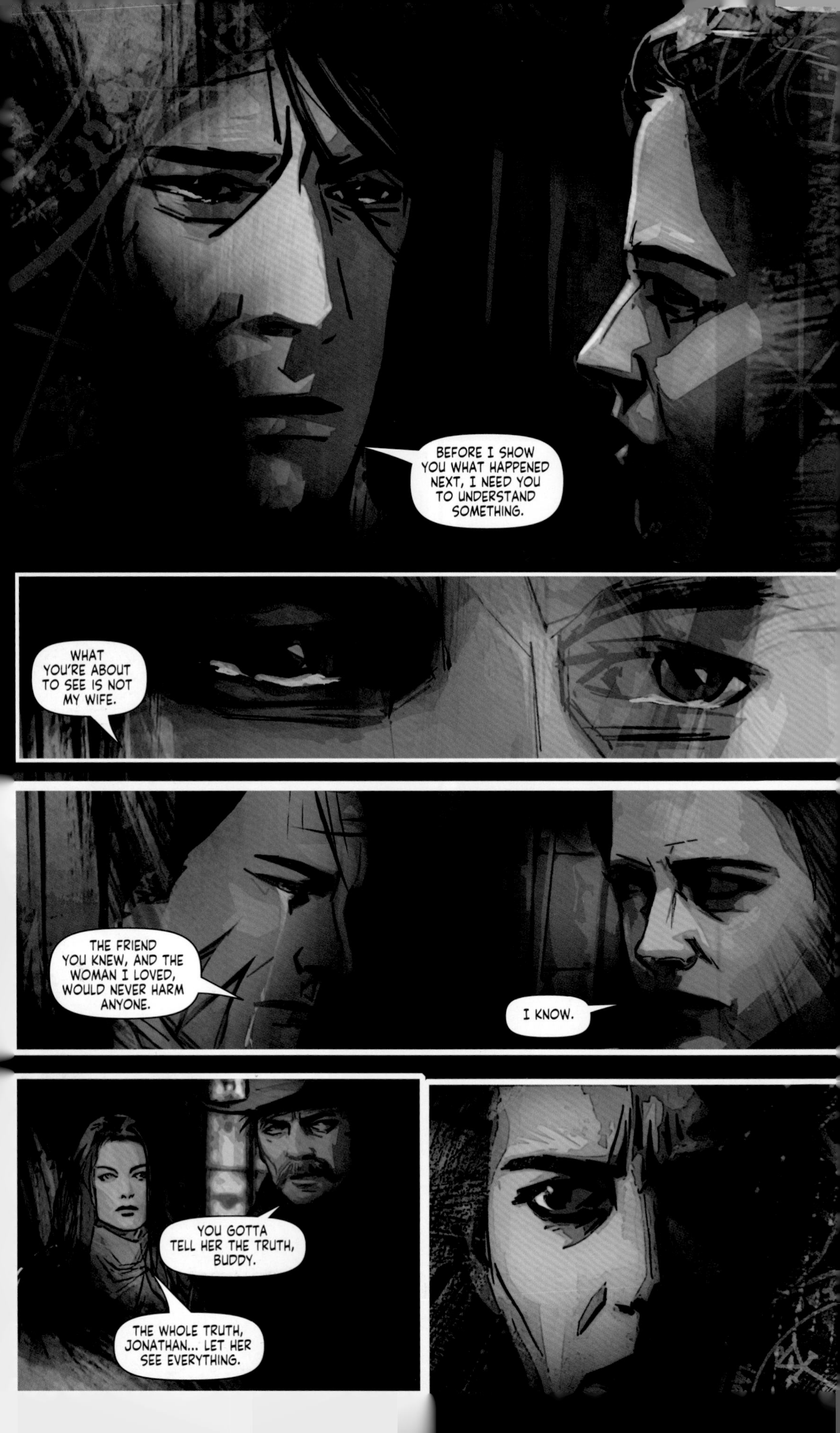

BEFORE I SHOW YOU WHAT HAPPENED NEXT, I NEED YOU TO UNDERSTAND SOMETHING.
WHAT YOU'RE ABOUT TO SEE IS NOT MY WIFE.
THE FRIEND YOU KNEW, AND THE WOMAN I LOVED, WOULD NEVER HARM ANYONE.
I KNOW.
YOU GOTTA TELL HER THE TRUTH, BUDDY.
THE WHOLE TRUTH, JONATHAN... LET HER SEE EVERYTHING.

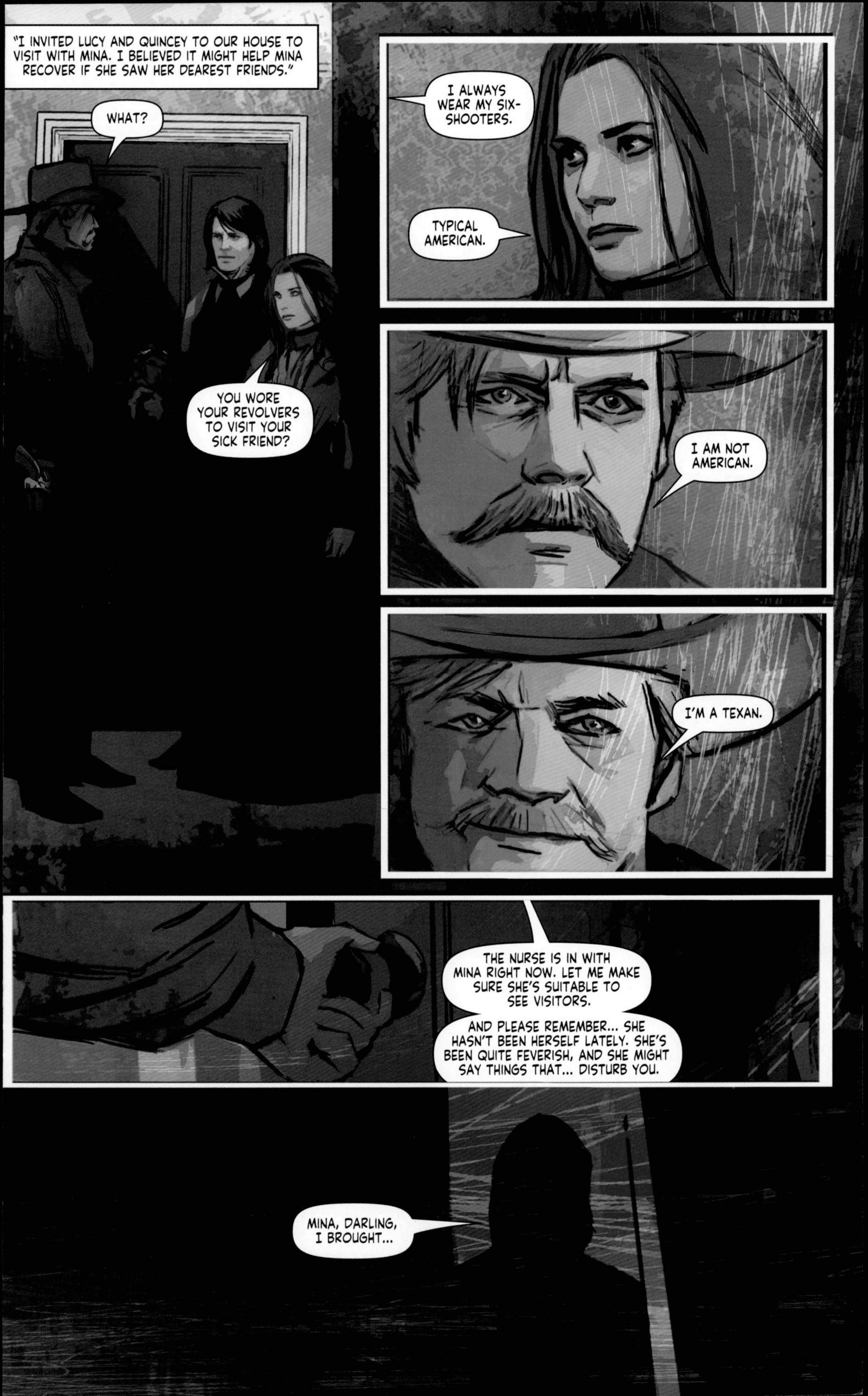
"I INVITED LUCY AND QUINCEY TO OUR HOUSE TO VISIT WITH MINA. I BELIEVED IT MIGHT HELP MINA RECOVER IF SHE SAW HER DEAREST FRIENDS."
WHAT?
YOU WORE YOUR REVOLVERS TO VISIT YOUR SICK FRIEND?
I ALWAYS WEAR MY SIX-SHOOTERS.
TYPICAL AMERICAN.
I AM NOT AMERICAN.
I'M A TEXAN.
THE NURSE IS IN WITH MINA RIGHT NOW. LET ME MAKE SURE SHE'S SUITABLE TO SEE VISITORS.
AND PLEASE REMEMBER... SHE HASN'T BEEN HERSELF LATELY. SHE'S BEEN QUITE FEVERISH, AND SHE MIGHT SAY THINGS THAT... DISTURB YOU.
MINA, DARLING, I BROUGHT...

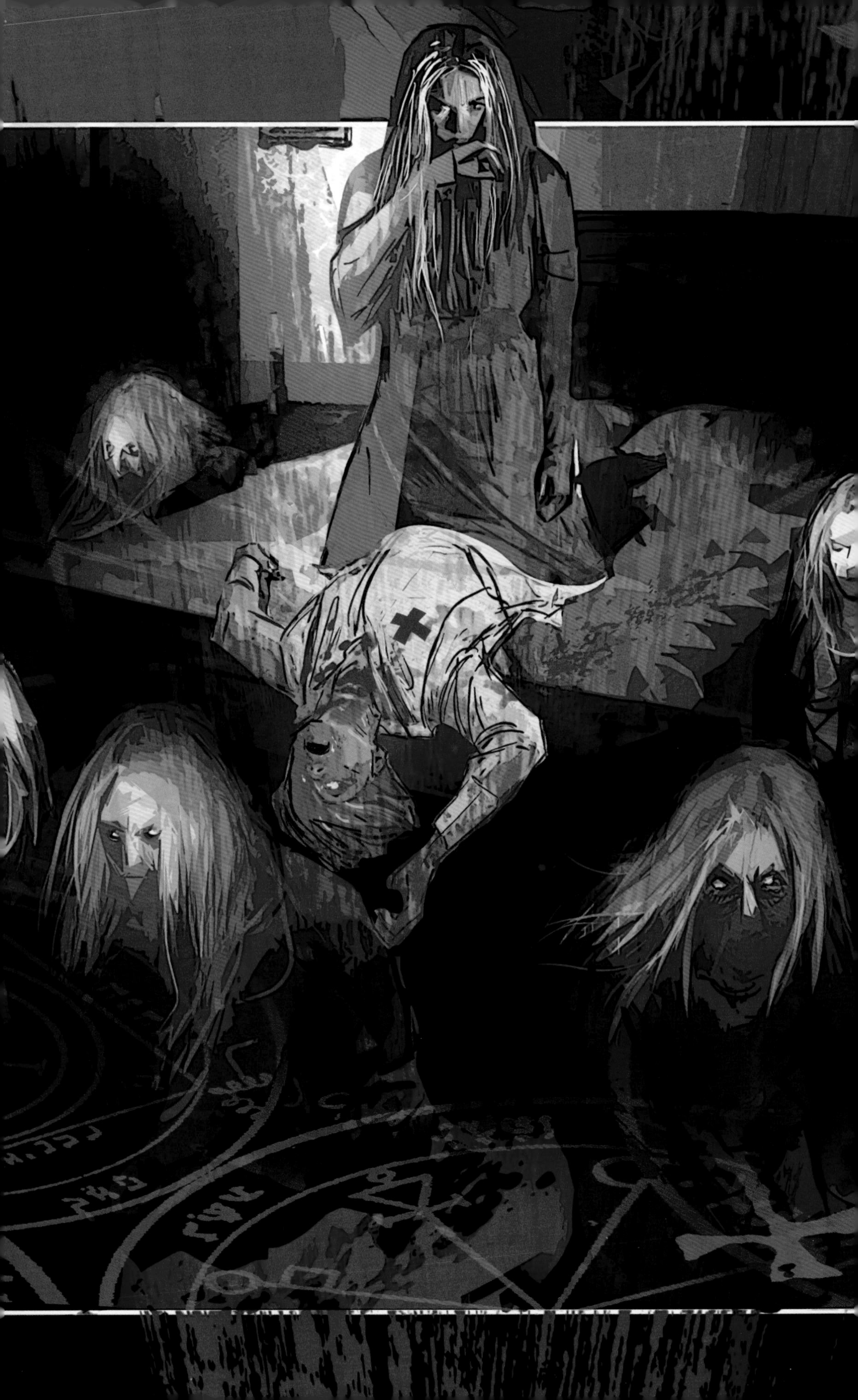

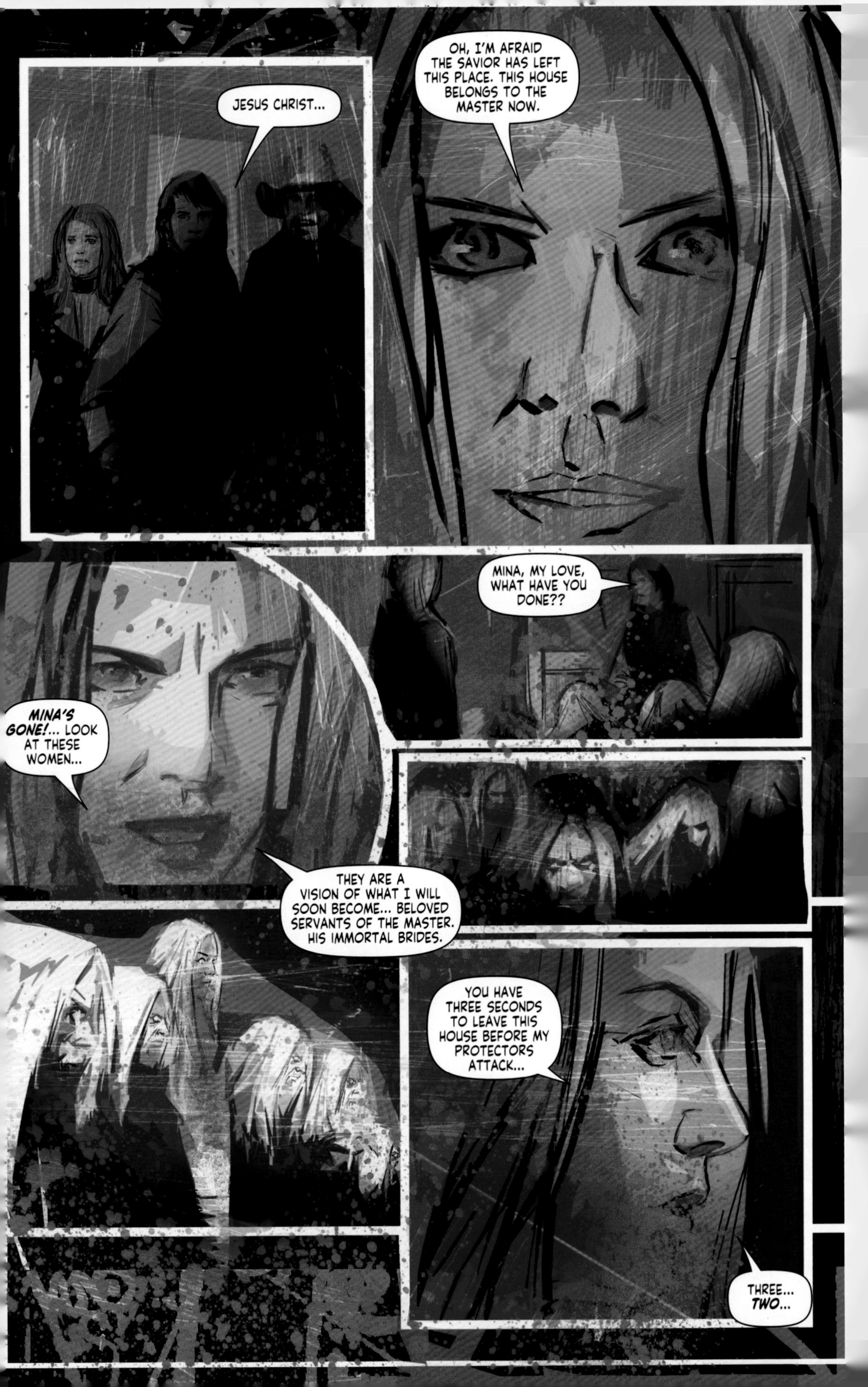
JESUS CHRIST...
OH, I'M AFRAID THE SAVIOR HAS LEFT THIS PLACE. THIS HOUSE BELONGS TO THE MASTER NOW.
MINA, MY LOVE, WHAT HAVE YOU DONE??
MINA'S GONE!... LOOK AT THESE WOMEN...
THEY ARE A VISION OF WHAT I WILL SOON BECOME... BELOVED SERVANTS OF THE MASTER. HIS IMMORTAL BRIDES.
YOU HAVE THREE SECONDS TO LEAVE THIS HOUSE BEFORE MY PROTECTORS ATTACK...
THREE... TWO...

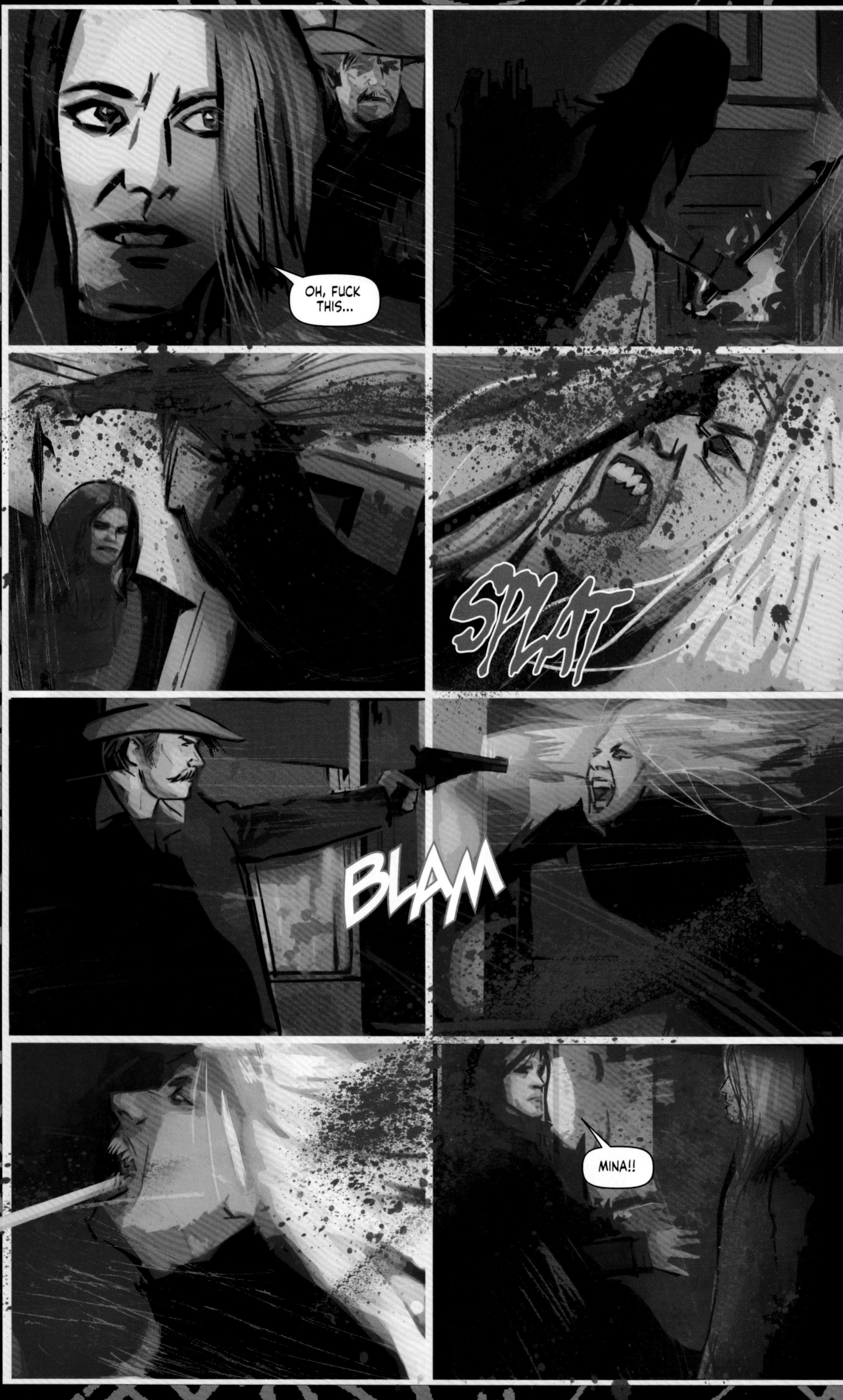
OH, FUCK THIS...
SPLAT
BLAM
MINA!!

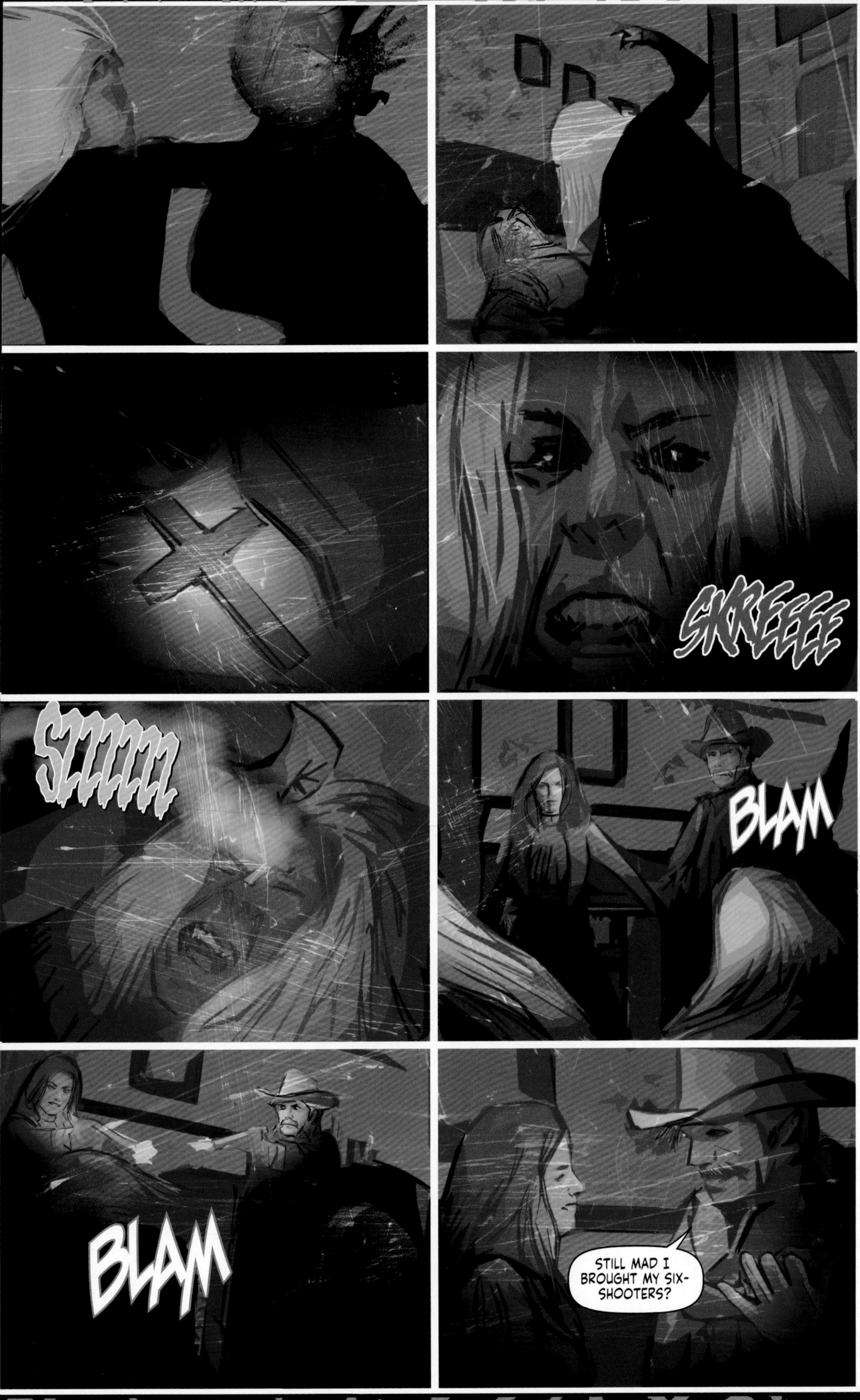
SKREEEE
SZZZZZZ
BLAM
BLAM
STILL MAD I BROUGHT MY SIX-SHOOTERS?

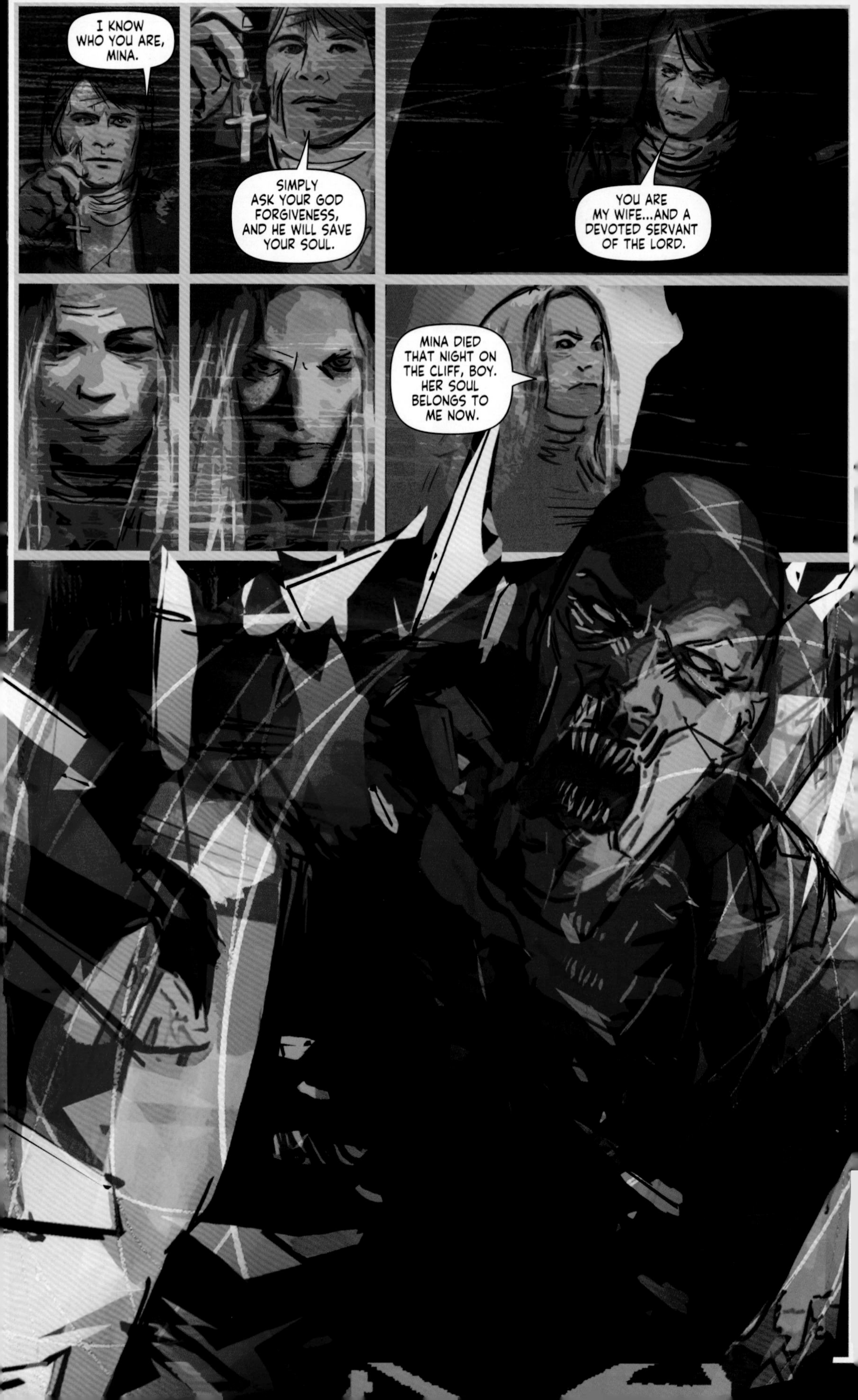
I KNOW WHO YOU ARE, MINA.
SIMPLY ASK YOUR GOD FORGIVENESS, AND HE WILL SAVE YOUR SOUL.
YOU ARE MY WIFE...AND A DEVOTED SERVANT OF THE LORD.
MINA DIED THAT NIGHT ON THE CLIFF, BOY. HER SOUL BELONGS TO ME NOW.

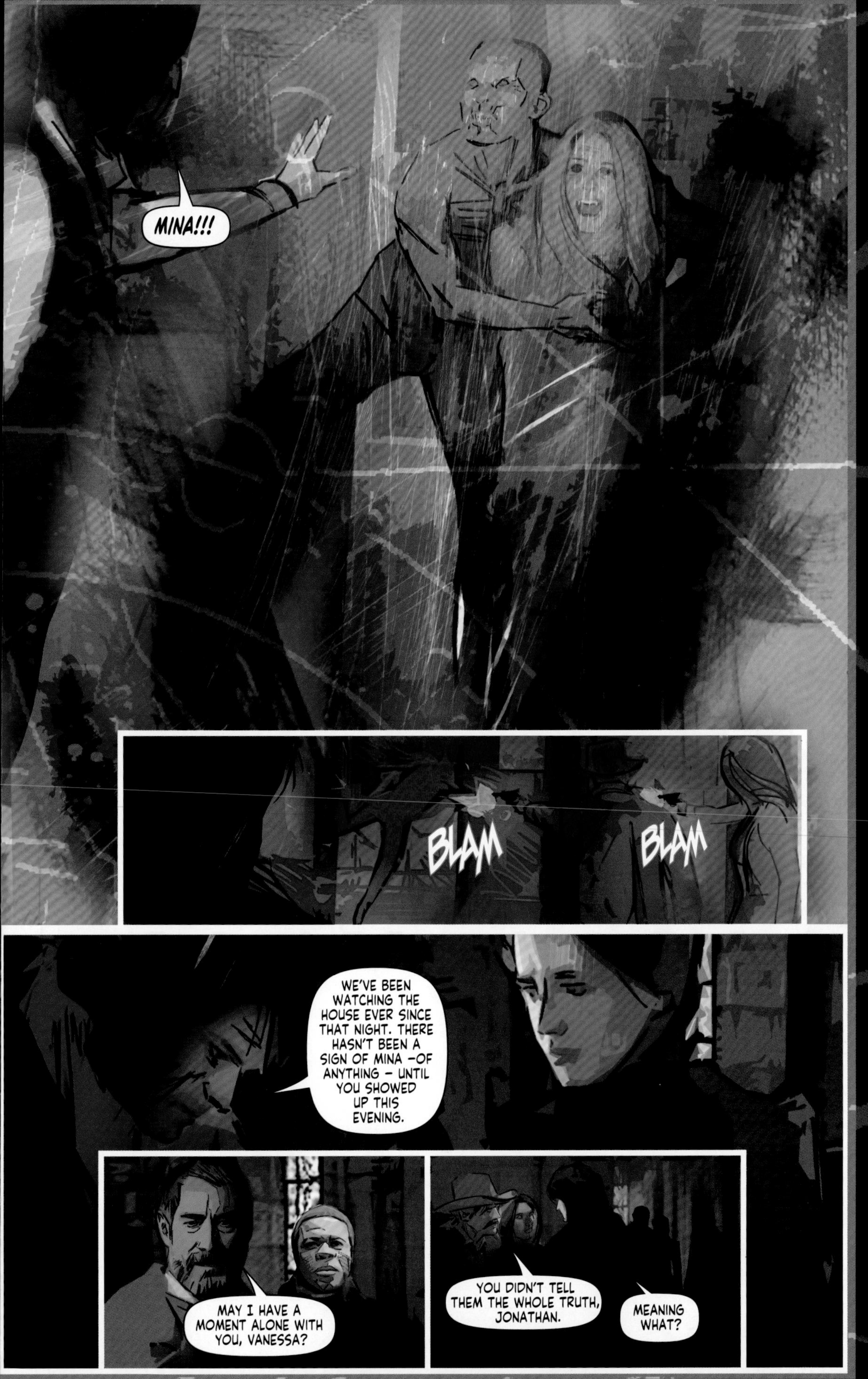
MINA!!!
BLAM
BLAM
WE'VE BEEN WATCHING THE HOUSE EVER SINCE THAT NIGHT. THERE HASN'T BEEN A SIGN OF MINA –OF ANYTHING – UNTIL YOU SHOWED UP THIS EVENING.
MAY I HAVE A MOMENT ALONE WITH YOU, VANESSA?
YOU DIDN'T TELL THEM THE WHOLE TRUTH, JONATHAN.
MEANING WHAT?

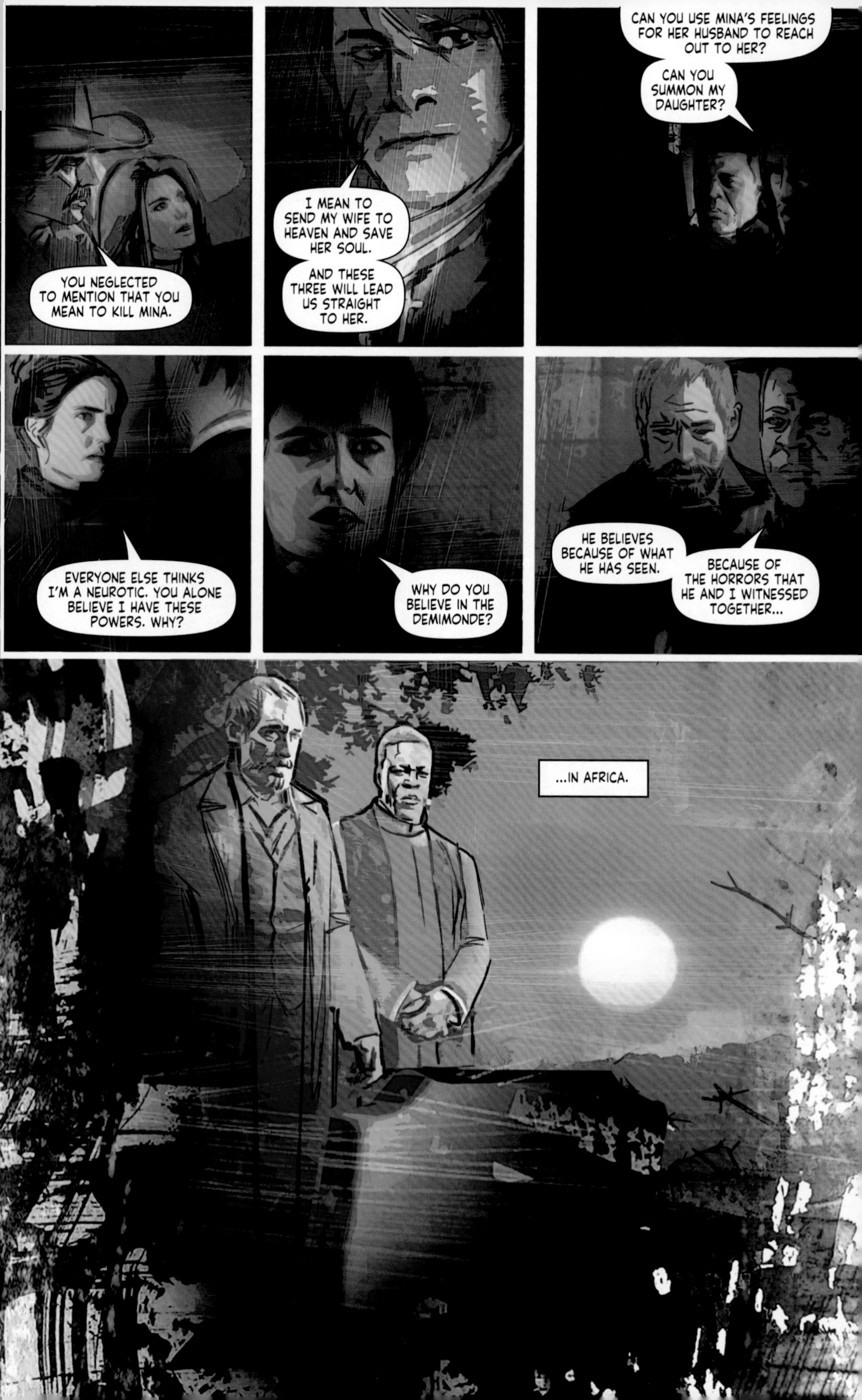
YOU NEGLECTED TO MENTION THAT YOU MEAN TO KILL MINA.
I MEAN TO SEND MY WIFE TO HEAVEN AND SAVE HER SOUL.
AND THESE THREE WILL LEAD US STRAIGHT TO HER.
CAN YOU USE MINA'S FEELINGS FOR HER HUSBAND TO REACH OUT TO HER?
CAN YOU SUMMON MY DAUGHTER?
EVERYONE ELSE THINKS I'M A NEUROTIC. YOU ALONE BELIEVE I HAVE THESE POWERS. WHY?
WHY DO YOU BELIEVE IN THE DEMIMONDE?
HE BELIEVES BECAUSE OF WHAT HE HAS SEEN.
BECAUSE OF THE HORRORS THAT HE AND I WITNESSED TOGETHER...
...IN AFRICA.

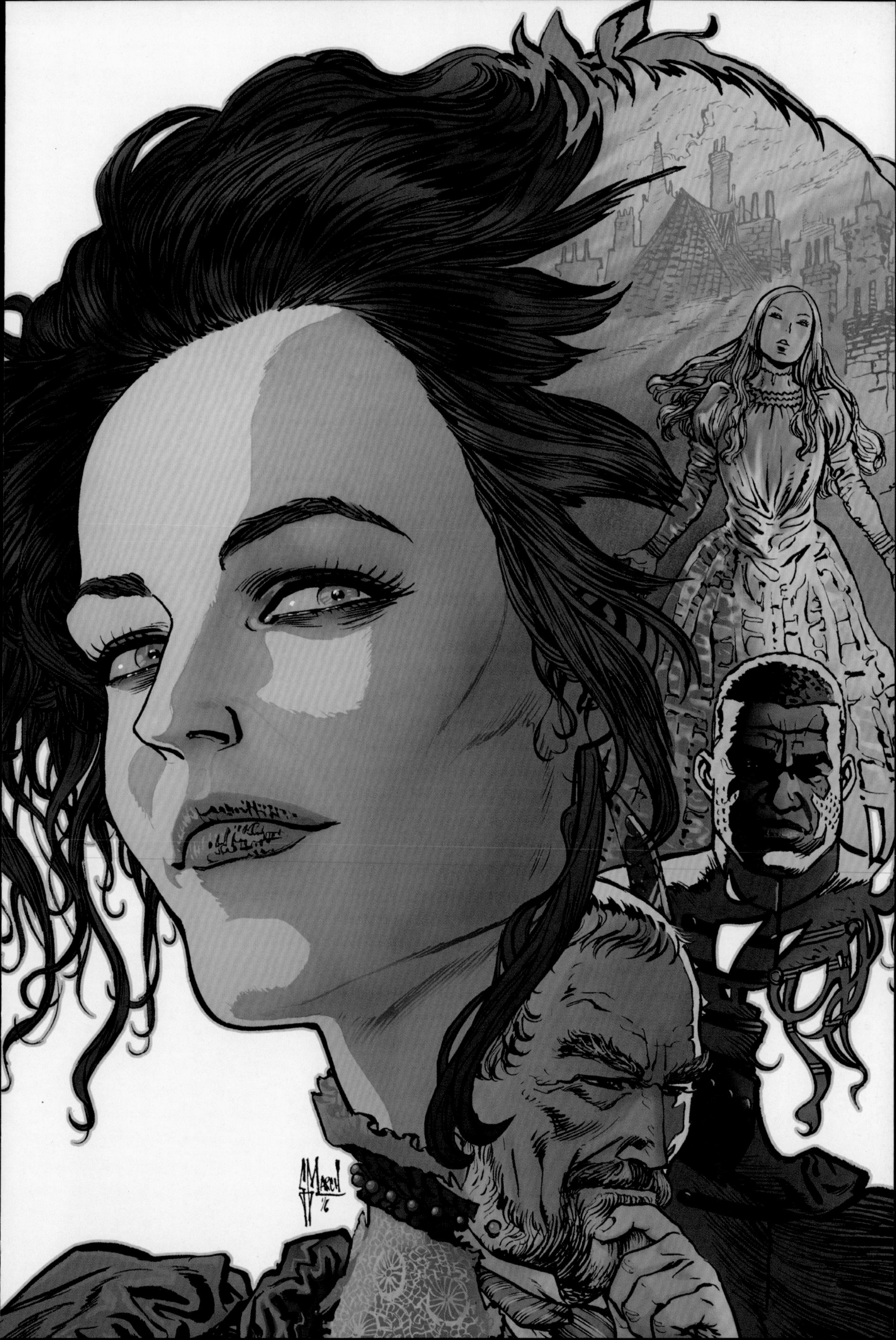
March
'16

#3 COVER A - GUILLEM MARCH

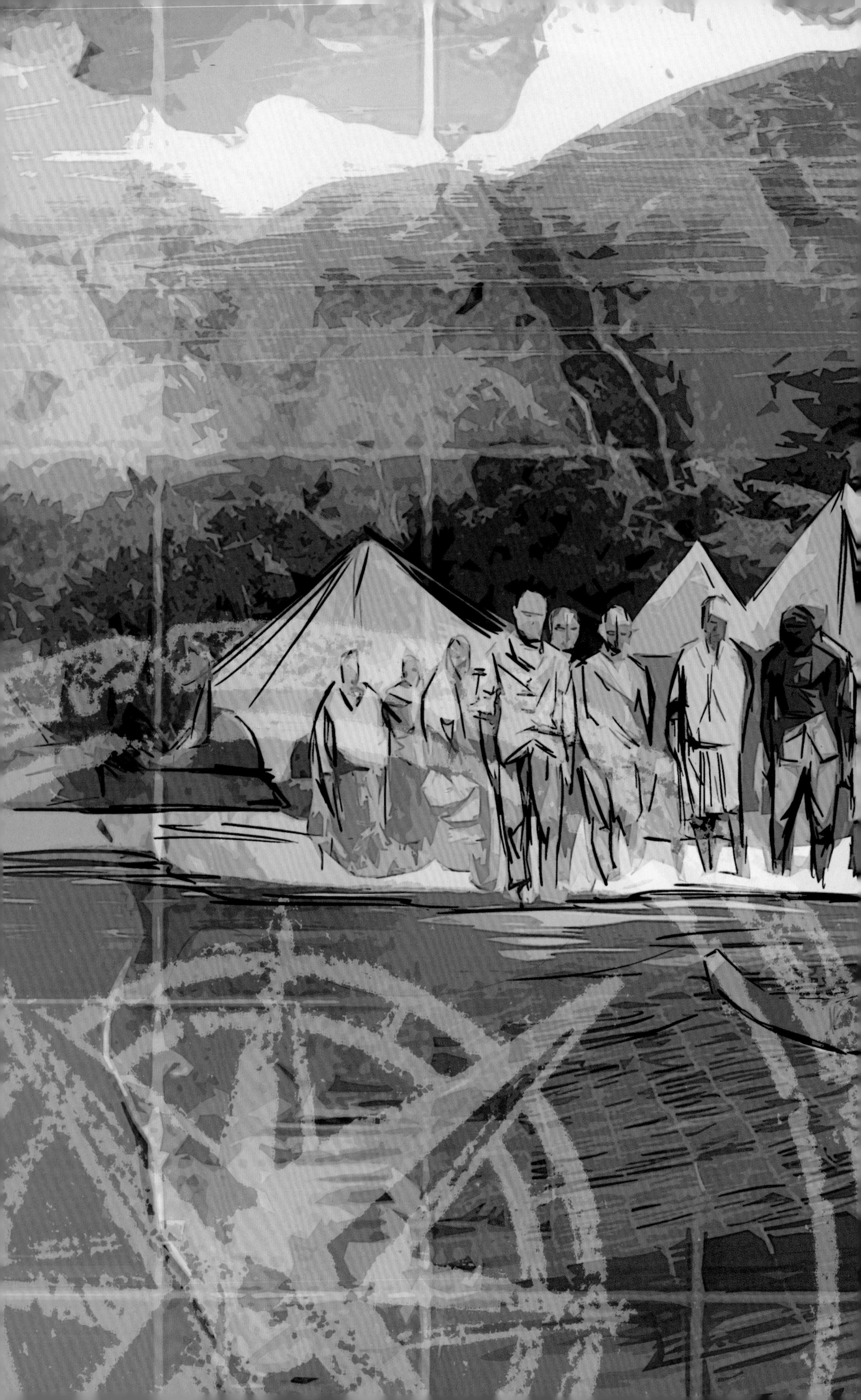

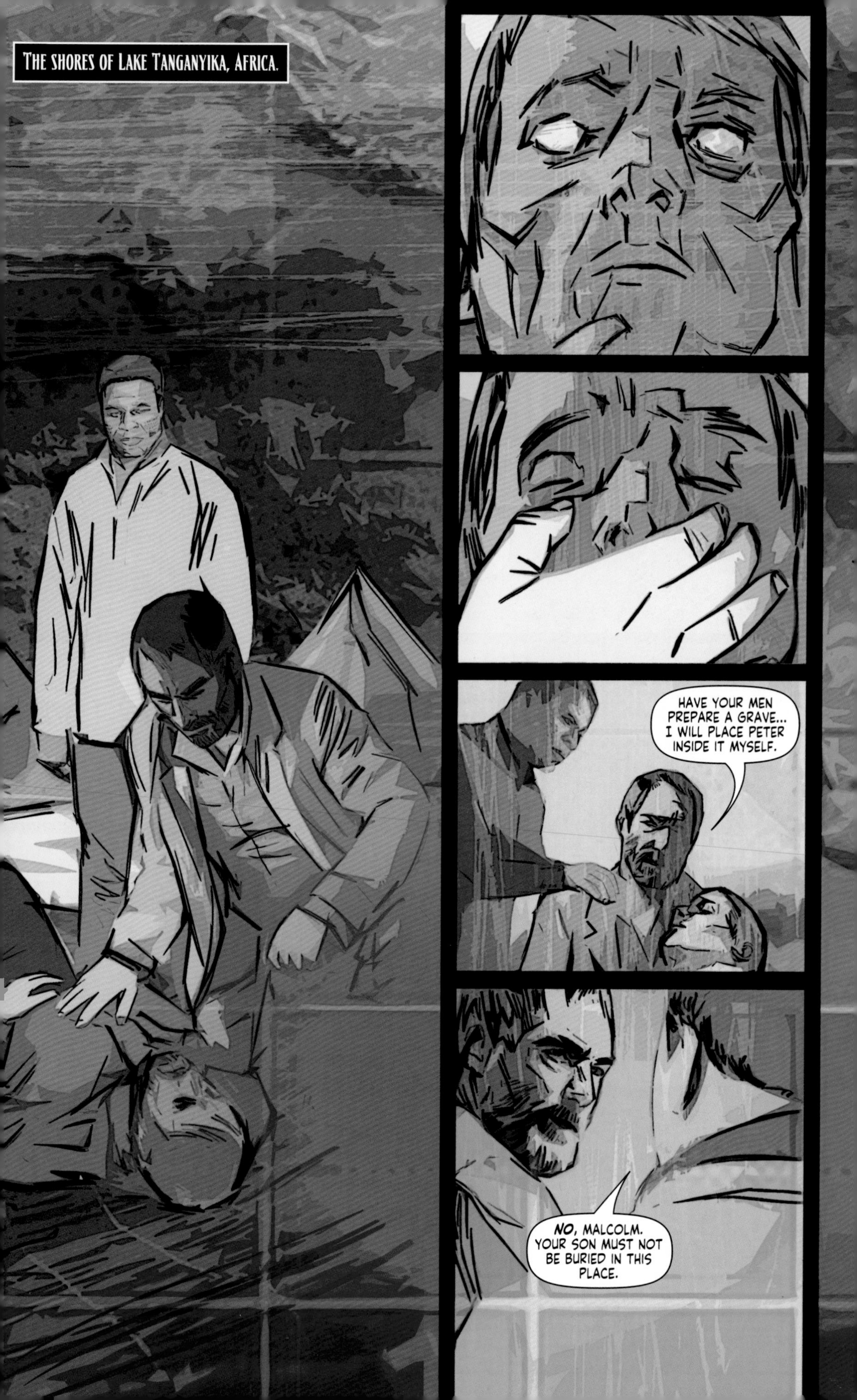
THE SHORES OF LAKE TANGANYIKA, AFRICA.
HAVE YOUR MEN PREPARE A GRAVE... I WILL PLACE PETER INSIDE IT MYSELF.
NO, MALCOLM. YOUR SON MUST NOT BE BURIED IN THIS PLACE.

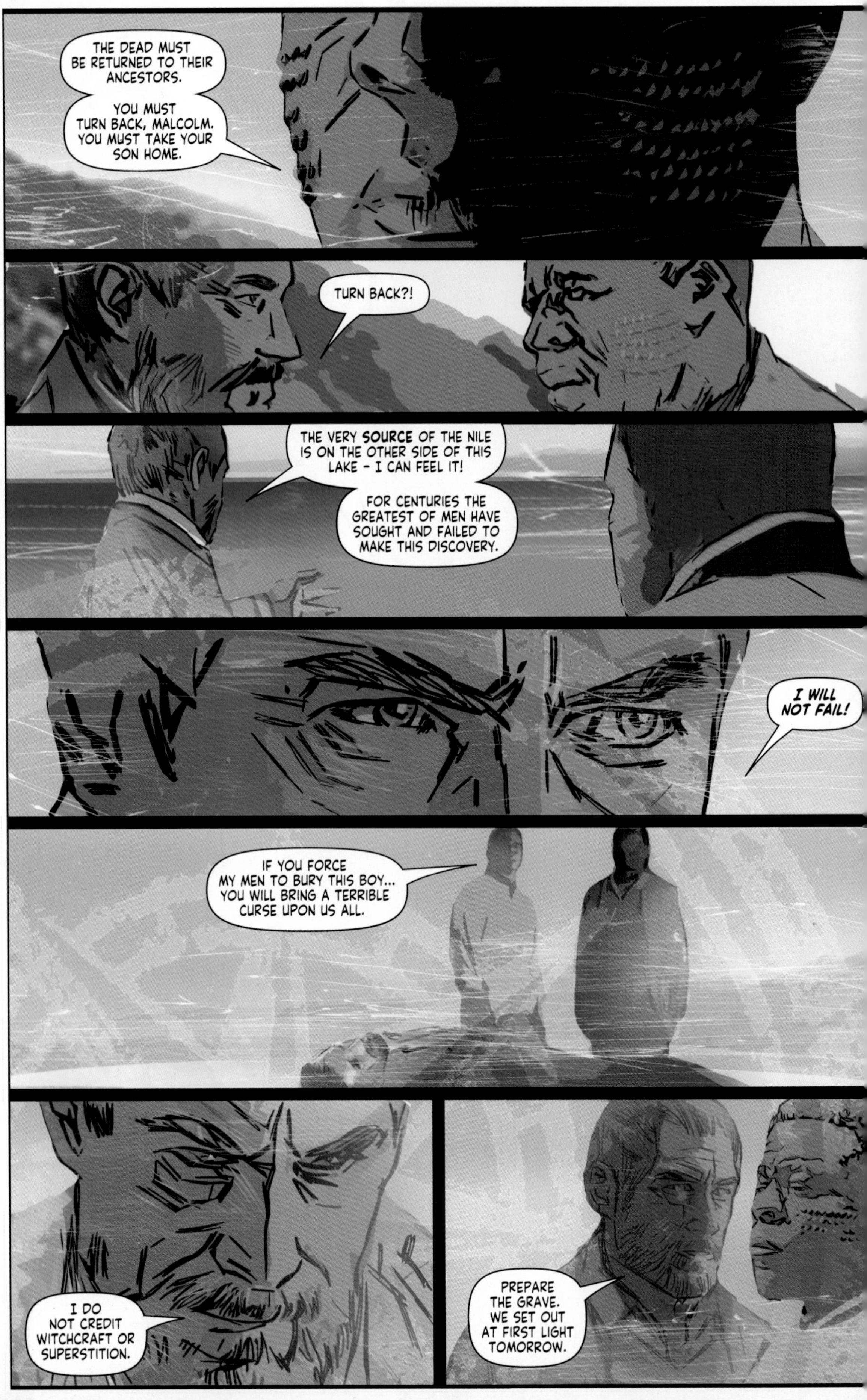
THE DEAD MUST BE RETURNED TO THEIR ANCESTORS.
YOU MUST TURN BACK, MALCOLM. YOU MUST TAKE YOUR SON HOME.
TURN BACK?!
THE VERY SOURCE OF THE NILE IS ON THE OTHER SIDE OF THIS LAKE – I CAN FEEL IT!
FOR CENTURIES THE GREATEST OF MEN HAVE SOUGHT AND FAILED TO MAKE THIS DISCOVERY.
I WILL NOT FAIL!
IF YOU FORCE MY MEN TO BURY THIS BOY... YOU WILL BRING A TERRIBLE CURSE UPON US ALL.
I DO NOT CREDIT WITCHCRAFT OR SUPERSTITION.
PREPARE THE GRAVE. WE SET OUT AT FIRST LIGHT TOMORROW.

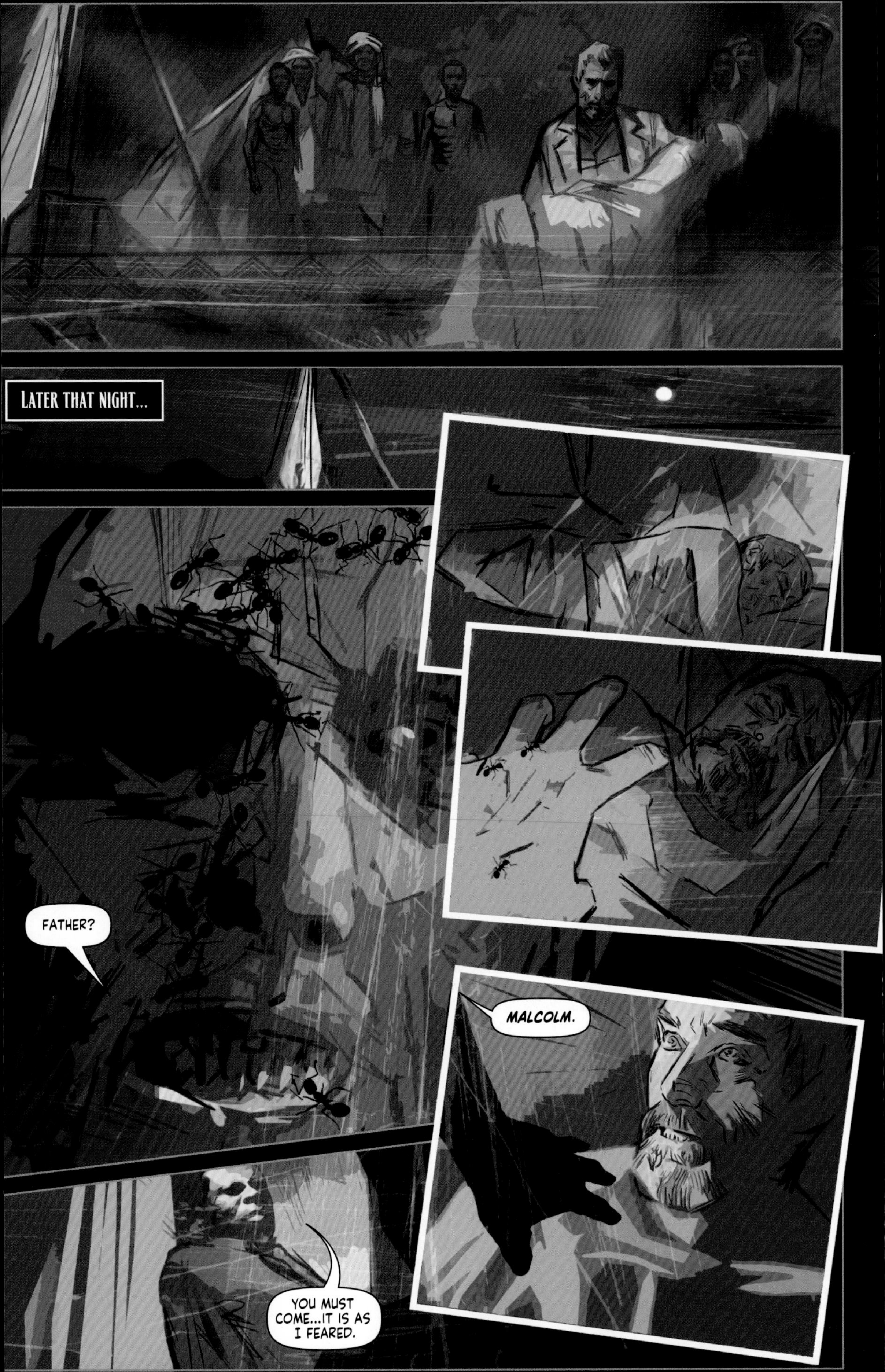
LATER THAT NIGHT...
FATHER?
MALCOLM.
YOU MUST COME...IT IS AS I FEARED.

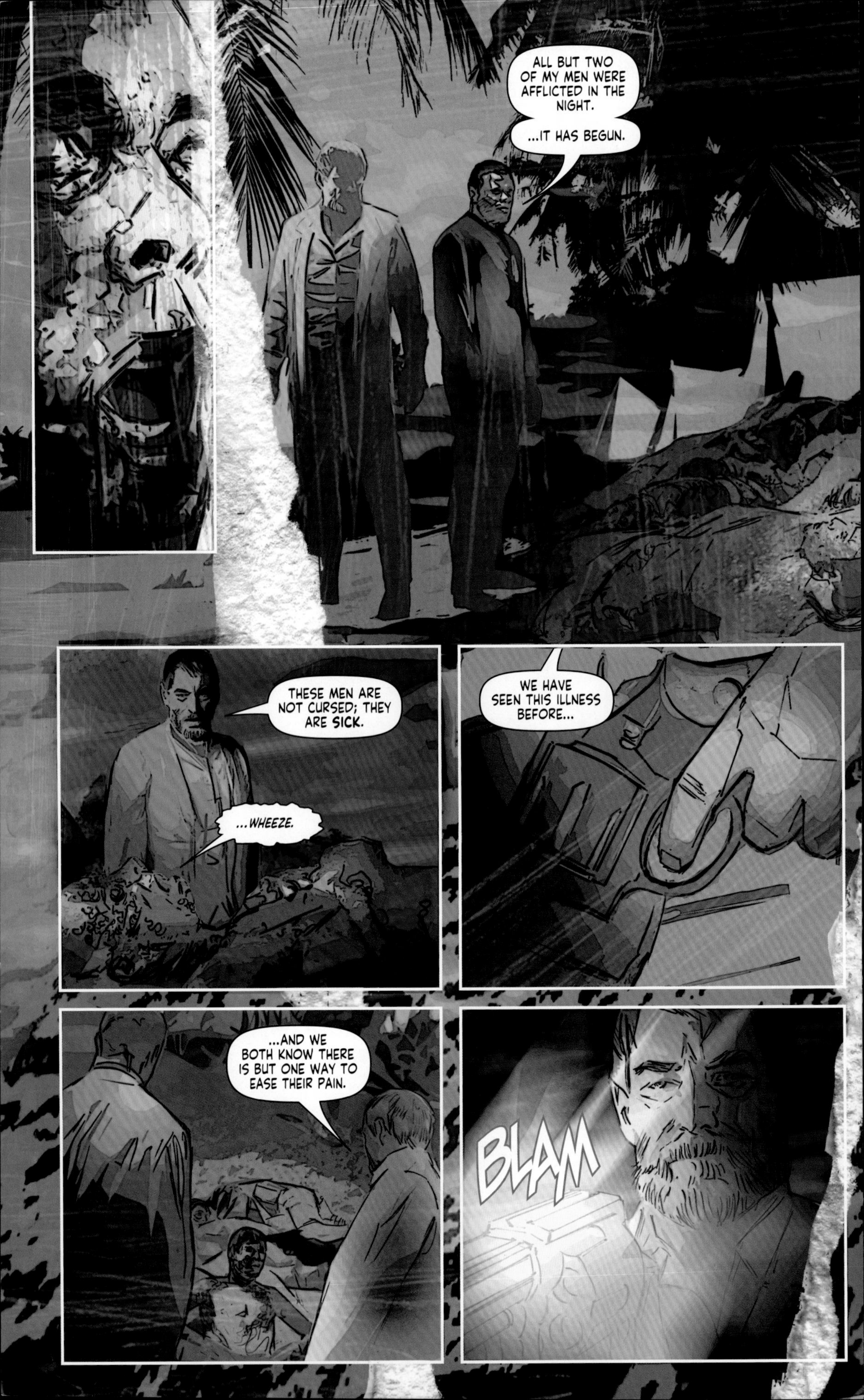
ALL BUT TWO OF MY MEN WERE AFFLICTED IN THE NIGHT.
...IT HAS BEGUN.
THESE MEN ARE NOT CURSED; THEY ARE SICK.
...WHEEZE.
WE HAVE SEEN THIS ILLNESS BEFORE...
...AND WE BOTH KNOW THERE IS BUT ONE WAY TO EASE THEIR PAIN.
BLAM

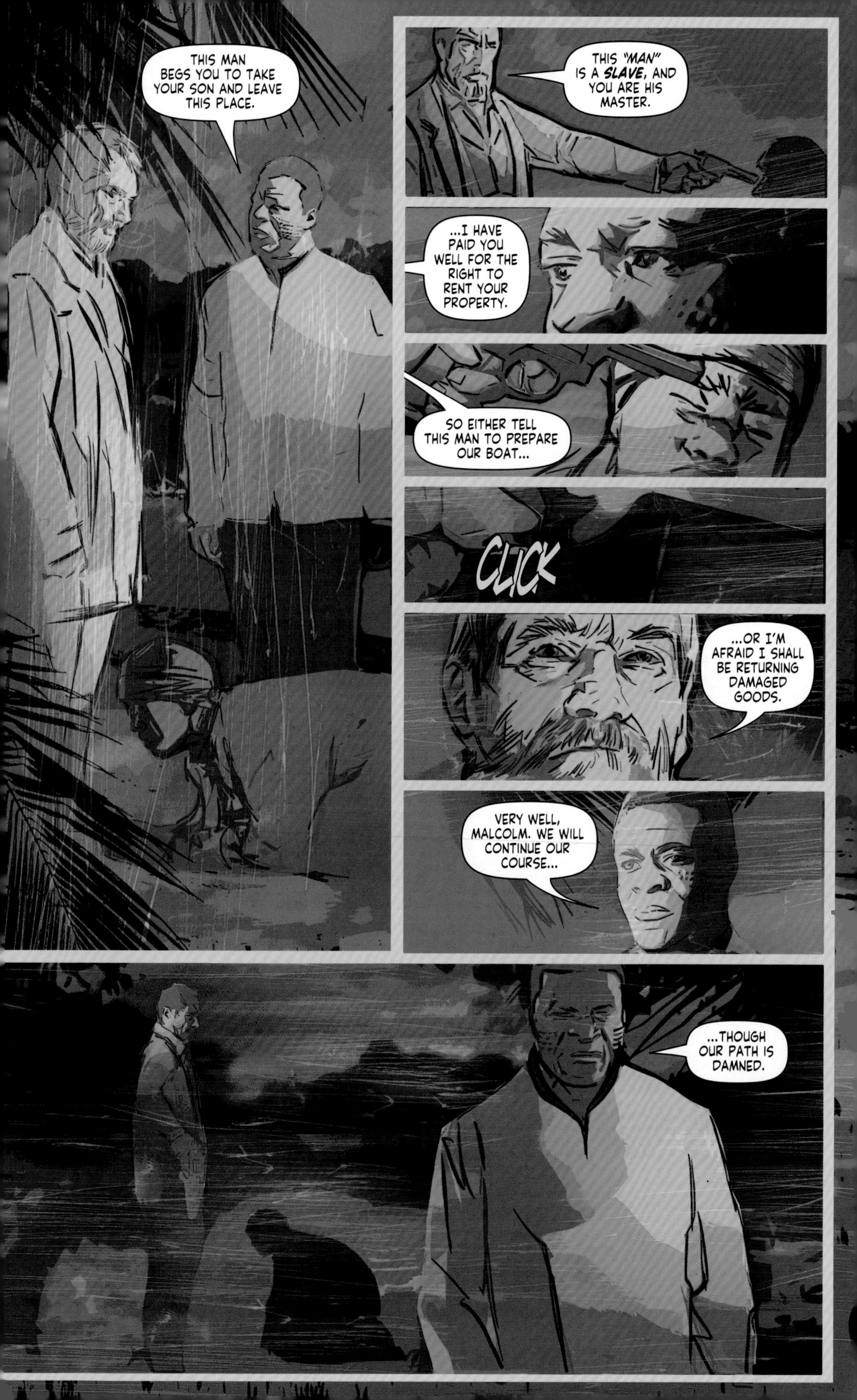
THIS MAN BEGS YOU TO TAKE YOUR SON AND LEAVE THIS PLACE.
THIS "MAN" IS A **SLAVE**, AND YOU ARE HIS MASTER.
...I HAVE PAID YOU WELL FOR THE RIGHT TO RENT YOUR PROPERTY.
SO EITHER TELL THIS MAN TO PREPARE OUR BOAT...
CLICK
...OR I'M AFRAID I SHALL BE RETURNING DAMAGED GOODS.
VERY WELL, MALCOLM. WE WILL CONTINUE OUR COURSE...
...THOUGH OUR PATH IS DAMNED.

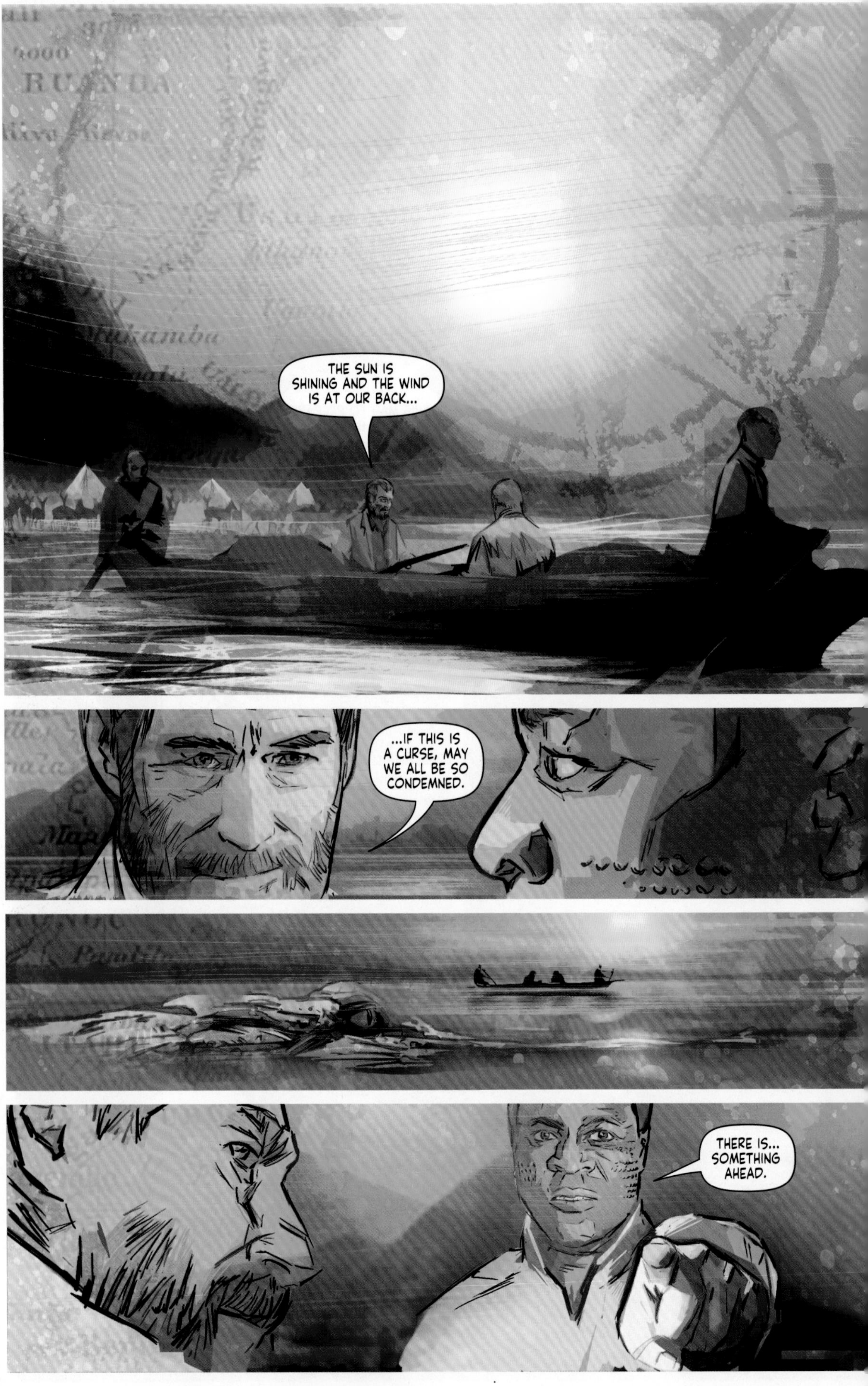
THE SUN IS SHINING AND THE WIND IS AT OUR BACK...
...IF THIS IS A CURSE, MAY WE ALL BE SO CONDEMNED.
THERE IS... SOMETHING AHEAD.

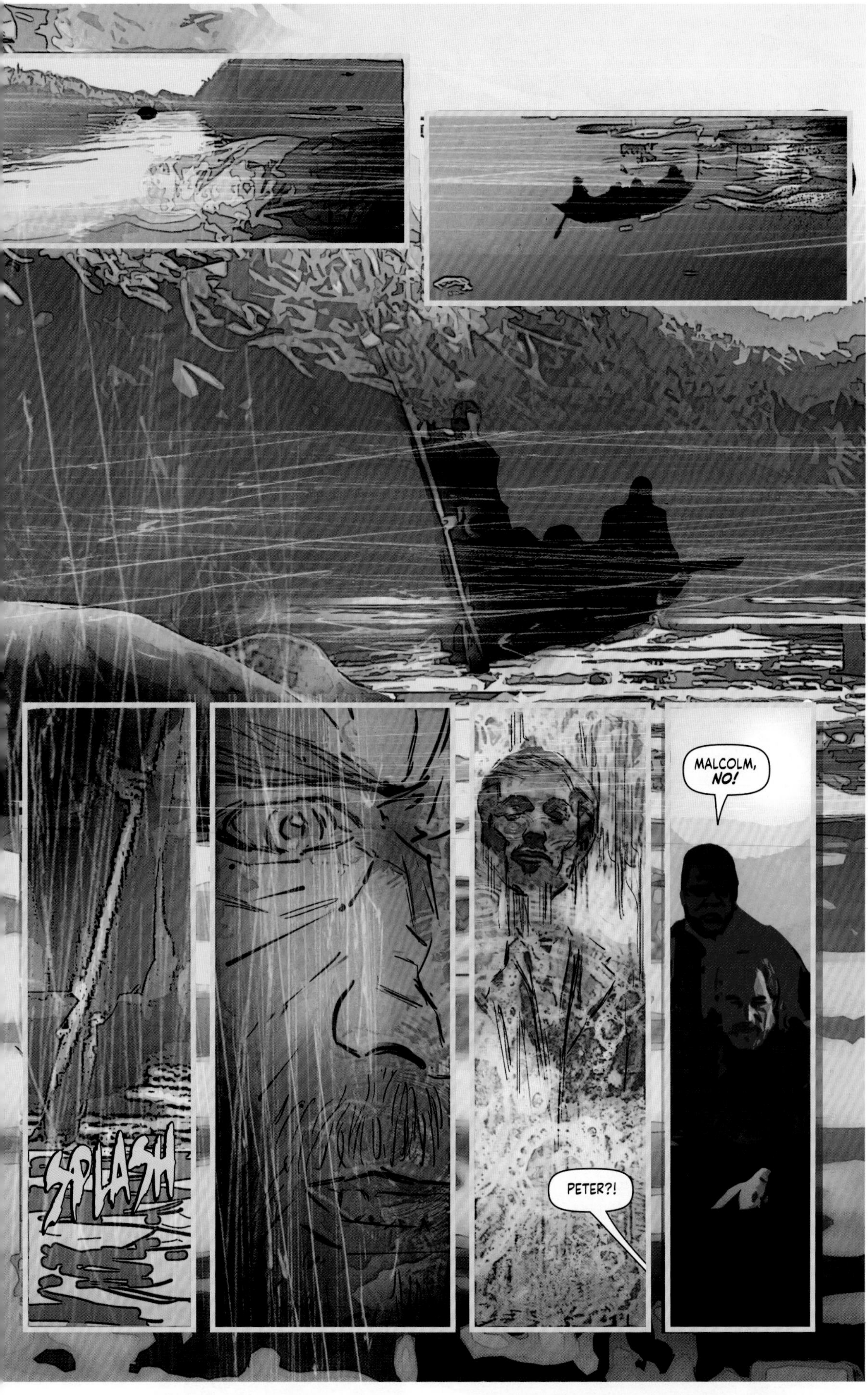
SPLASH
PETER?!
MALCOLM, NO!

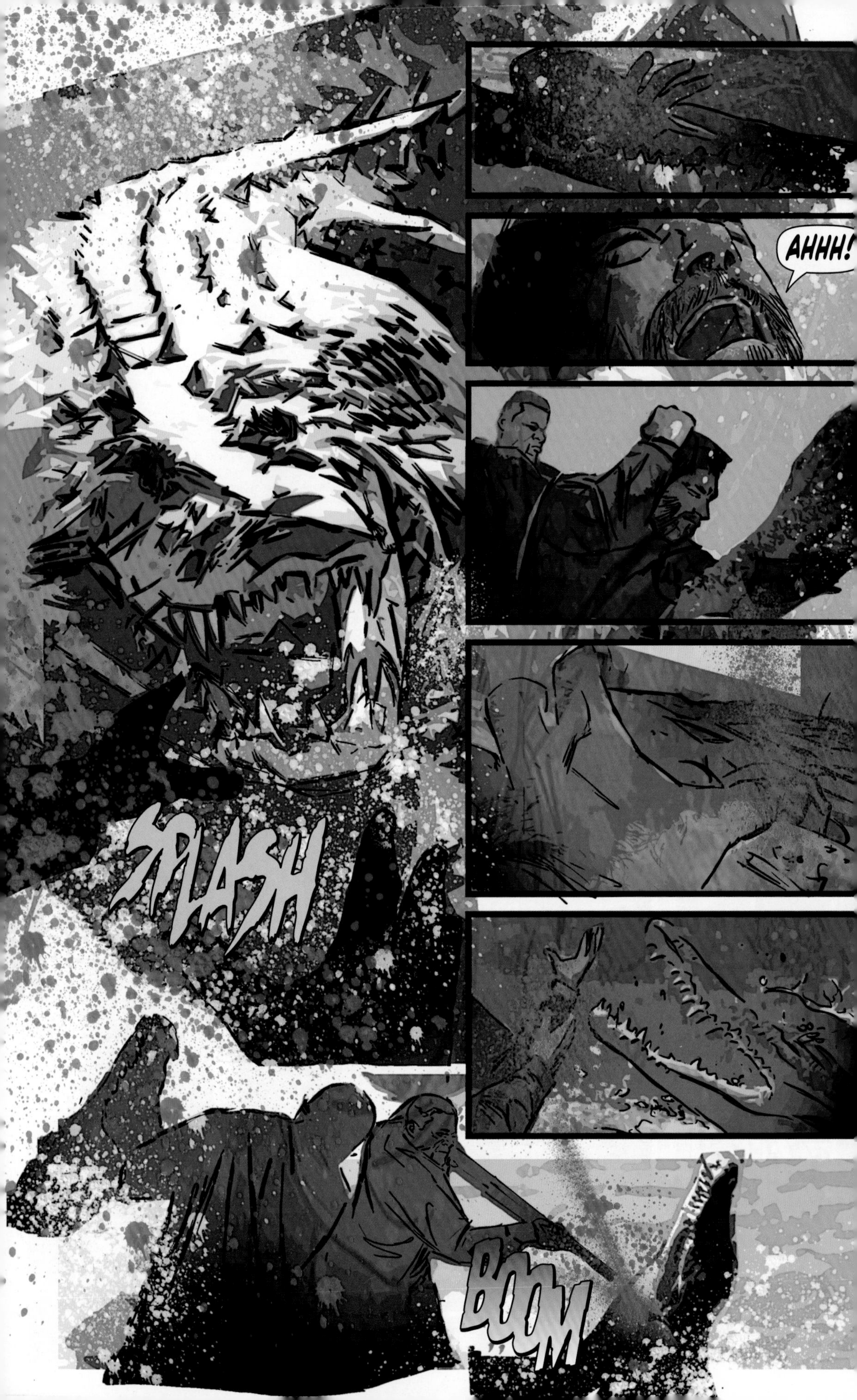
AHHH!
SPLASH
BOOM

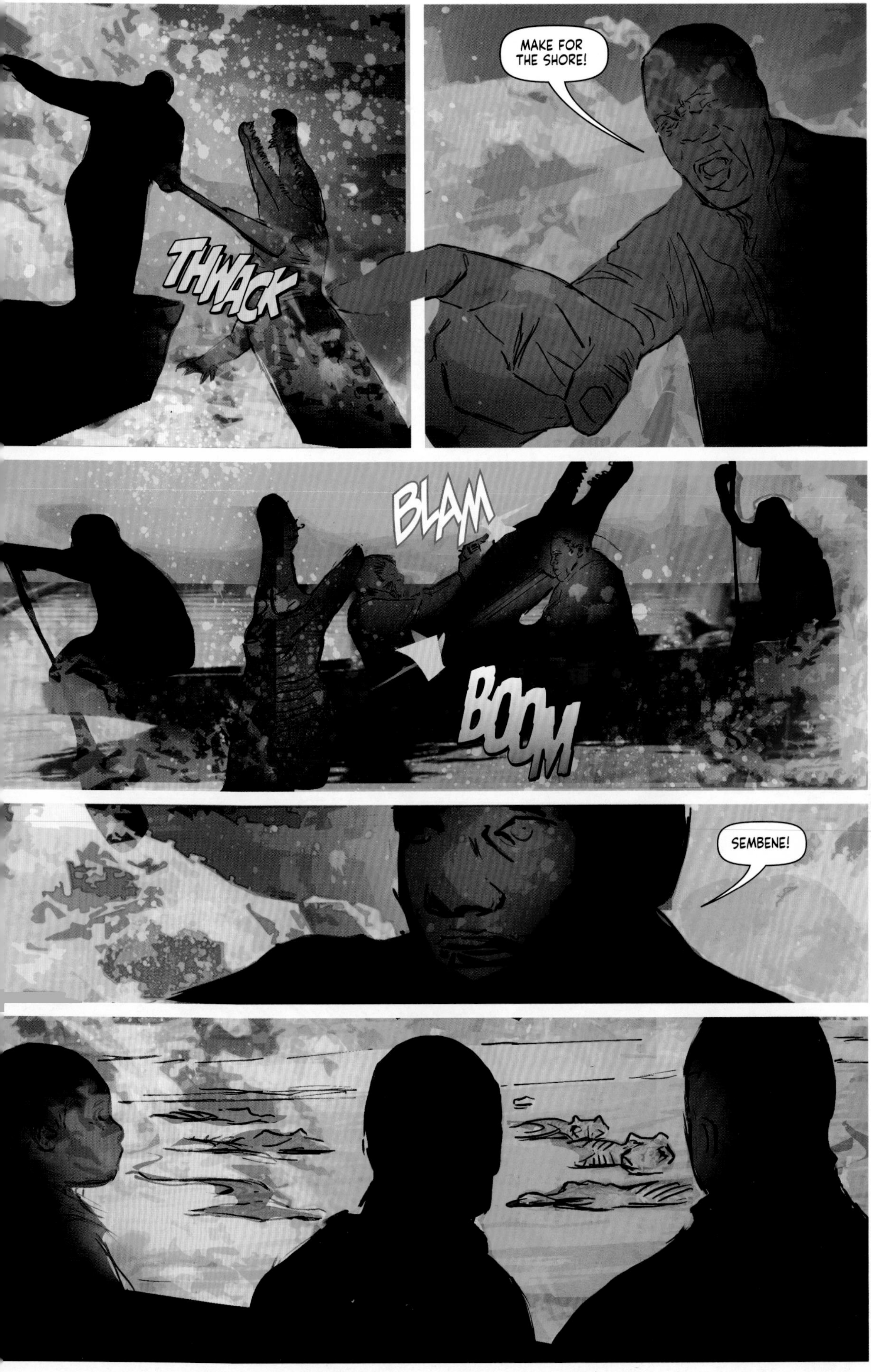
THWACK
MAKE FOR THE SHORE!
BLAM
BOOM
SEMBENE!

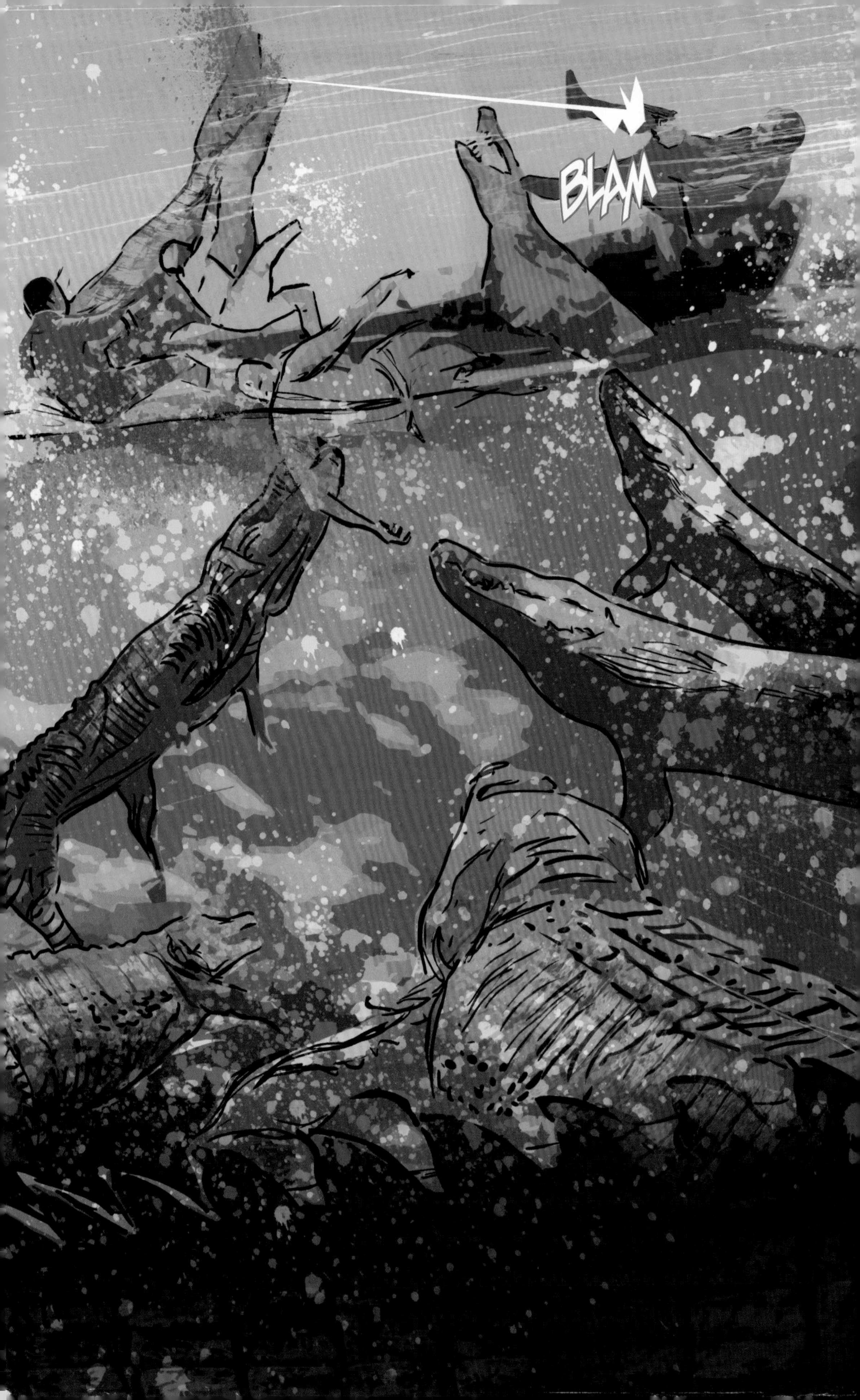
BLAM

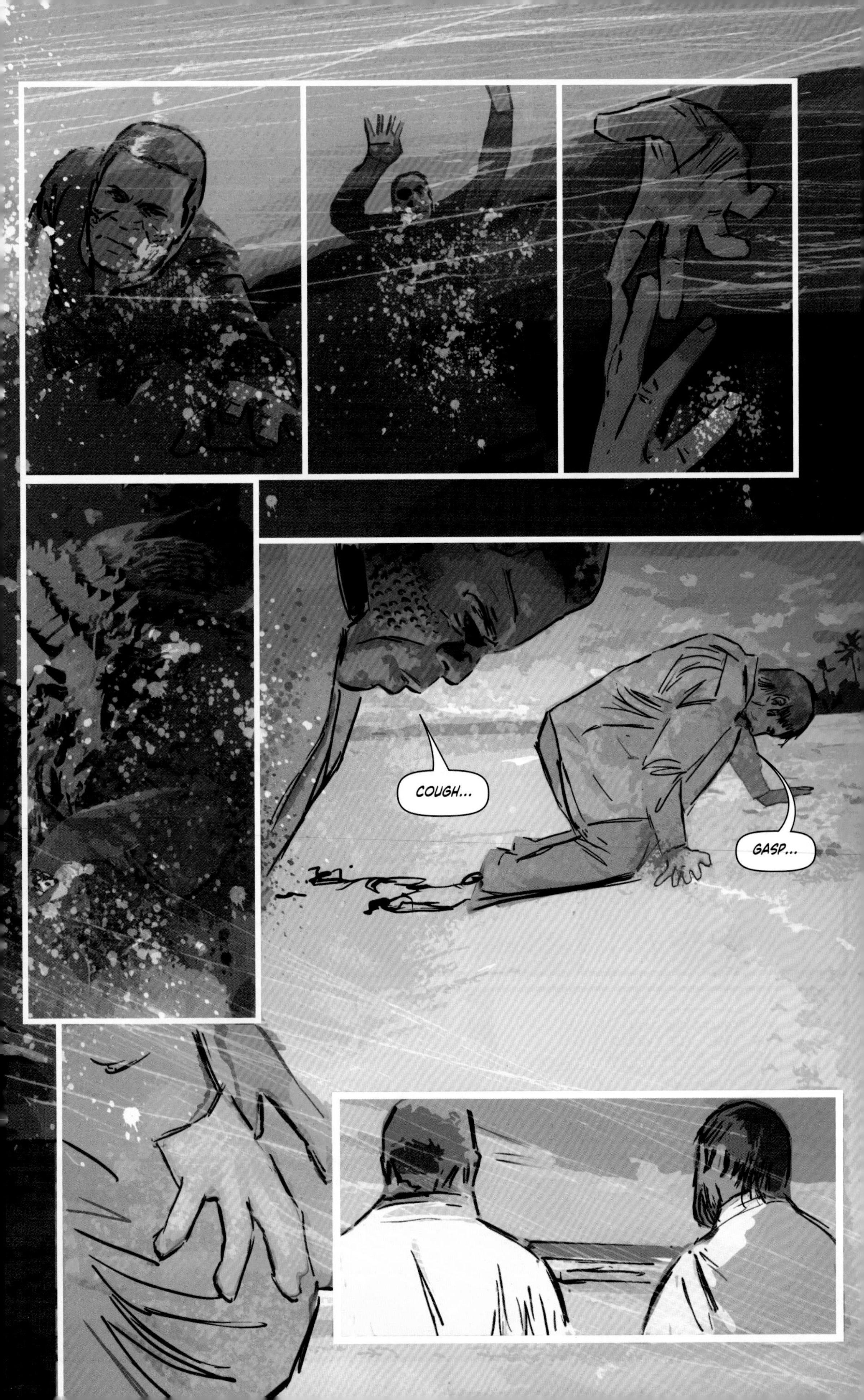
COUGH...
GASP...

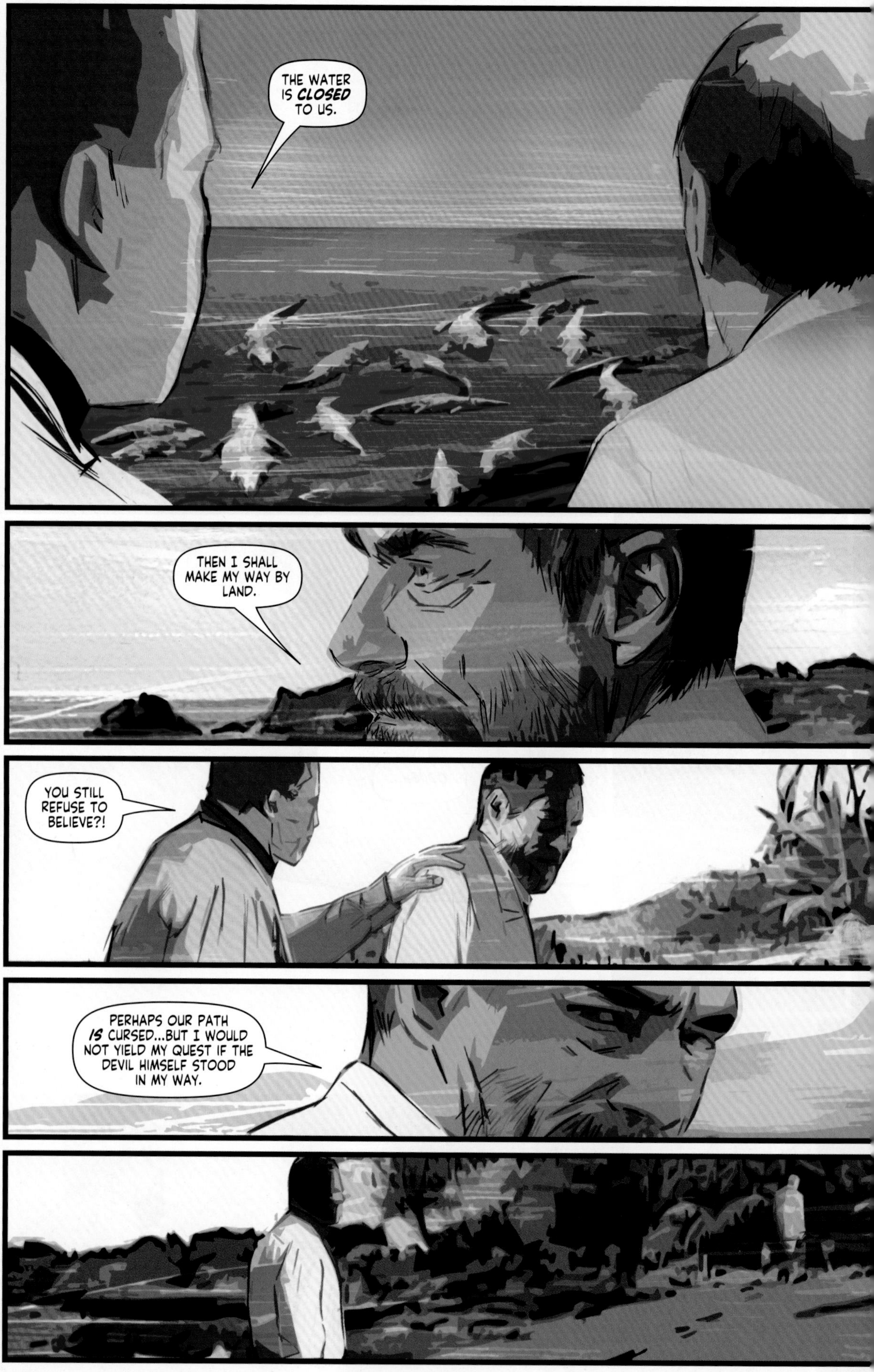
THE WATER IS CLOSED TO US.
THEN I SHALL MAKE MY WAY BY LAND.
YOU STILL REFUSE TO BELIEVE?!
PERHAPS OUR PATH IS CURSED...BUT I WOULD NOT YIELD MY QUEST IF THE DEVIL HIMSELF STOOD IN MY WAY.

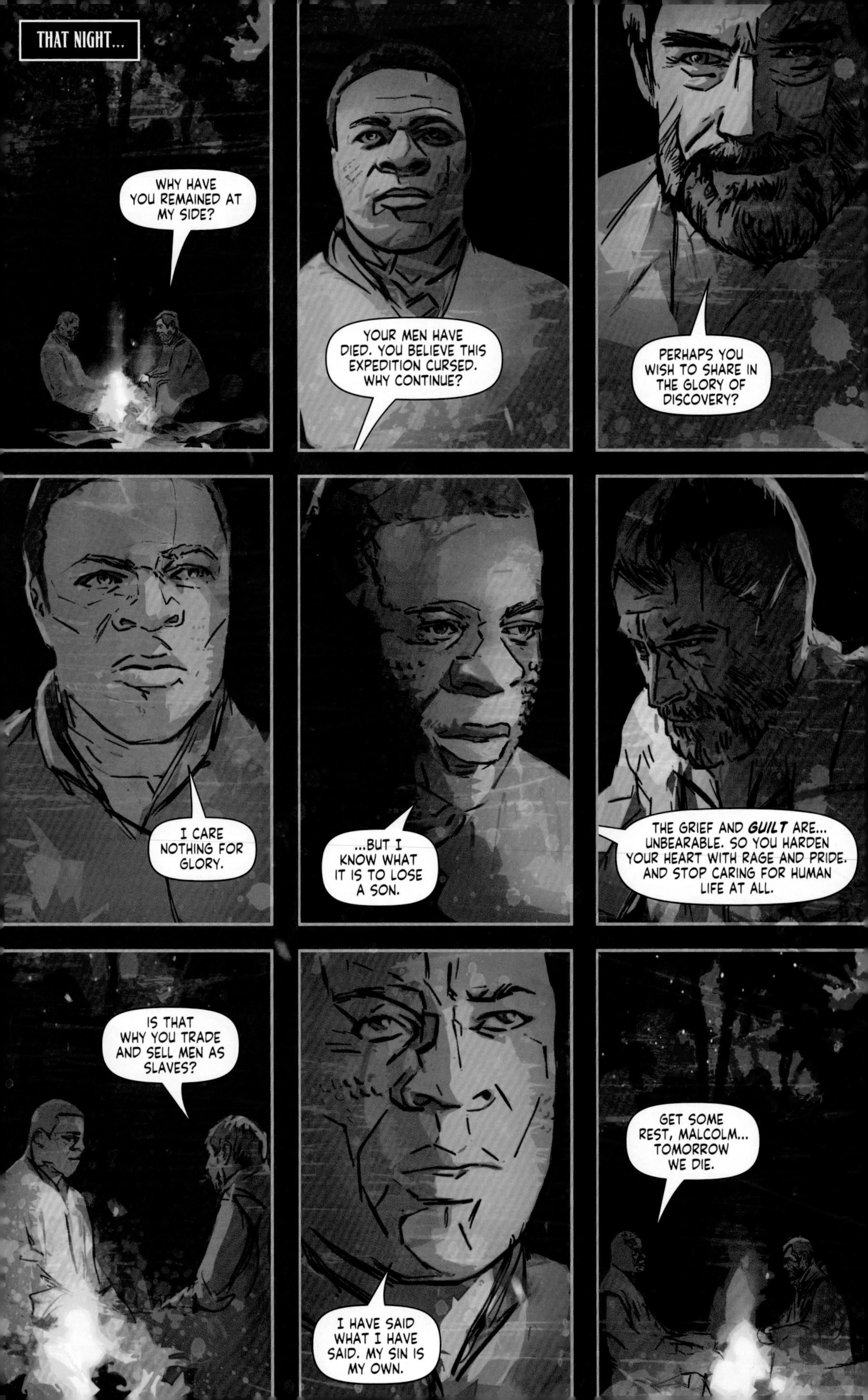
THAT NIGHT...
WHY HAVE YOU REMAINED AT MY SIDE?
YOUR MEN HAVE DIED. YOU BELIEVE THIS EXPEDITION CURSED. WHY CONTINUE?
PERHAPS YOU WISH TO SHARE IN THE GLORY OF DISCOVERY?
I CARE NOTHING FOR GLORY.
...BUT I KNOW WHAT IT IS TO LOSE A SON.
THE GRIEF AND *GUILT* ARE... UNBEARABLE. SO YOU HARDEN YOUR HEART WITH RAGE AND PRIDE. AND STOP CARING FOR HUMAN LIFE AT ALL.
IS THAT WHY YOU TRADE AND SELL MEN AS SLAVES?
I HAVE SAID WHAT I HAVE SAID. MY SIN IS MY OWN.
GET SOME REST, MALCOLM... TOMORROW WE DIE.

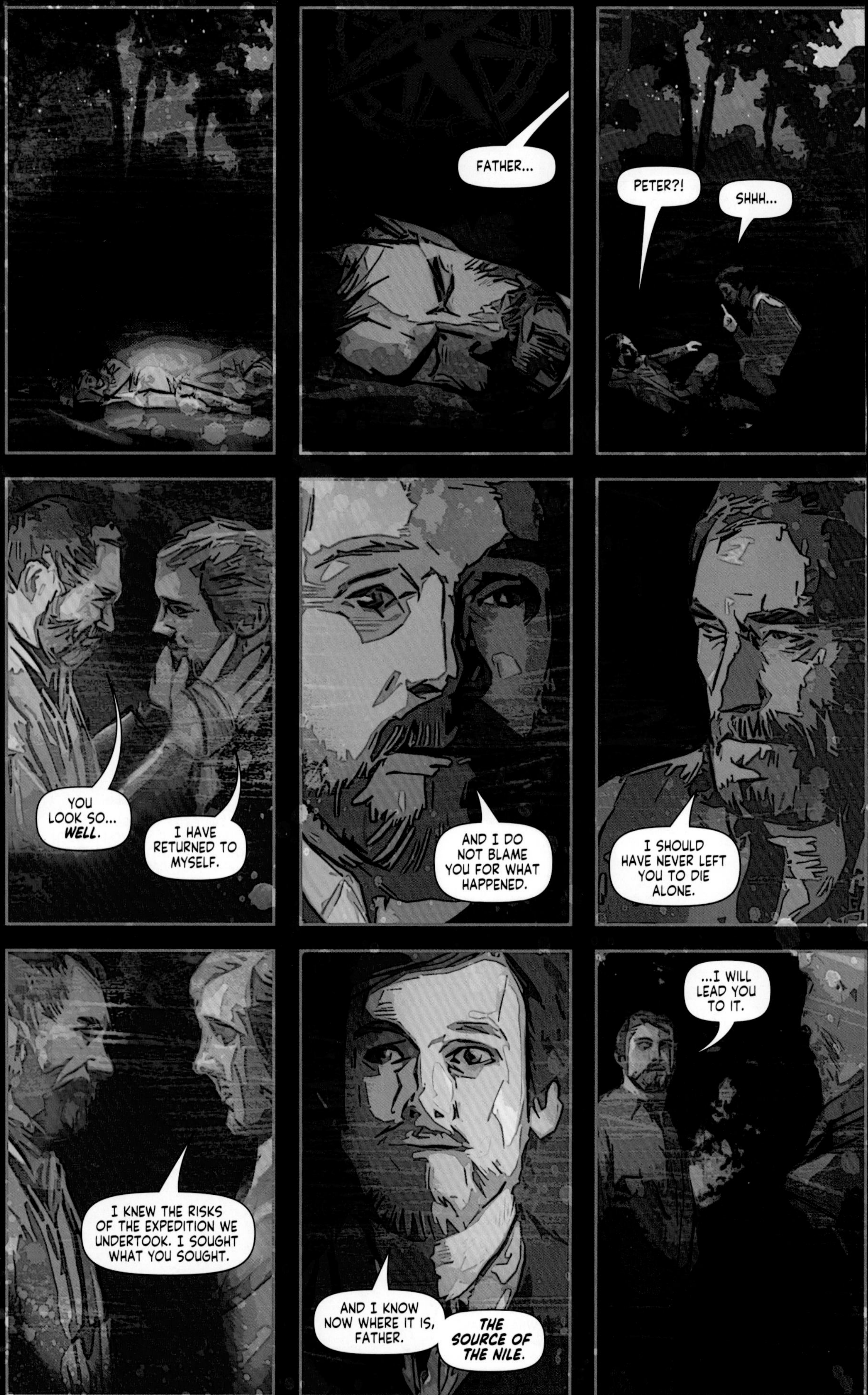
FATHER...
PETER?!
SHHH...
YOU LOOK SO... *WELL*.
I HAVE RETURNED TO MYSELF.
AND I DO NOT BLAME YOU FOR WHAT HAPPENED.
I SHOULD HAVE NEVER LEFT YOU TO DIE ALONE.
I KNEW THE RISKS OF THE EXPEDITION WE UNDERTOOK. I SOUGHT WHAT YOU SOUGHT.
AND I KNOW NOW WHERE IT IS, FATHER.
THE SOURCE OF THE NILE.
...I WILL LEAD YOU TO IT.

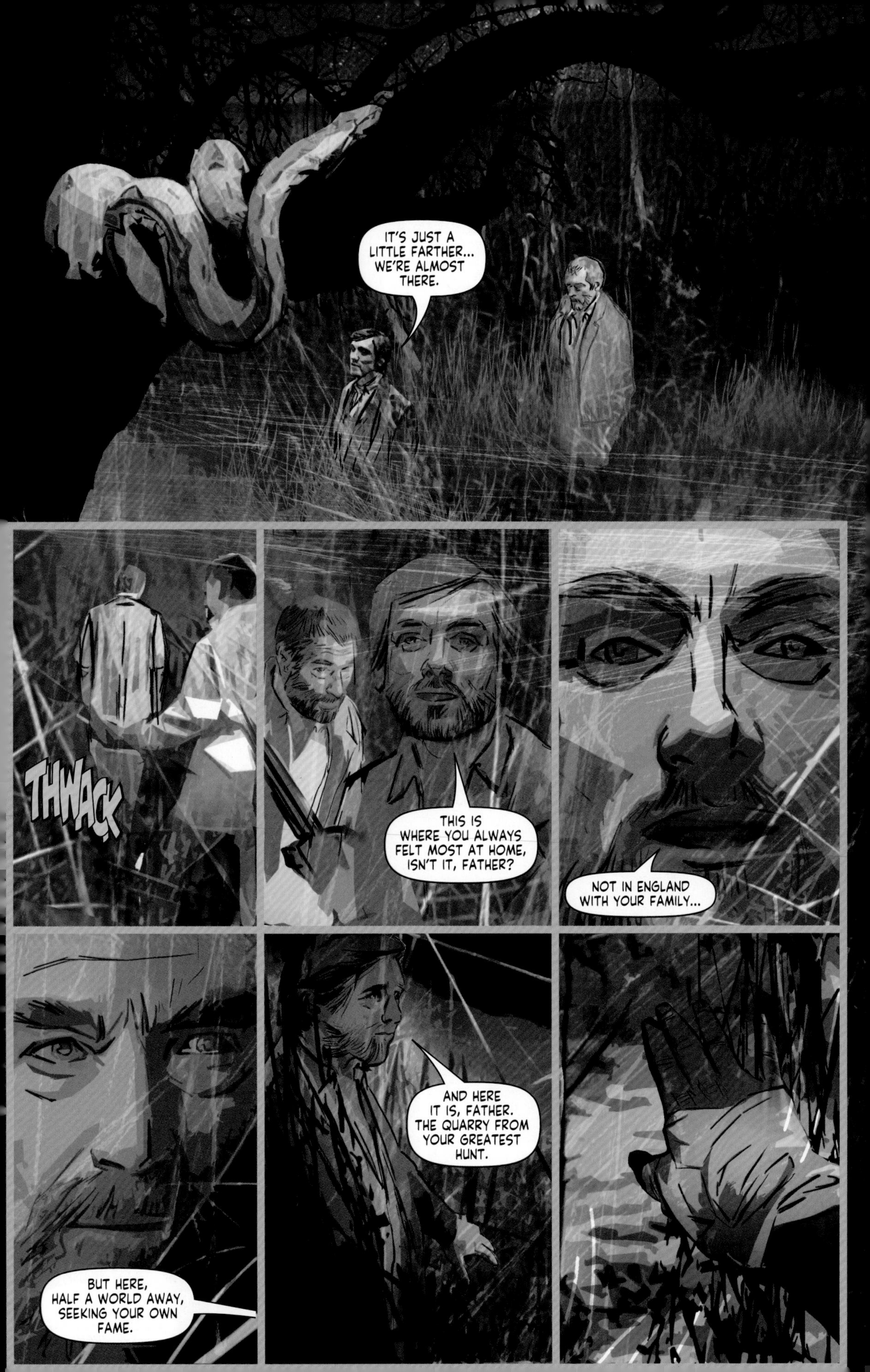
IT'S JUST A LITTLE FARTHER... WE'RE ALMOST THERE.
THWACK
THIS IS WHERE YOU ALWAYS FELT MOST AT HOME, ISN'T IT, FATHER?
NOT IN ENGLAND WITH YOUR FAMILY...
BUT HERE, HALF A WORLD AWAY, SEEKING YOUR OWN FAME.
AND HERE IT IS, FATHER. THE QUARRY FROM YOUR GREATEST HUNT.

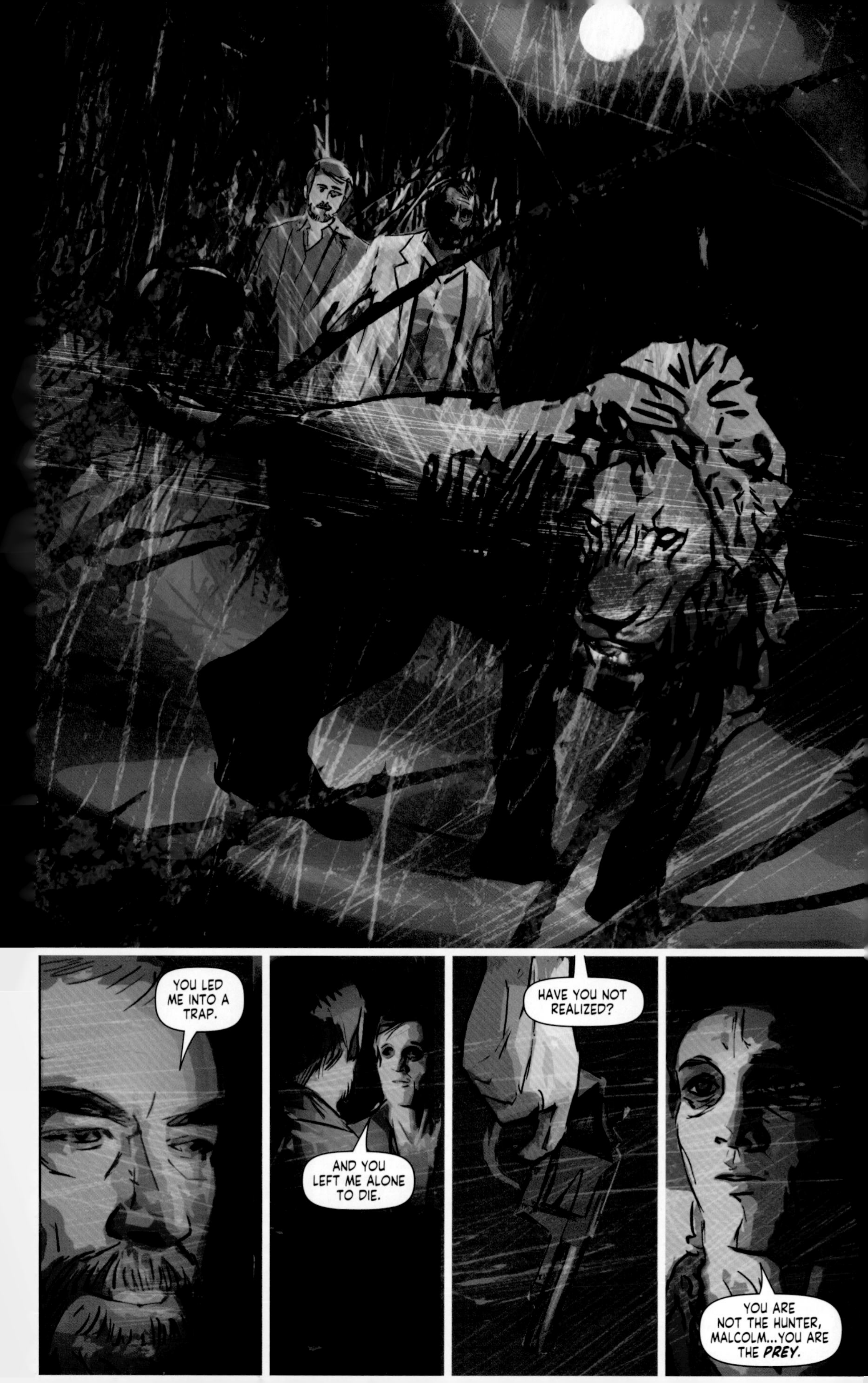
YOU LED ME INTO A TRAP.
AND YOU LEFT ME ALONE TO DIE.
HAVE YOU NOT REALIZED?
YOU ARE NOT THE HUNTER, MALCOLM...YOU ARE THE *PREY*.

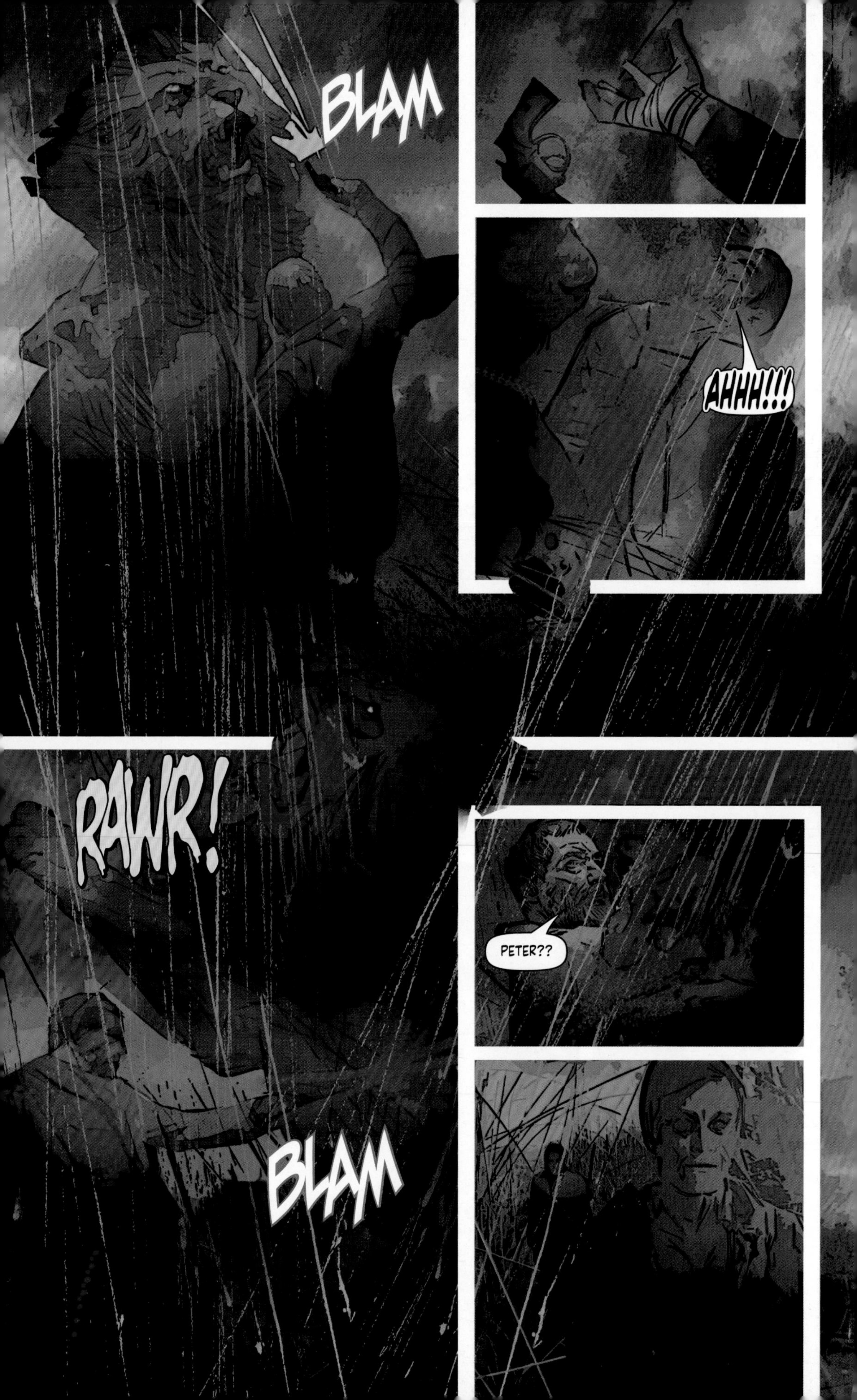
BLAM
AHHH!!!
RAWR!
BLAM
PETER??

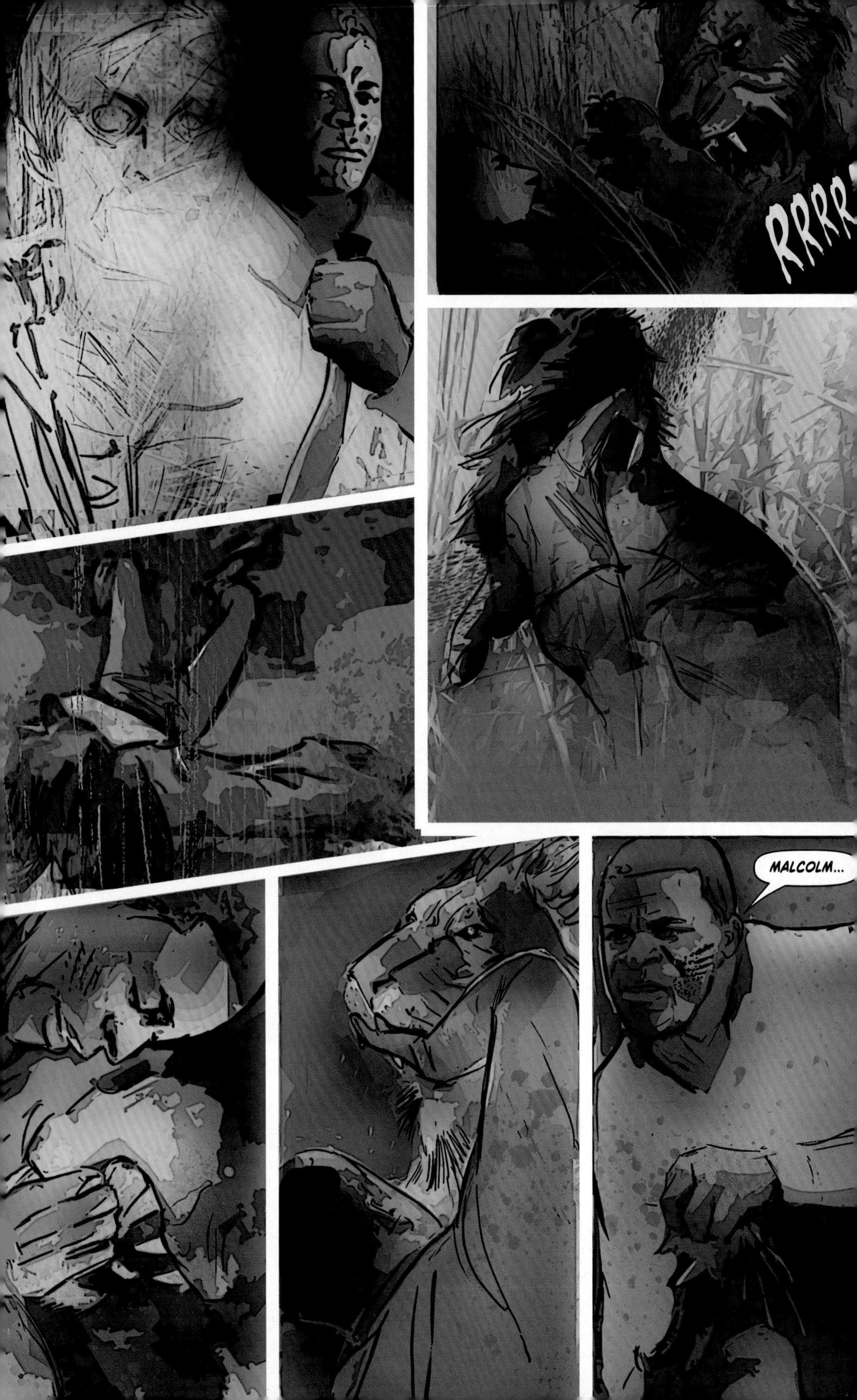
RRRR
MALCOLM...

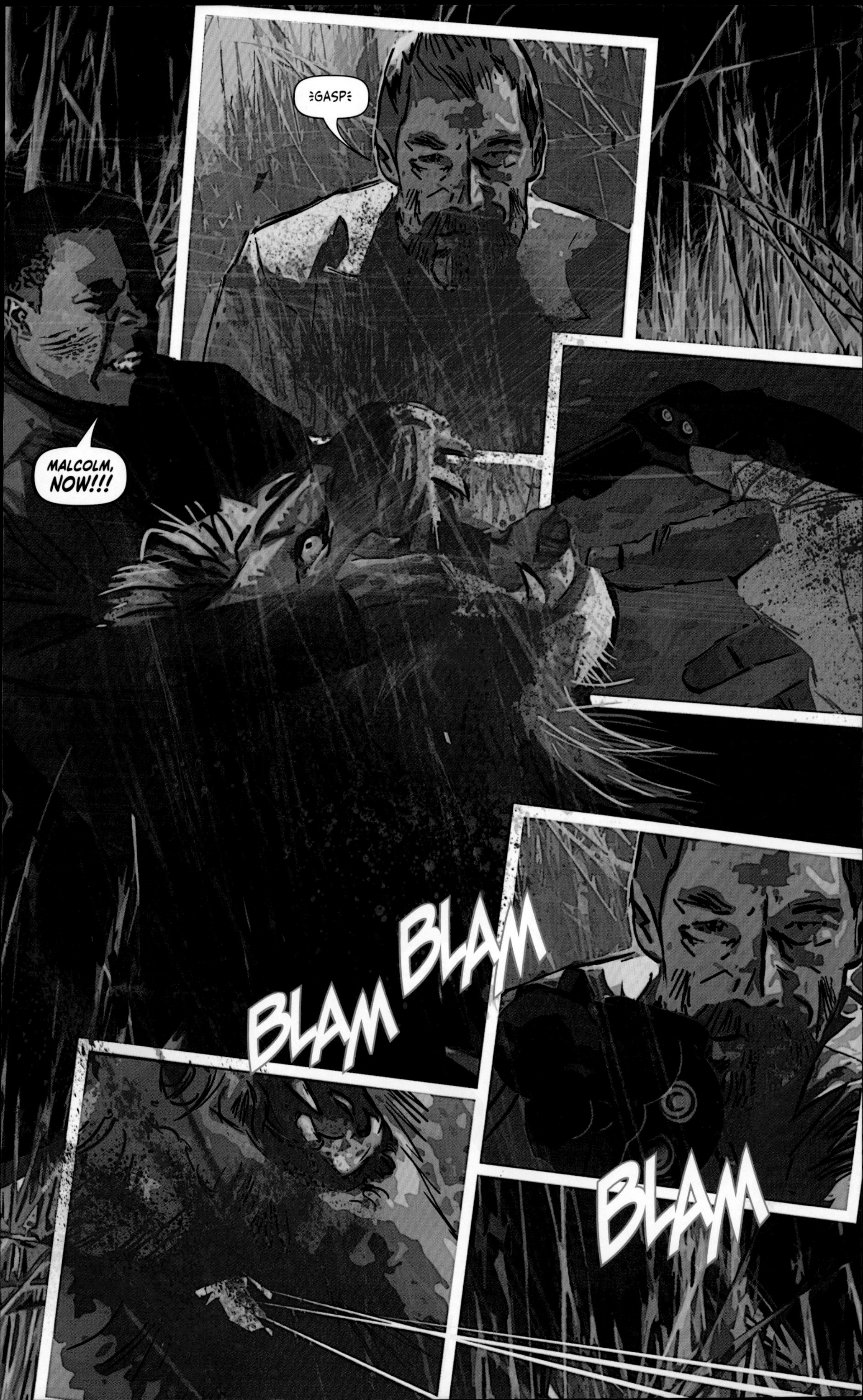

GASP
MALCOLM, NOW!!!
BLAM
BLAM
BLAM

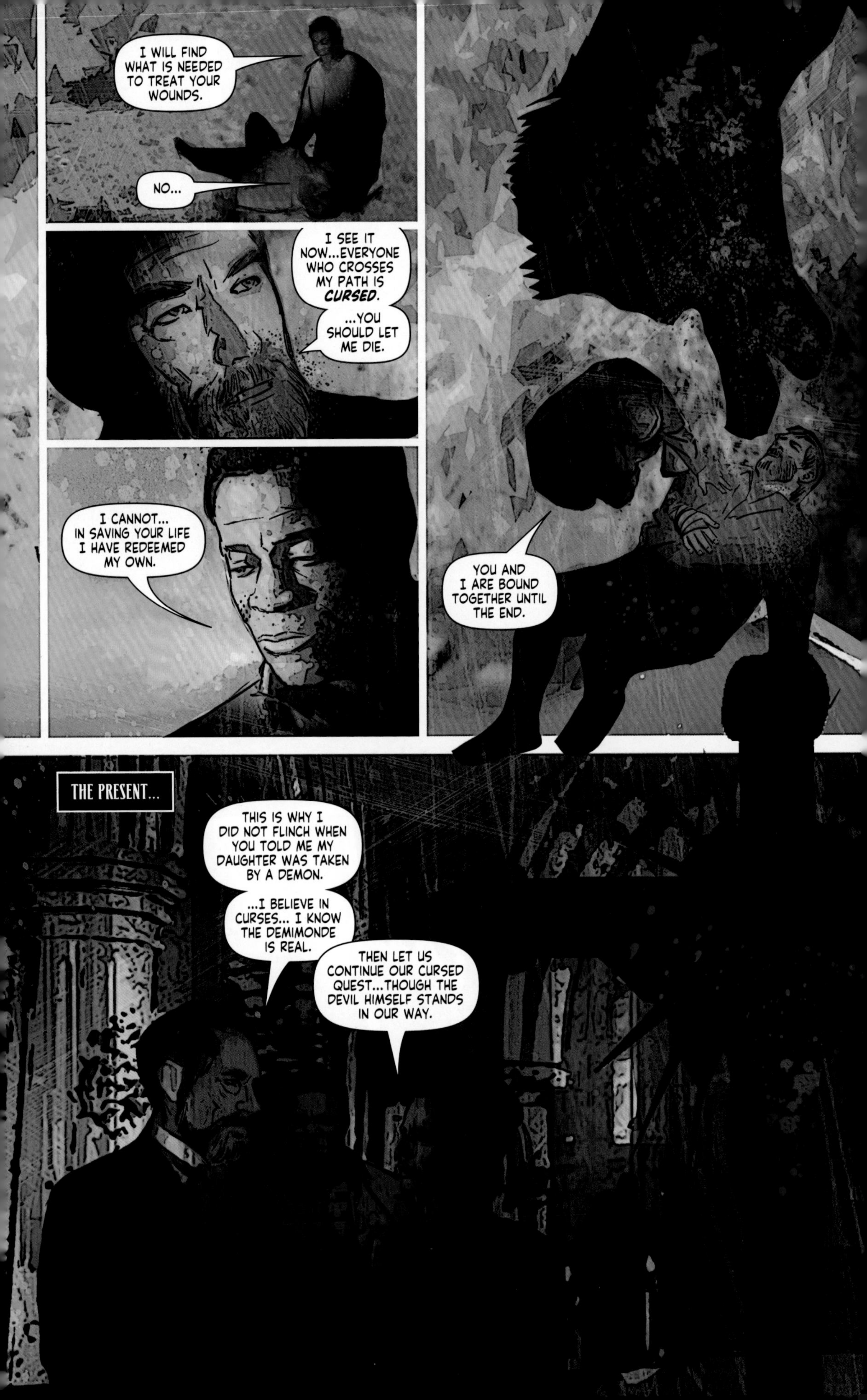
I WILL FIND WHAT IS NEEDED TO TREAT YOUR WOUNDS.
NO...
I SEE IT NOW...EVERYONE WHO CROSSES MY PATH IS *CURSED*.
...YOU SHOULD LET ME DIE.
I CANNOT... IN SAVING YOUR LIFE I HAVE REDEEMED MY OWN.
YOU AND I ARE BOUND TOGETHER UNTIL THE END.
THE PRESENT...
THIS IS WHY I DID NOT FLINCH WHEN YOU TOLD ME MY DAUGHTER WAS TAKEN BY A DEMON.
...I BELIEVE IN CURSES... I KNOW THE DEMIMONDE IS REAL.
THEN LET US CONTINUE OUR CURSED QUEST...THOUGH THE DEVIL HIMSELF STANDS IN OUR WAY.

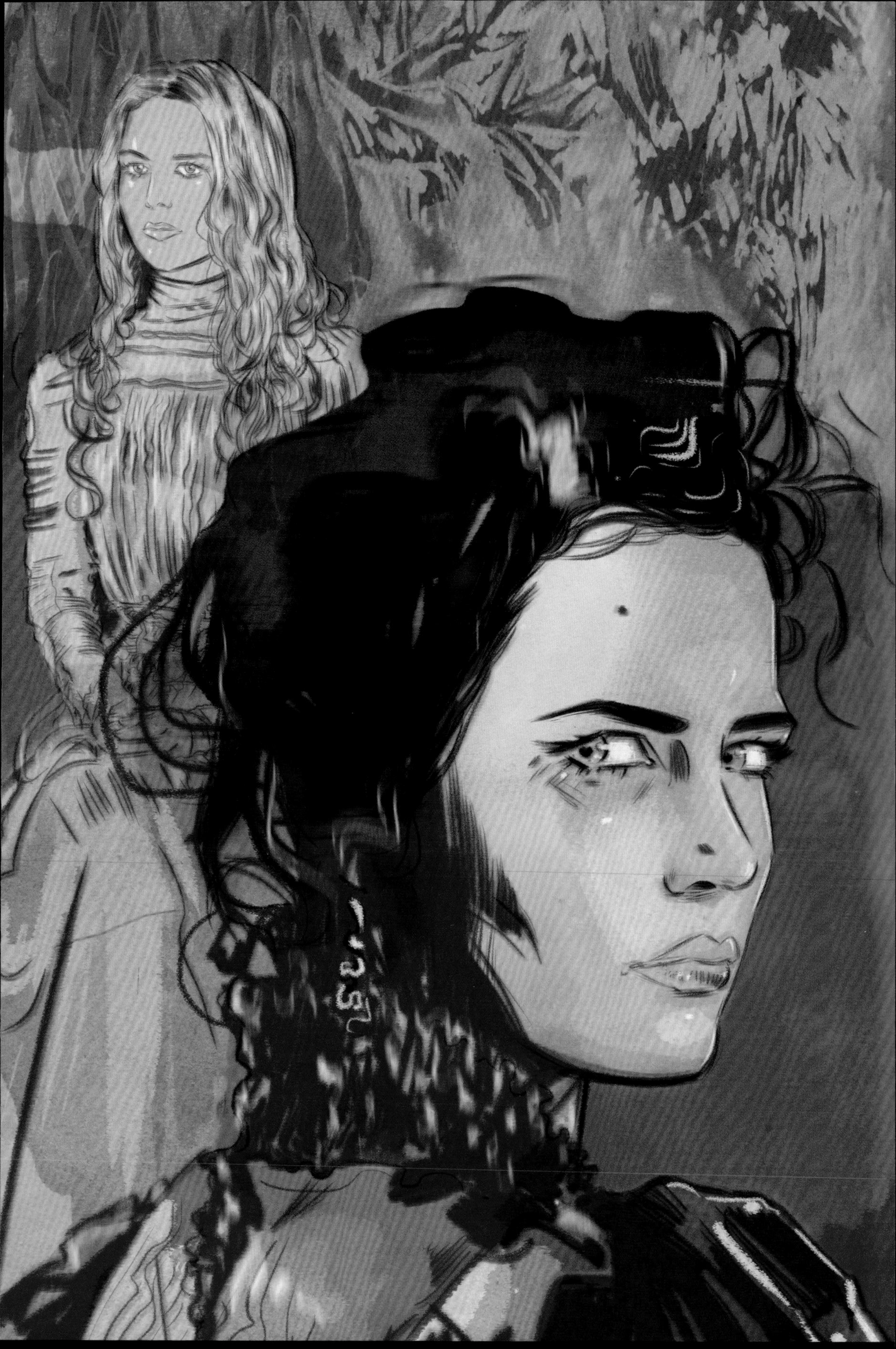

#4 COVER A - TULA LOTAY

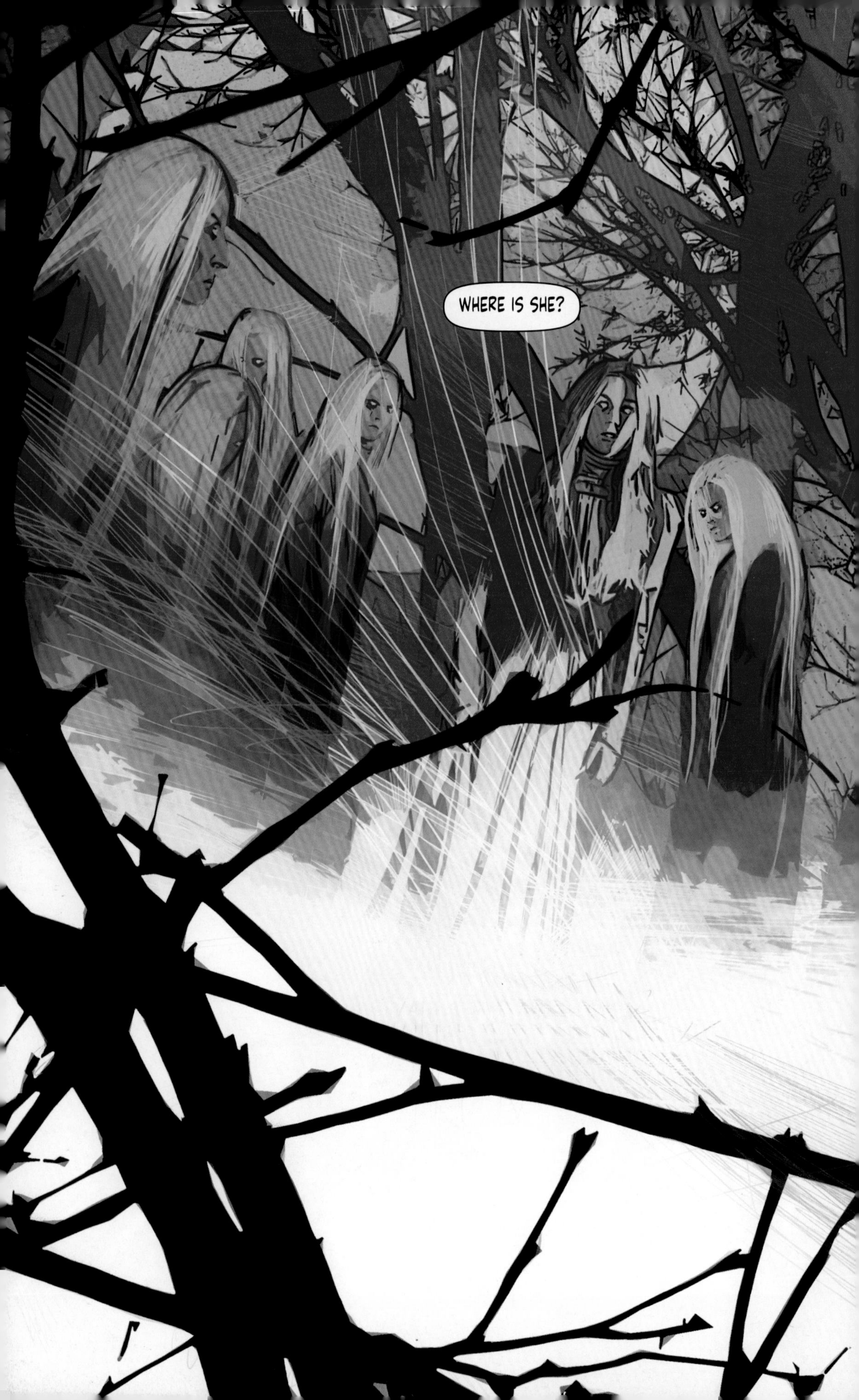
WHERE IS SHE?

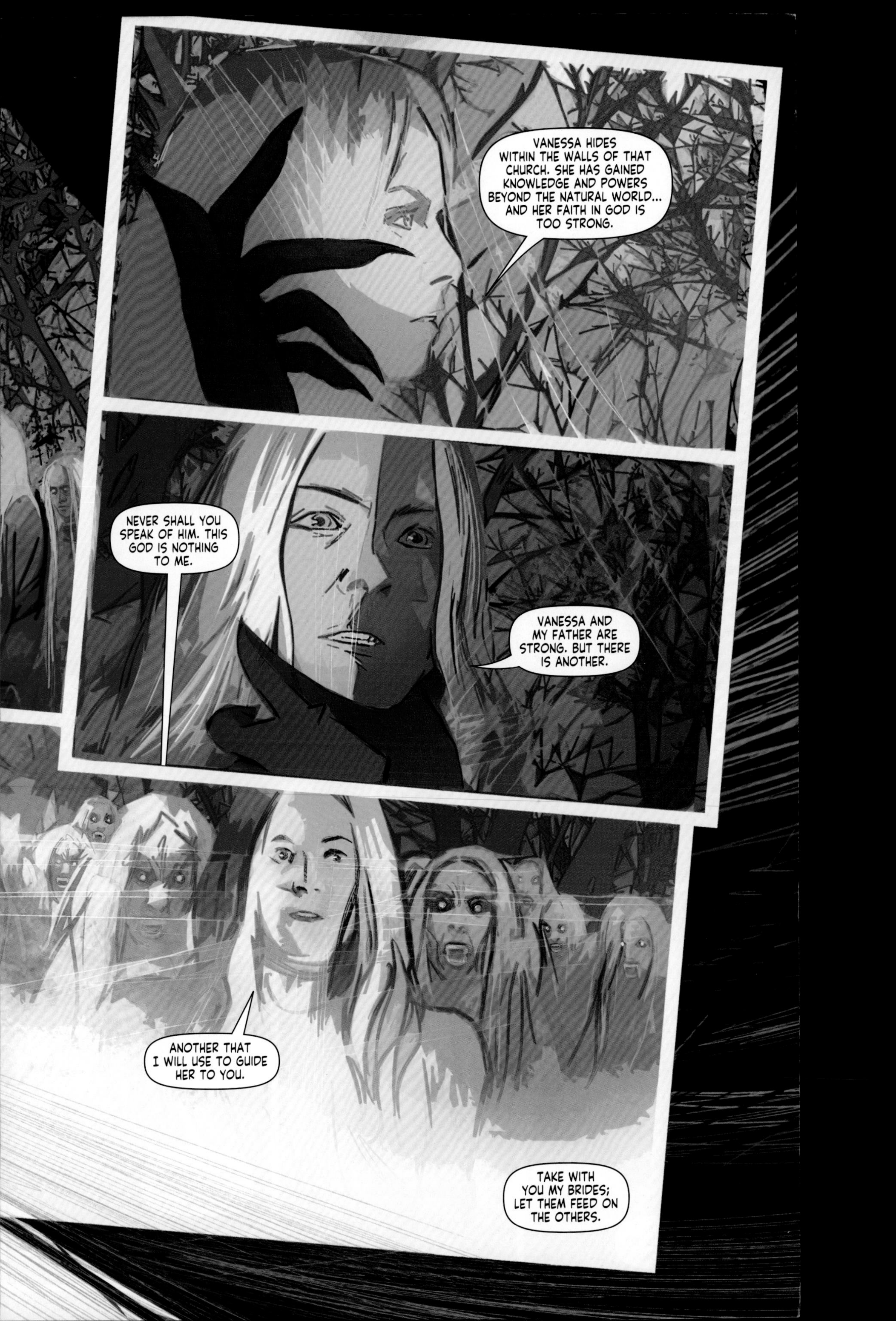
VANESSA HIDES WITHIN THE WALLS OF THAT CHURCH. SHE HAS GAINED KNOWLEDGE AND POWERS BEYOND THE NATURAL WORLD... AND HER FAITH IN GOD IS TOO STRONG.
NEVER SHALL YOU SPEAK OF HIM. THIS GOD IS NOTHING TO ME.
VANESSA AND MY FATHER ARE STRONG. BUT THERE IS ANOTHER.
ANOTHER THAT I WILL USE TO GUIDE HER TO YOU.
TAKE WITH YOU MY BRIDES; LET THEM FEED ON THE OTHERS.

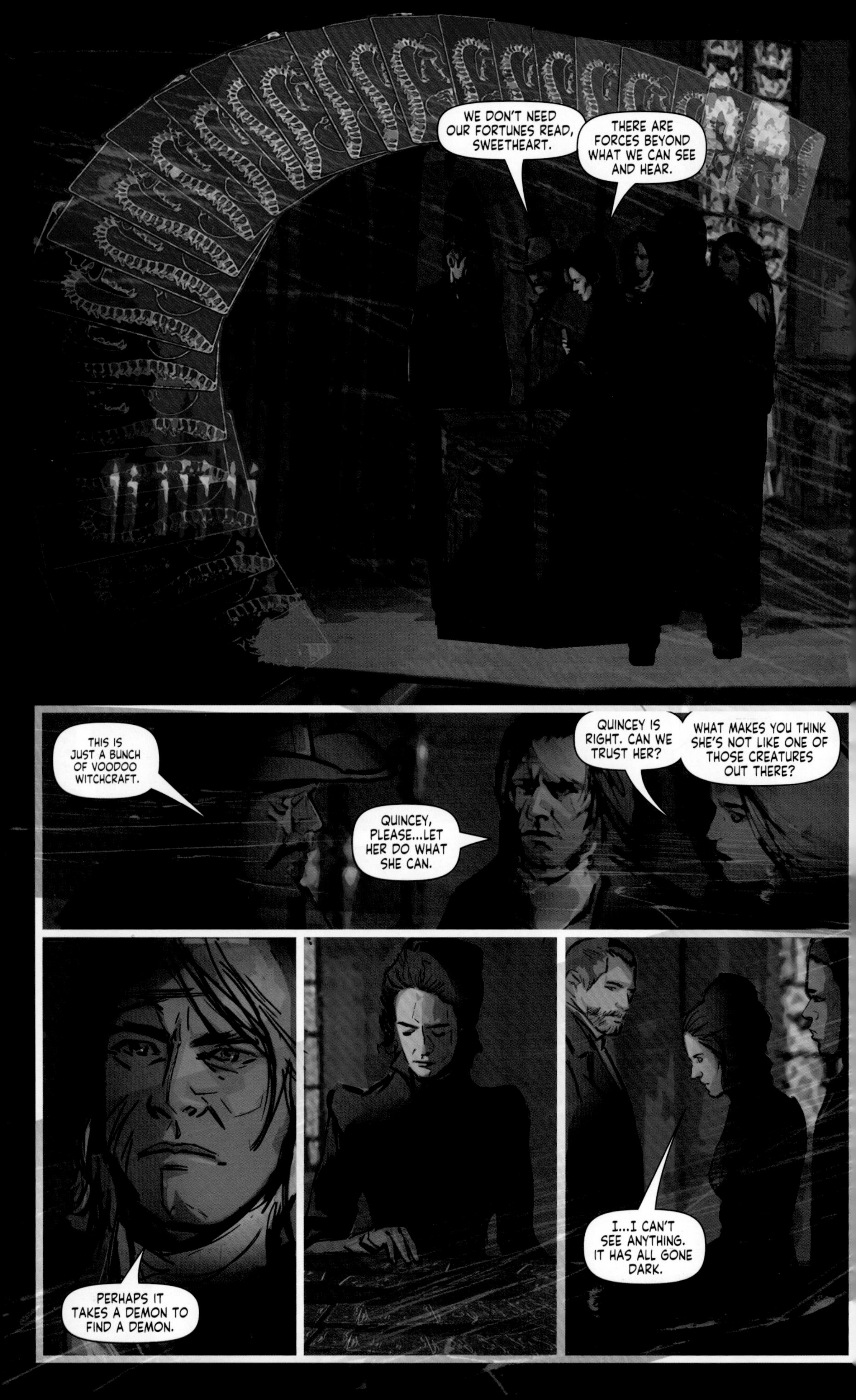
WE DON'T NEED OUR FORTUNES READ, SWEETHEART.
THERE ARE FORCES BEYOND WHAT WE CAN SEE AND HEAR.
THIS IS JUST A BUNCH OF VOODOO WITCHCRAFT.
QUINCEY, PLEASE...LET HER DO WHAT SHE CAN.
QUINCEY IS RIGHT. CAN WE TRUST HER?
WHAT MAKES YOU THINK SHE'S NOT LIKE ONE OF THOSE CREATURES OUT THERE?
PERHAPS IT TAKES A DEMON TO FIND A DEMON.
I...I CAN'T SEE ANYTHING. IT HAS ALL GONE DARK.

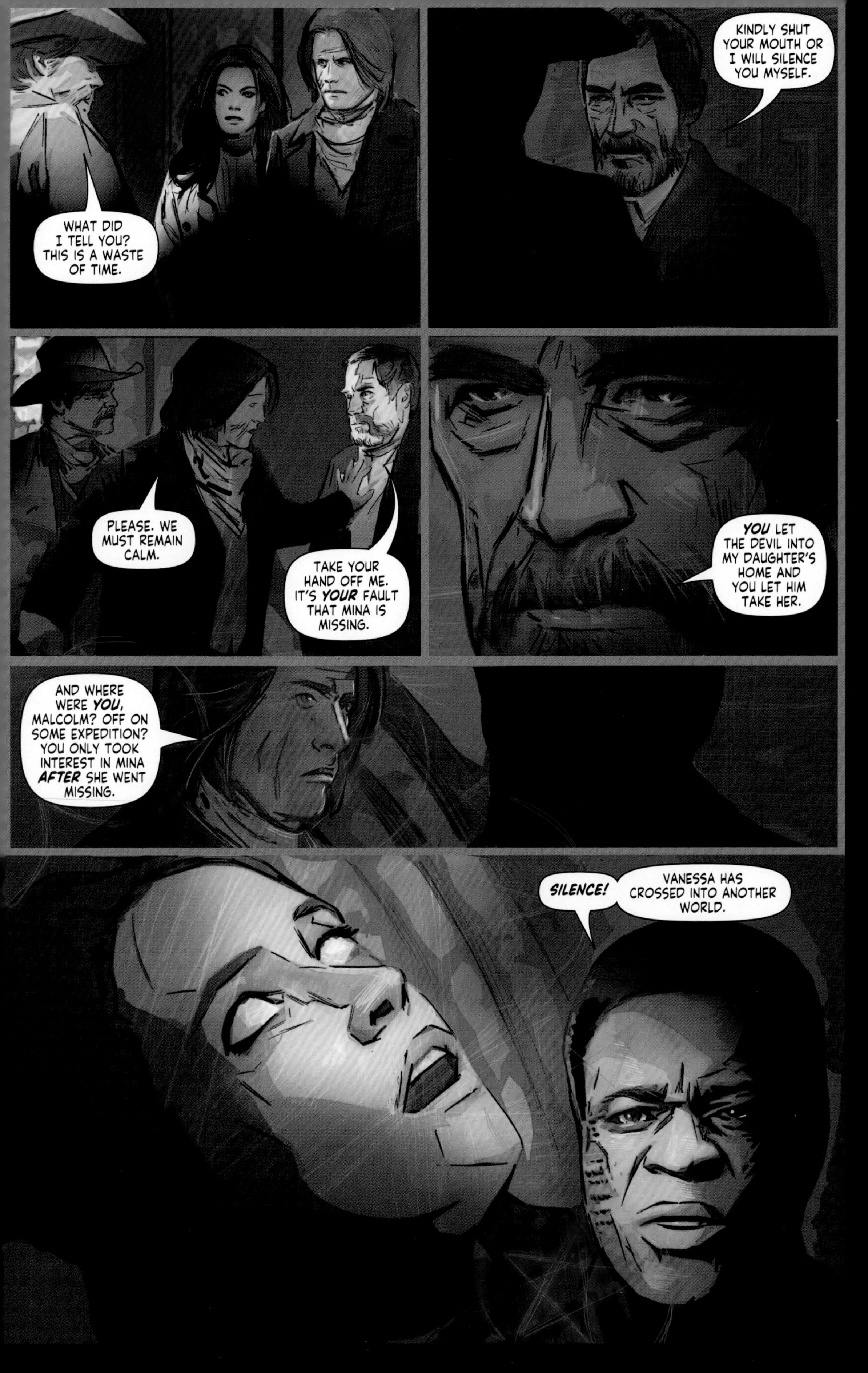
WHAT DID I TELL YOU? THIS IS A WASTE OF TIME.
KINDLY SHUT YOUR MOUTH OR I WILL SILENCE YOU MYSELF.
PLEASE. WE MUST REMAIN CALM.
TAKE YOUR HAND OFF ME. IT'S *YOUR* FAULT THAT MINA IS MISSING.
YOU LET THE DEVIL INTO MY DAUGHTER'S HOME AND YOU LET HIM TAKE HER.
AND WHERE WERE *YOU*, MALCOLM? OFF ON SOME EXPEDITION? YOU ONLY TOOK INTEREST IN MINA *AFTER* SHE WENT MISSING.
SILENCE!
VANESSA HAS CROSSED INTO ANOTHER WORLD.

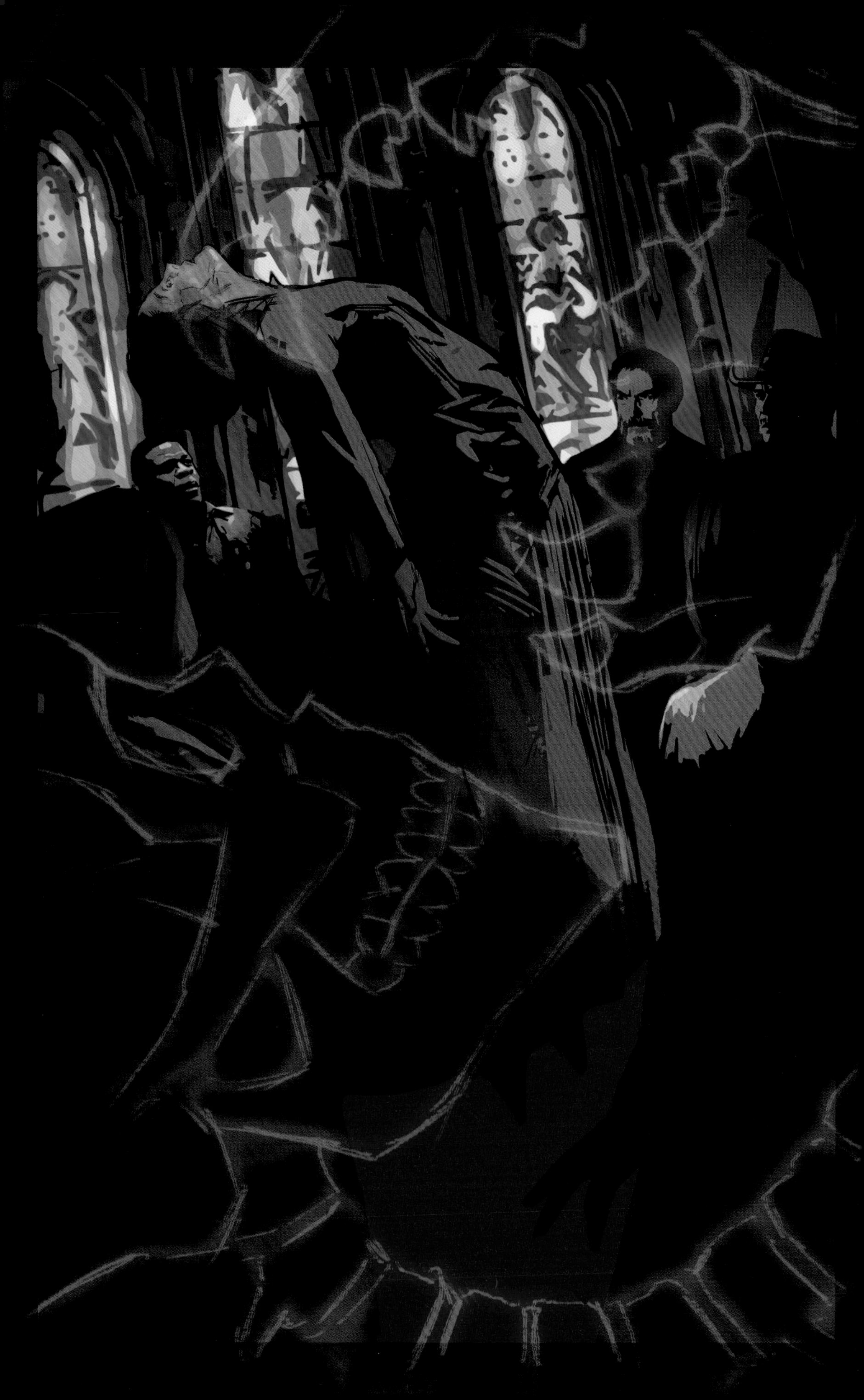

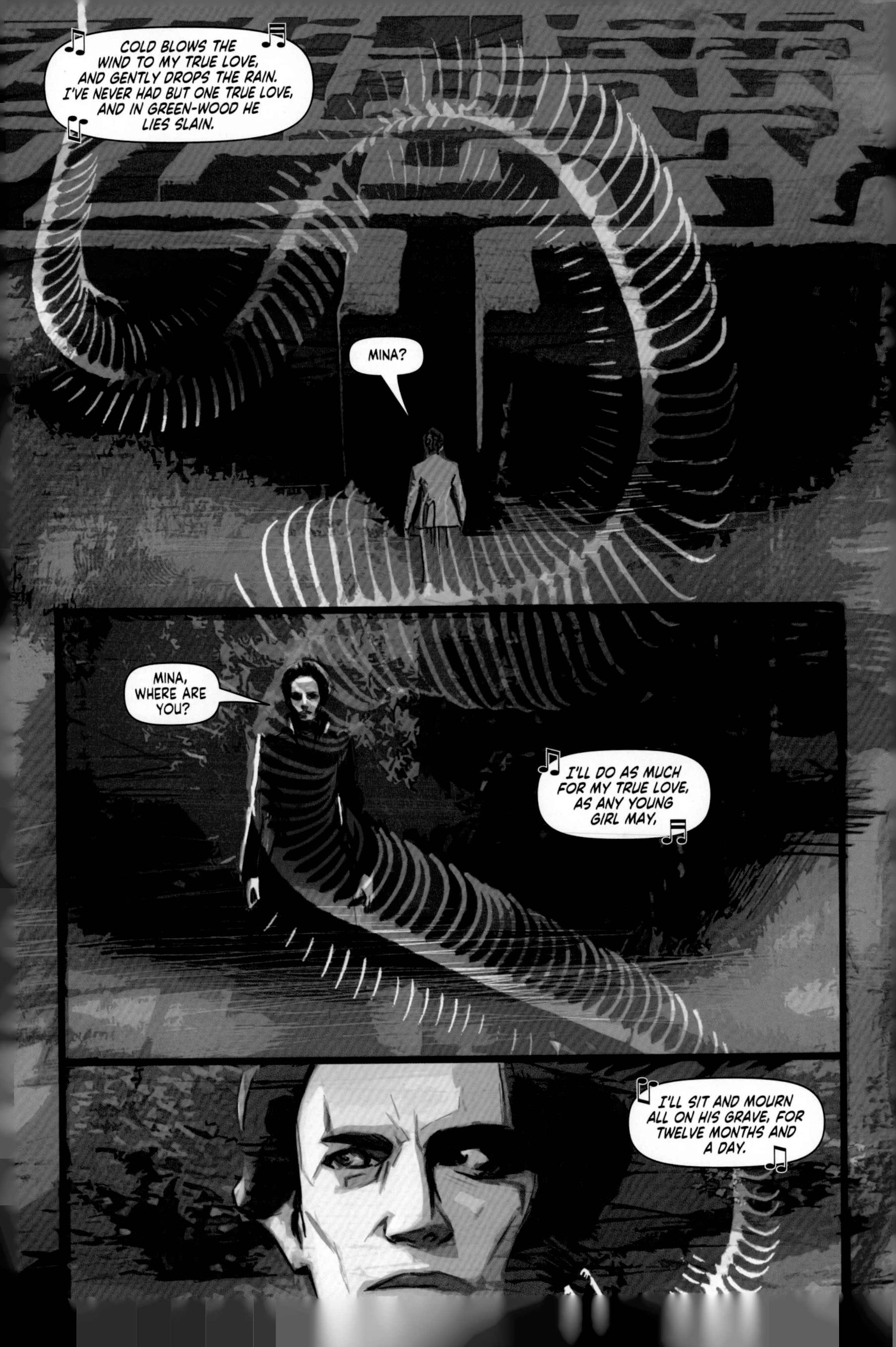
COLD BLOWS THE WIND TO MY TRUE LOVE, AND GENTLY DROPS THE RAIN. I'VE NEVER HAD BUT ONE TRUE LOVE, AND IN GREEN-WOOD HE LIES SLAIN.
MINA?
MINA, WHERE ARE YOU?
I'LL DO AS MUCH FOR MY TRUE LOVE, AS ANY YOUNG GIRL MAY,
I'LL SIT AND MOURN ALL ON HIS GRAVE, FOR TWELVE MONTHS AND A DAY.

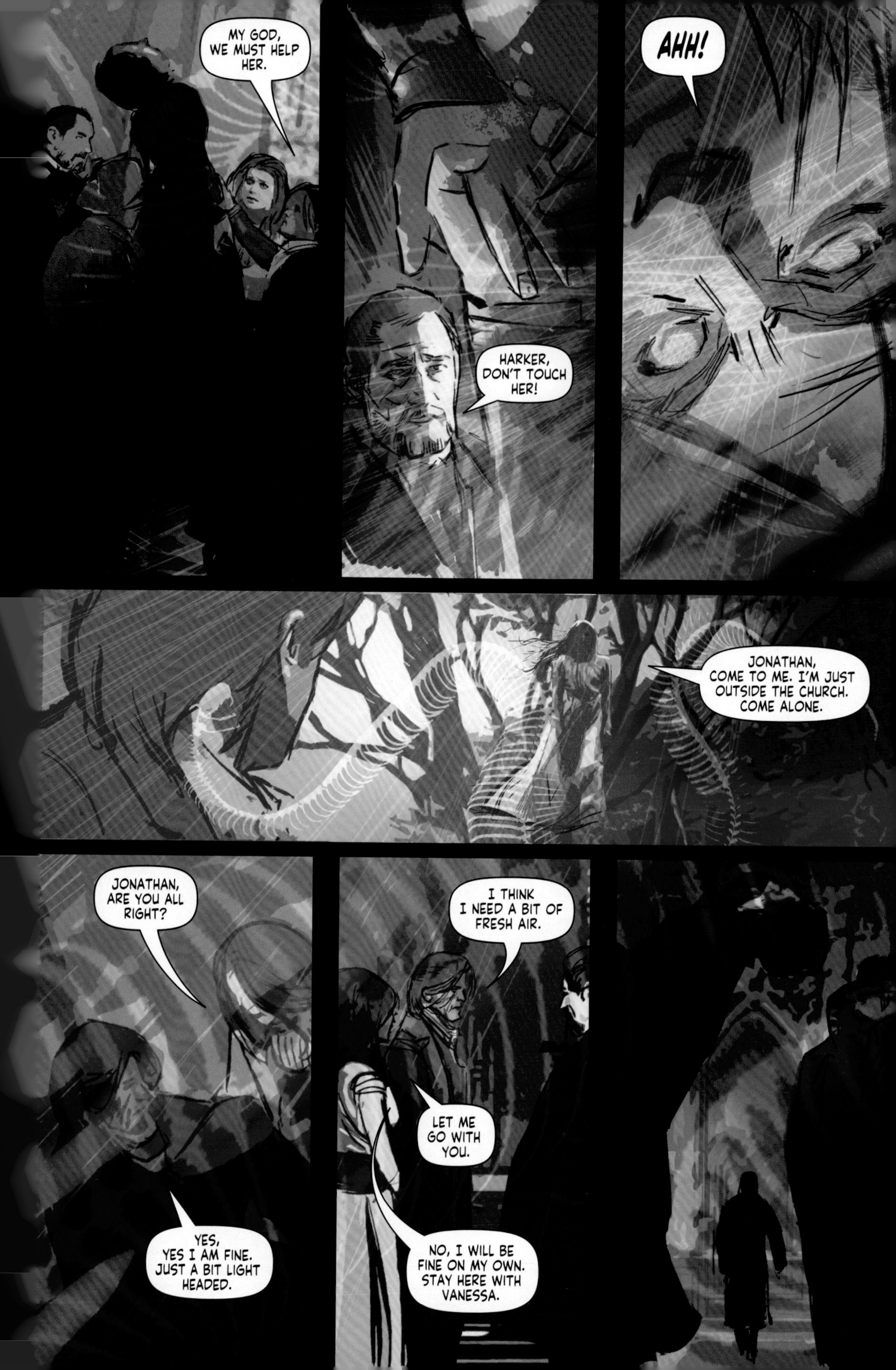
MY GOD, WE MUST HELP HER.
HARKER, DON'T TOUCH HER!
AHH!
JONATHAN, COME TO ME. I'M JUST OUTSIDE THE CHURCH. COME ALONE.
JONATHAN, ARE YOU ALL RIGHT?
YES, YES I AM FINE. JUST A BIT LIGHT HEADED.
I THINK I NEED A BIT OF FRESH AIR.
LET ME GO WITH YOU.
NO, I WILL BE FINE ON MY OWN. STAY HERE WITH VANESSA.

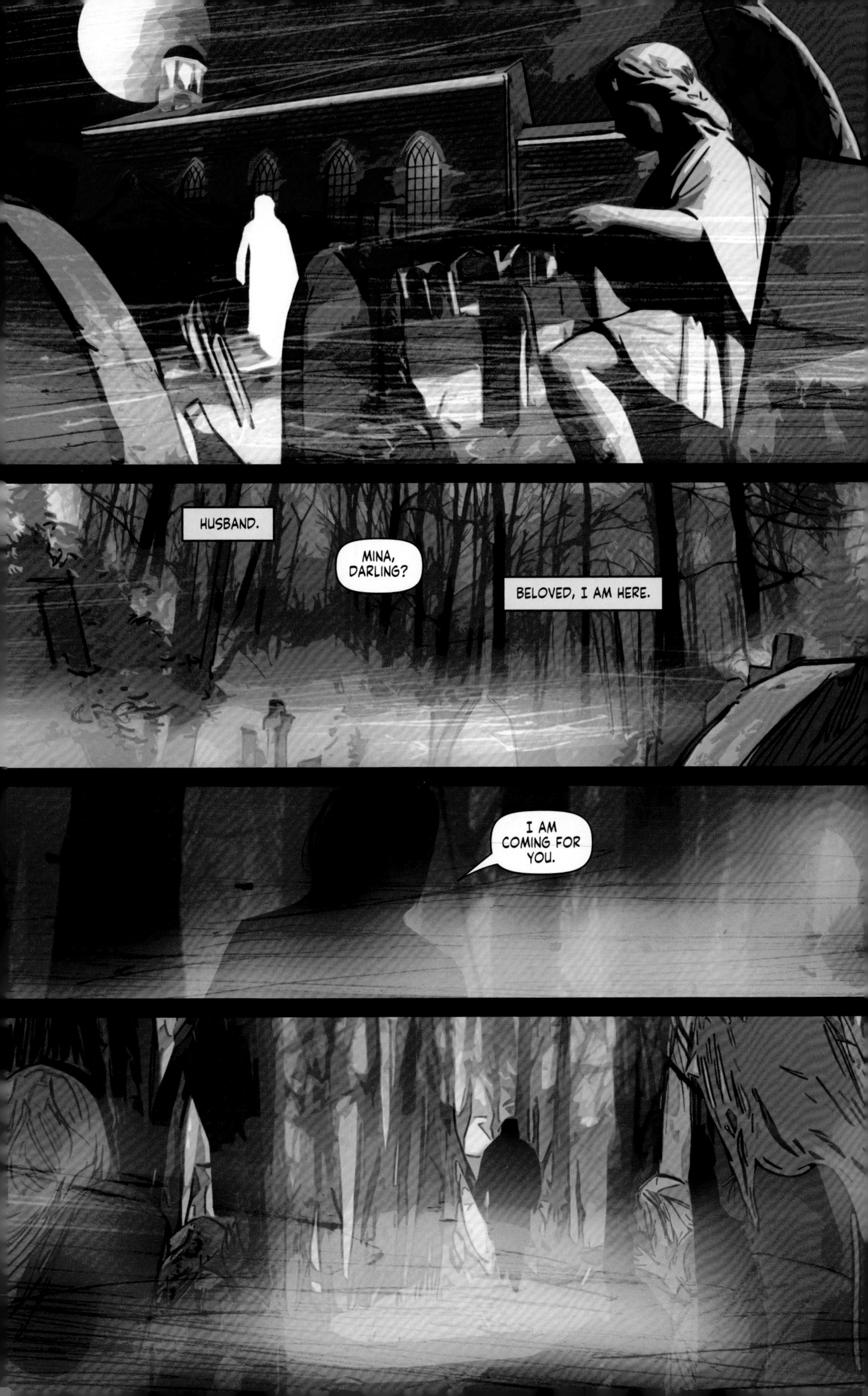
HUSBAND.
MINA, DARLING?
BELOVED, I AM HERE.
I AM COMING FOR YOU.

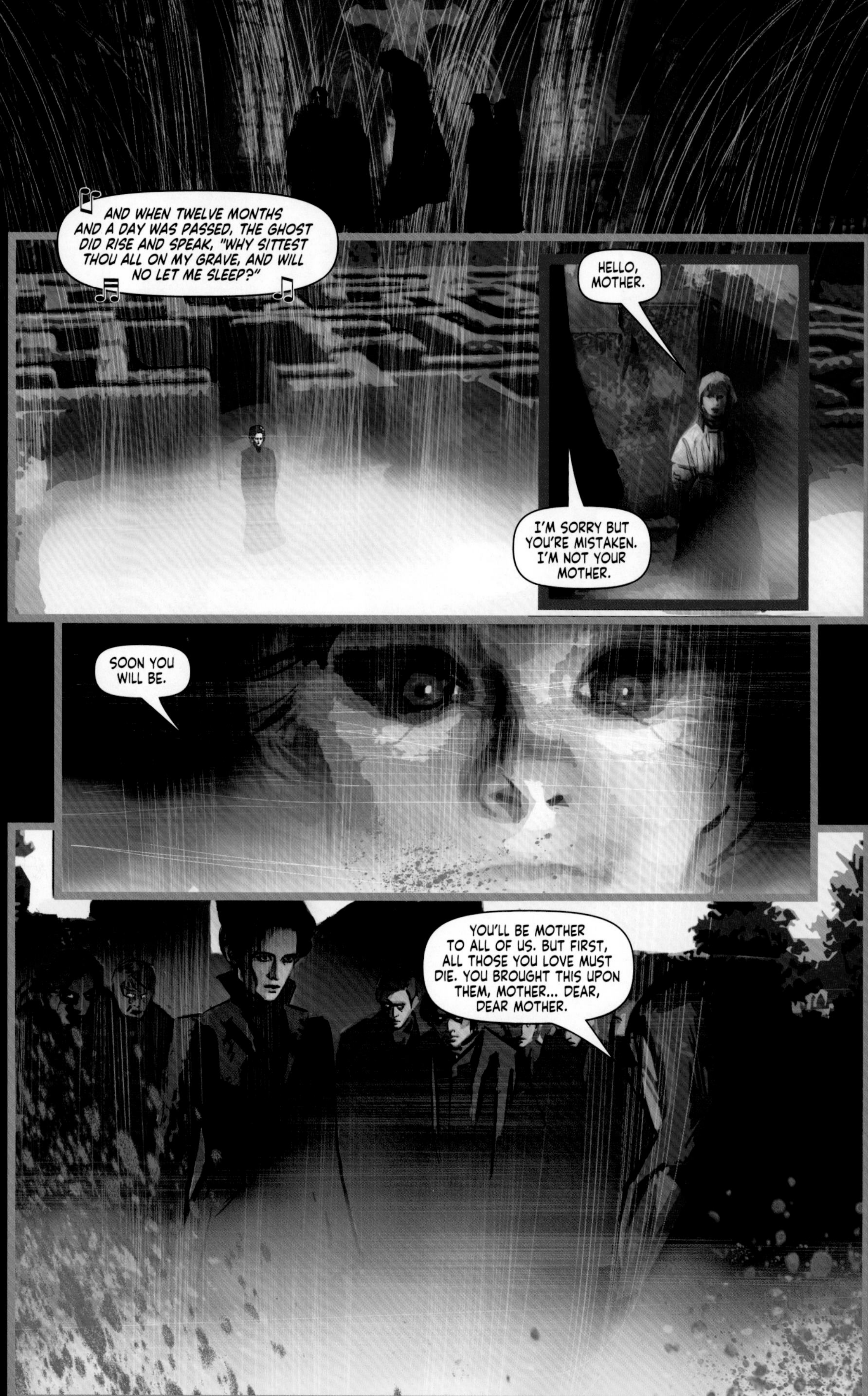
AND WHEN TWELVE MONTHS AND A DAY WAS PASSED, THE GHOST DID RISE AND SPEAK, "WHY SITTEST THOU ALL ON MY GRAVE, AND WILL NO LET ME SLEEP?"
HELLO, MOTHER.
I'M SORRY BUT YOU'RE MISTAKEN. I'M NOT YOUR MOTHER.
SOON YOU WILL BE.
YOU'LL BE MOTHER TO ALL OF US. BUT FIRST, ALL THOSE YOU LOVE MUST DIE. YOU BROUGHT THIS UPON THEM, MOTHER... DEAR, DEAR MOTHER.

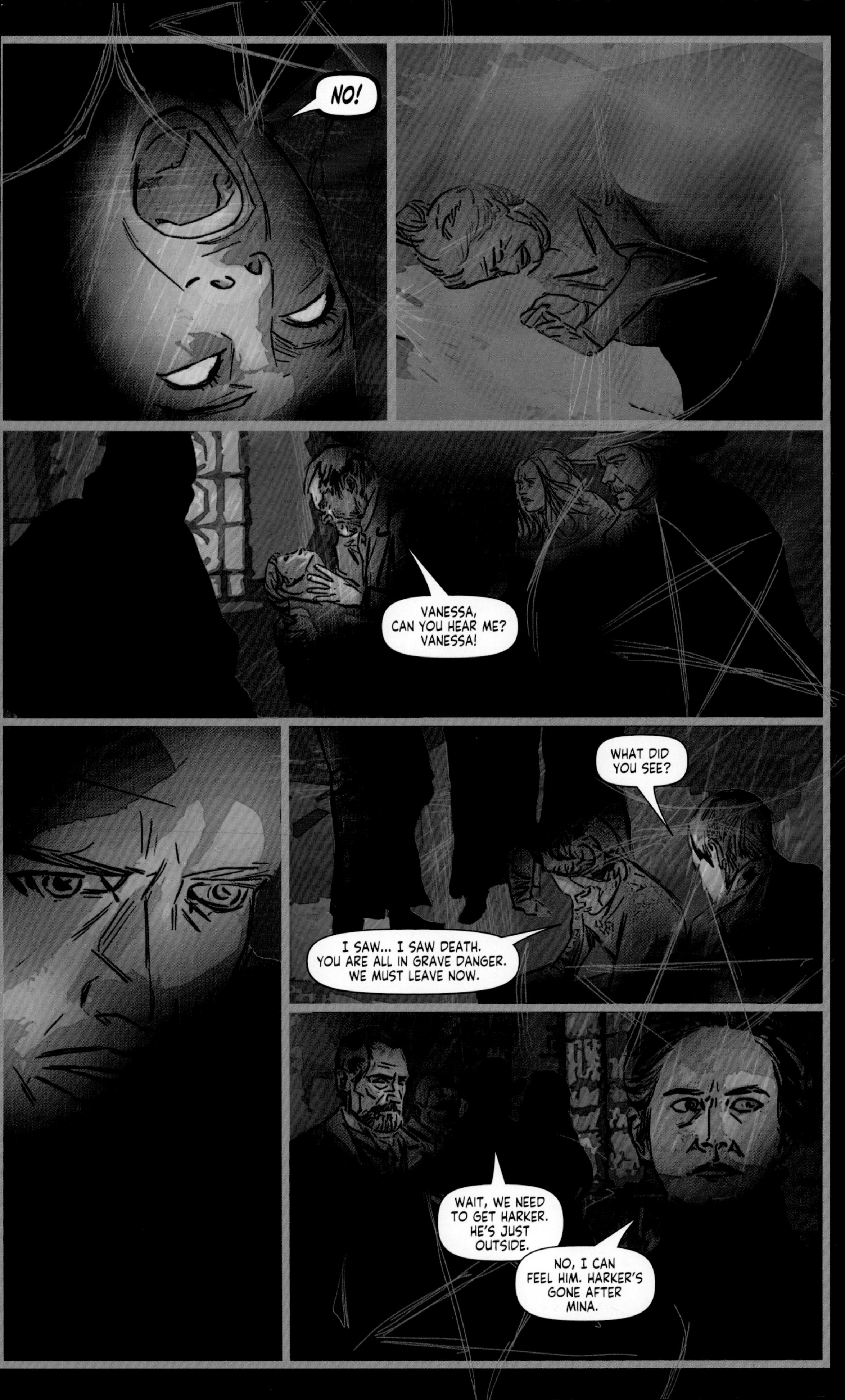
NO!
VANESSA, CAN YOU HEAR ME? VANESSA!
WHAT DID YOU SEE?
I SAW... I SAW DEATH. YOU ARE ALL IN GRAVE DANGER. WE MUST LEAVE NOW.
WAIT, WE NEED TO GET HARKER. HE'S JUST OUTSIDE.
NO, I CAN FEEL HIM. HARKER'S GONE AFTER MINA.

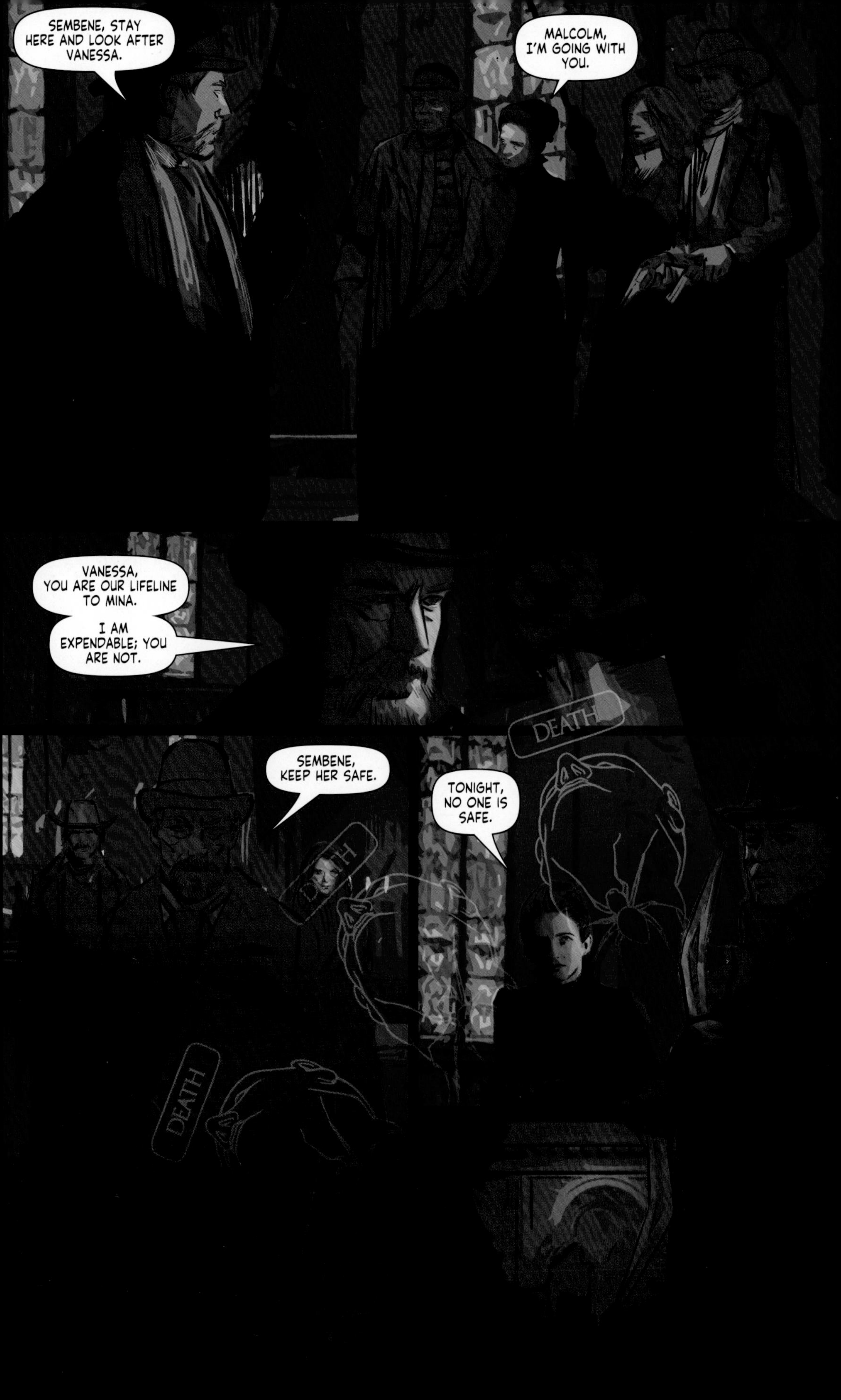
SEMBENE, STAY HERE AND LOOK AFTER VANESSA.
MALCOLM, I'M GOING WITH YOU.
VANESSA, YOU ARE OUR LIFELINE TO MINA.
I AM EXPENDABLE; YOU ARE NOT.
SEMBENE, KEEP HER SAFE.
TONIGHT, NO ONE IS SAFE.
DEATH
DEATH
DEATH

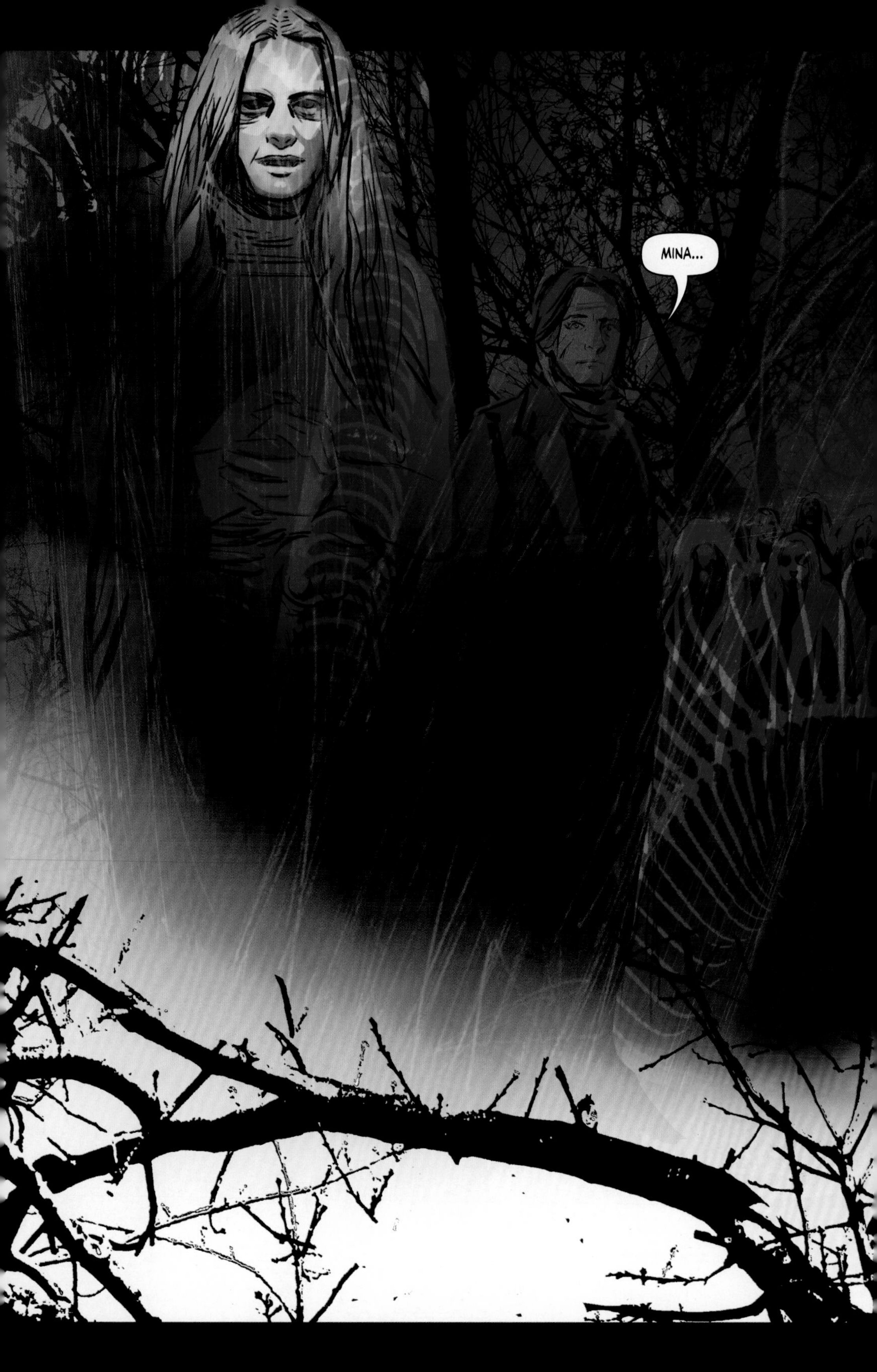
MINA...

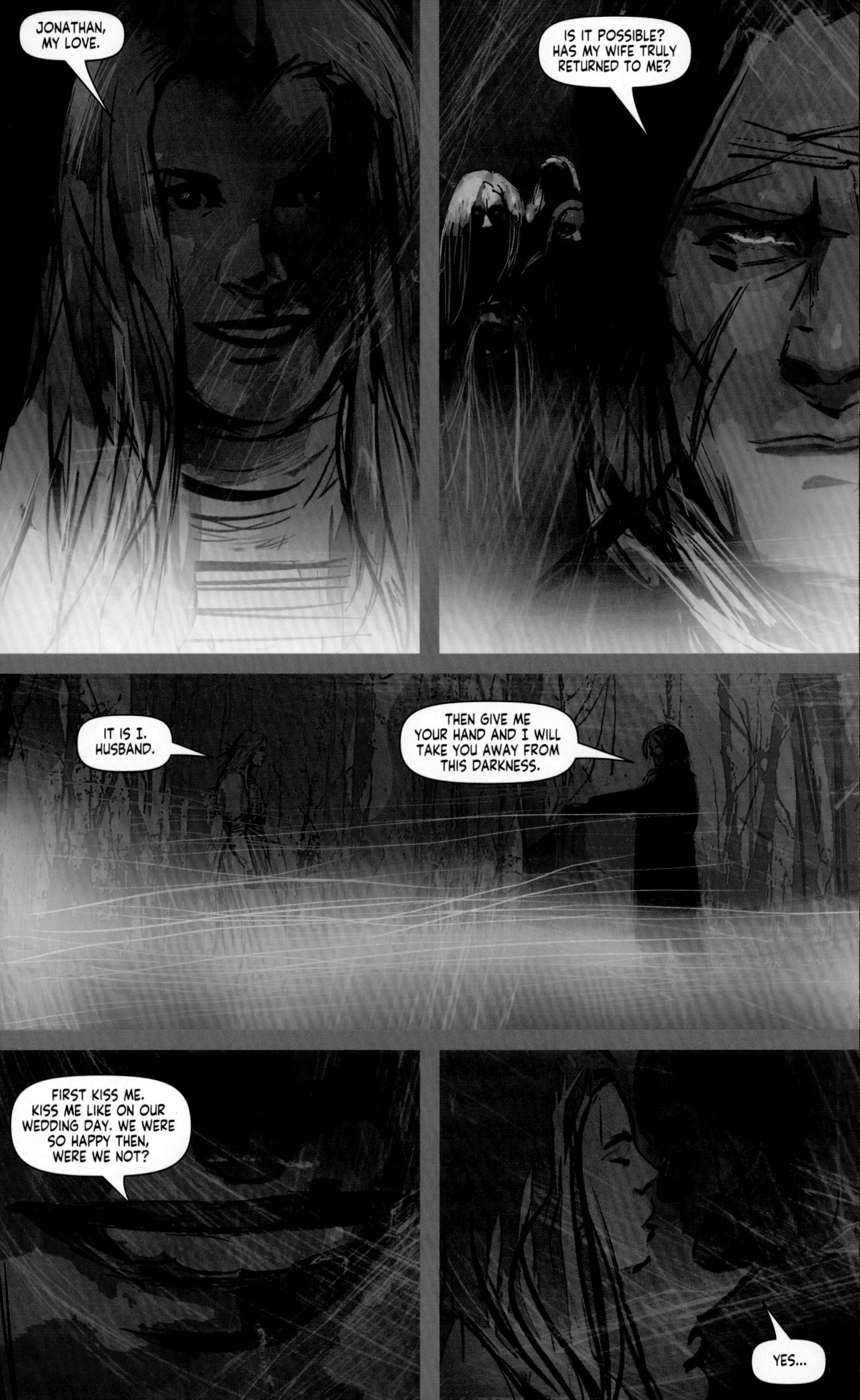
JONATHAN, MY LOVE.
IS IT POSSIBLE? HAS MY WIFE TRULY RETURNED TO ME?
IT IS I. HUSBAND.
THEN GIVE ME YOUR HAND AND I WILL TAKE YOU AWAY FROM THIS DARKNESS.
FIRST KISS ME. KISS ME LIKE ON OUR WEDDING DAY. WE WERE SO HAPPY THEN, WERE WE NOT?
YES...

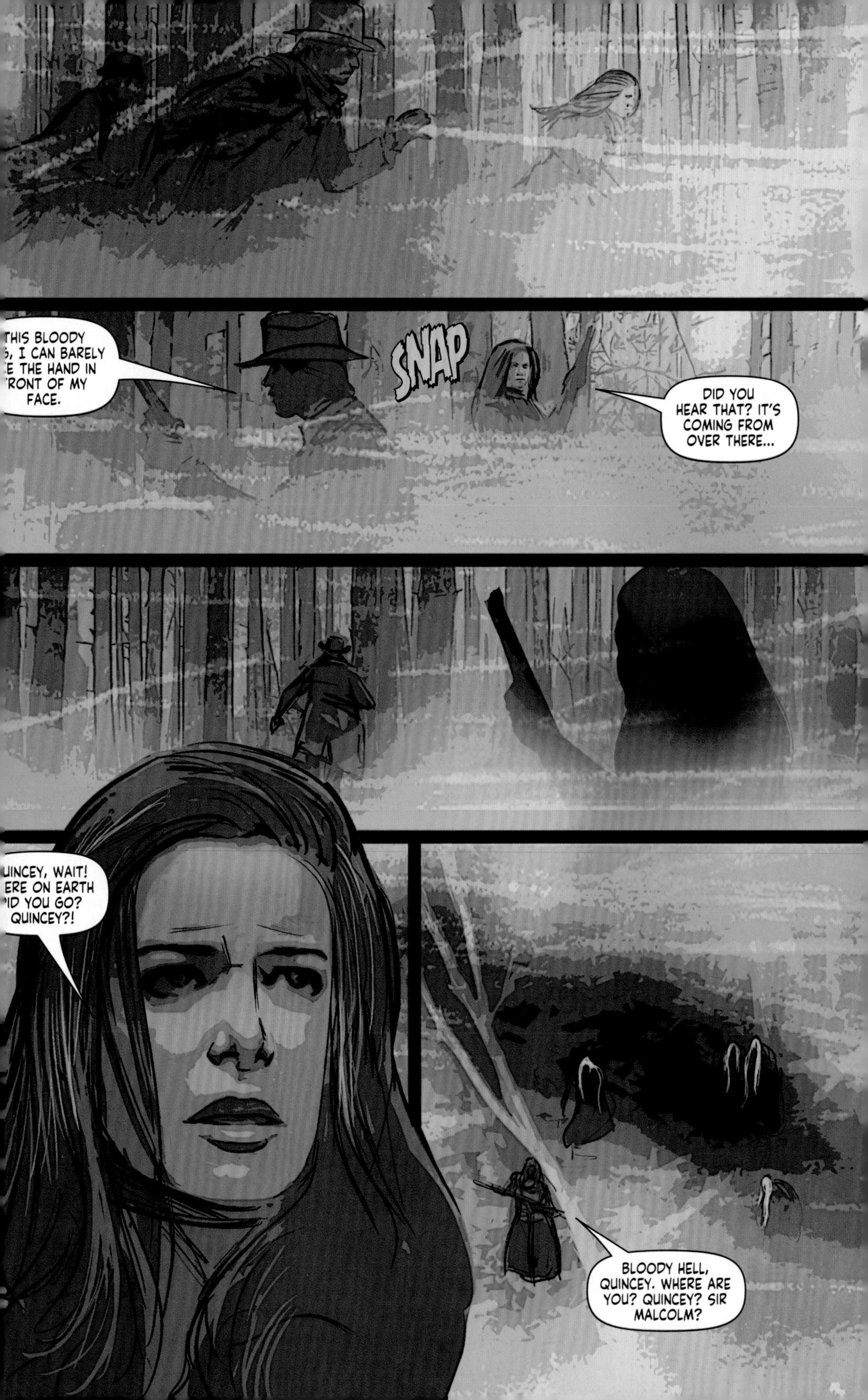
THIS BLOODY I CAN BARELY THE HAND IN RONT OF MY FACE.
SNAP
DID YOU HEAR THAT? IT'S COMING FROM OVER THERE...
QUINCEY, WAIT! ERE ON EARTH ID YOU GO? QUINCEY?!
BLOODY HELL, QUINCEY. WHERE ARE YOU? QUINCEY? SIR MALCOLM?

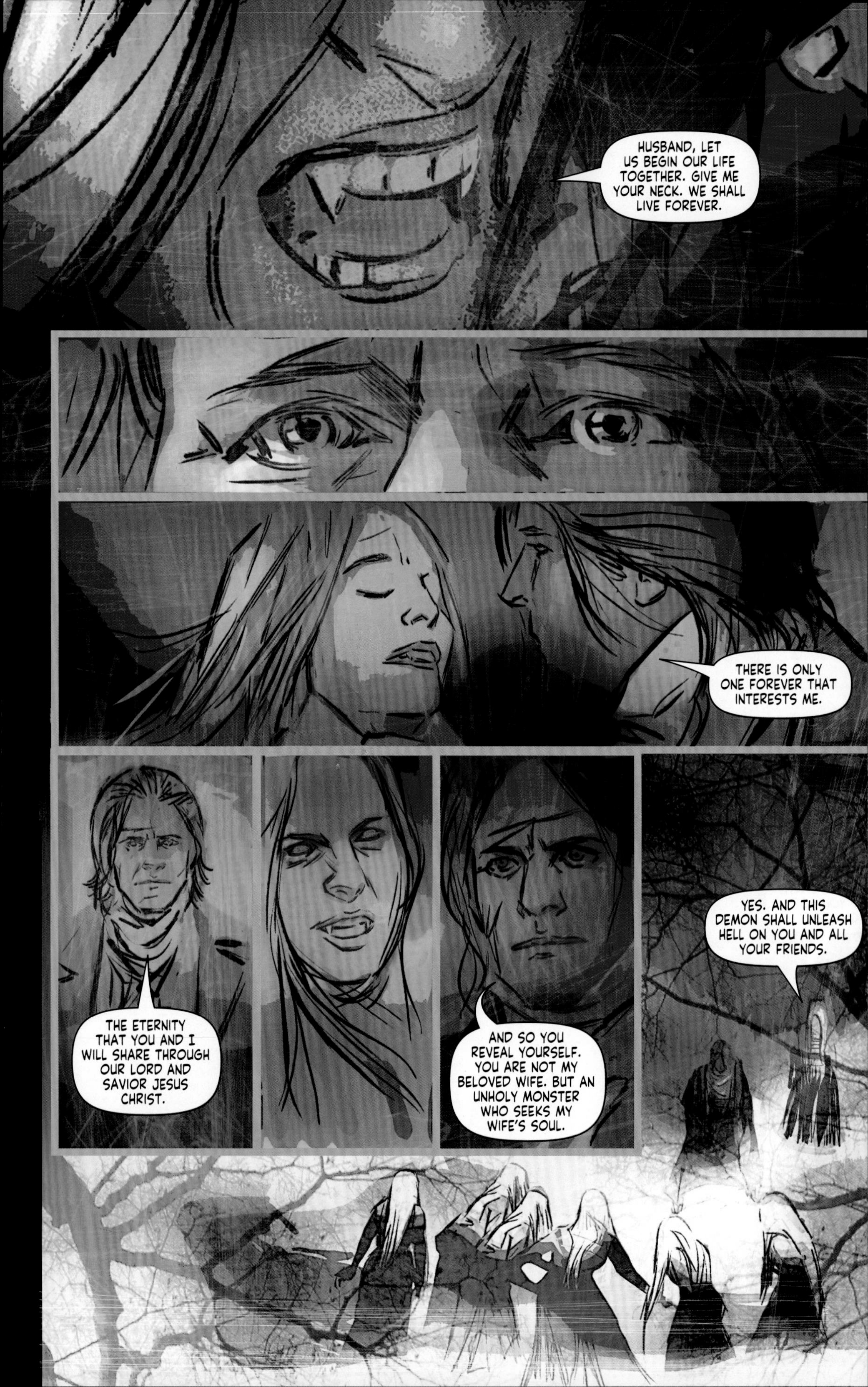
HUSBAND, LET US BEGIN OUR LIFE TOGETHER. GIVE ME YOUR NECK. WE SHALL LIVE FOREVER.
THERE IS ONLY ONE FOREVER THAT INTERESTS ME.
THE ETERNITY THAT YOU AND I WILL SHARE THROUGH OUR LORD AND SAVIOR JESUS CHRIST.
AND SO YOU REVEAL YOURSELF. YOU ARE NOT MY BELOVED WIFE. BUT AN UNHOLY MONSTER WHO SEEKS MY WIFE'S SOUL.
YES. AND THIS DEMON SHALL UNLEASH HELL ON YOU AND ALL YOUR FRIENDS.

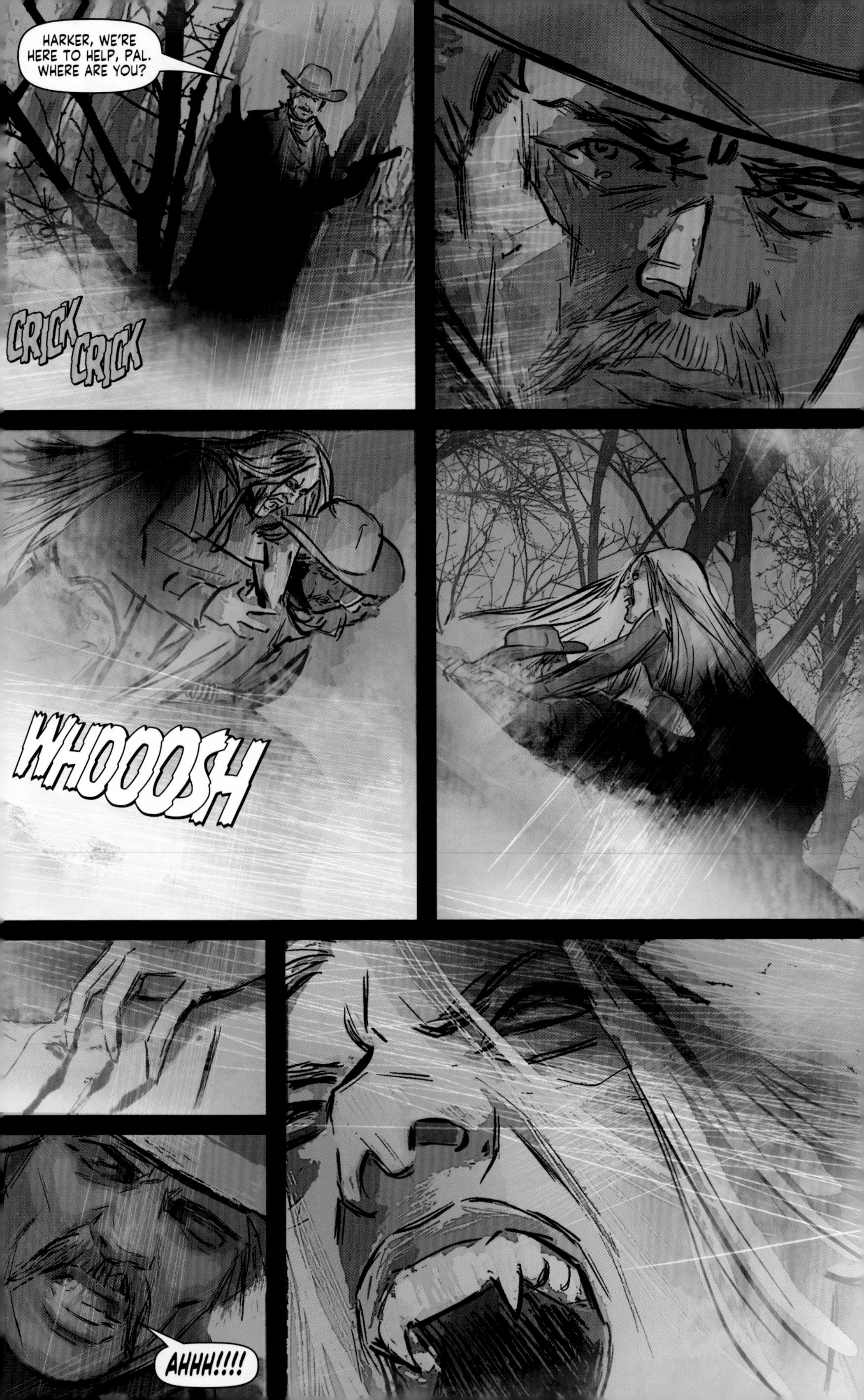
HARKER, WE'RE HERE TO HELP, PAL. WHERE ARE YOU?
CRICK CRICK
WHOOOSH
AHHH!!!!

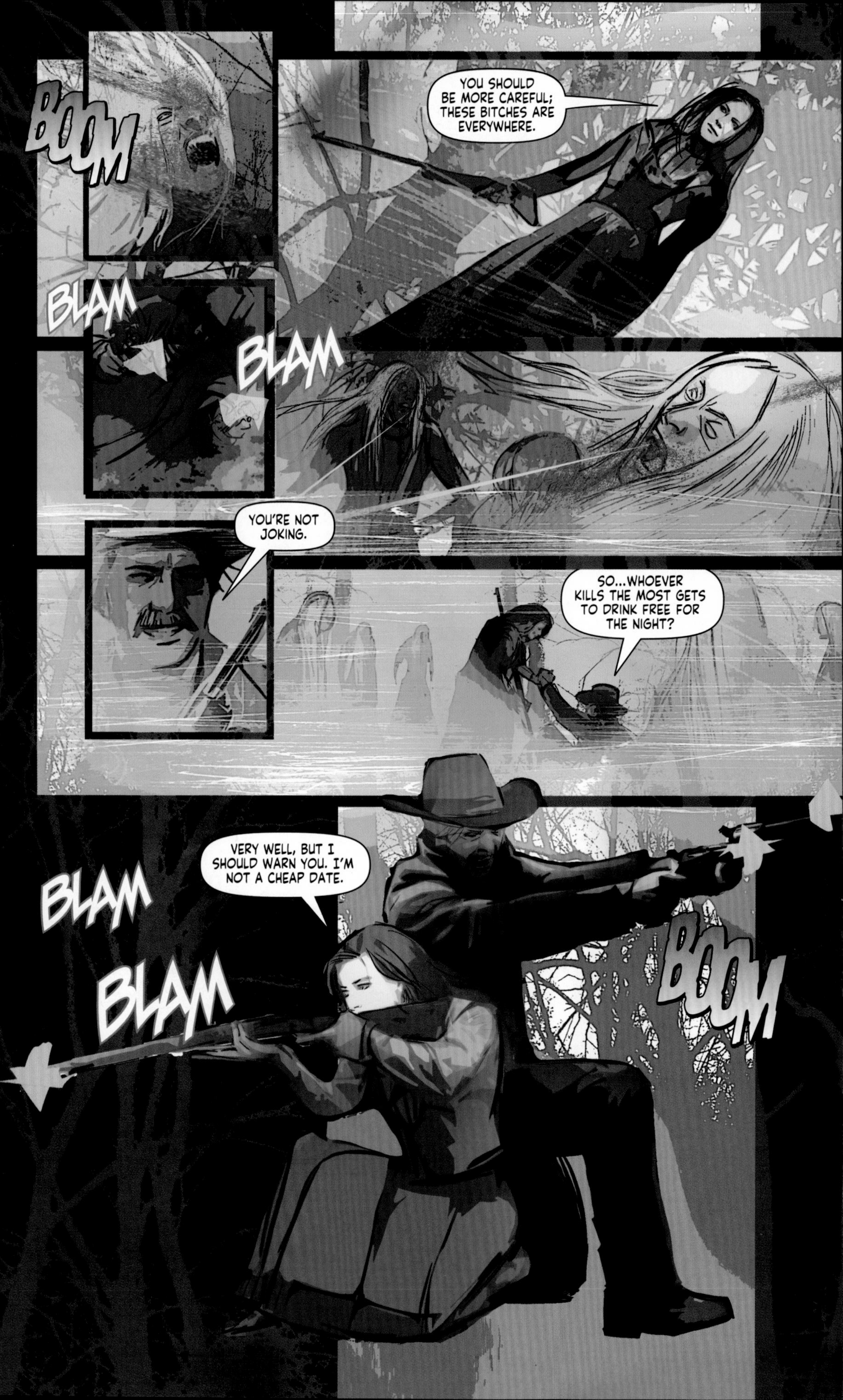
BOOM
YOU SHOULD BE MORE CAREFUL; THESE BITCHES ARE EVERYWHERE.
BLAM
BLAM
YOU'RE NOT JOKING.
SO...WHOEVER KILLS THE MOST GETS TO DRINK FREE FOR THE NIGHT?
VERY WELL, BUT I SHOULD WARN YOU. I'M NOT A CHEAP DATE.
BLAM
BLAM
BOOM

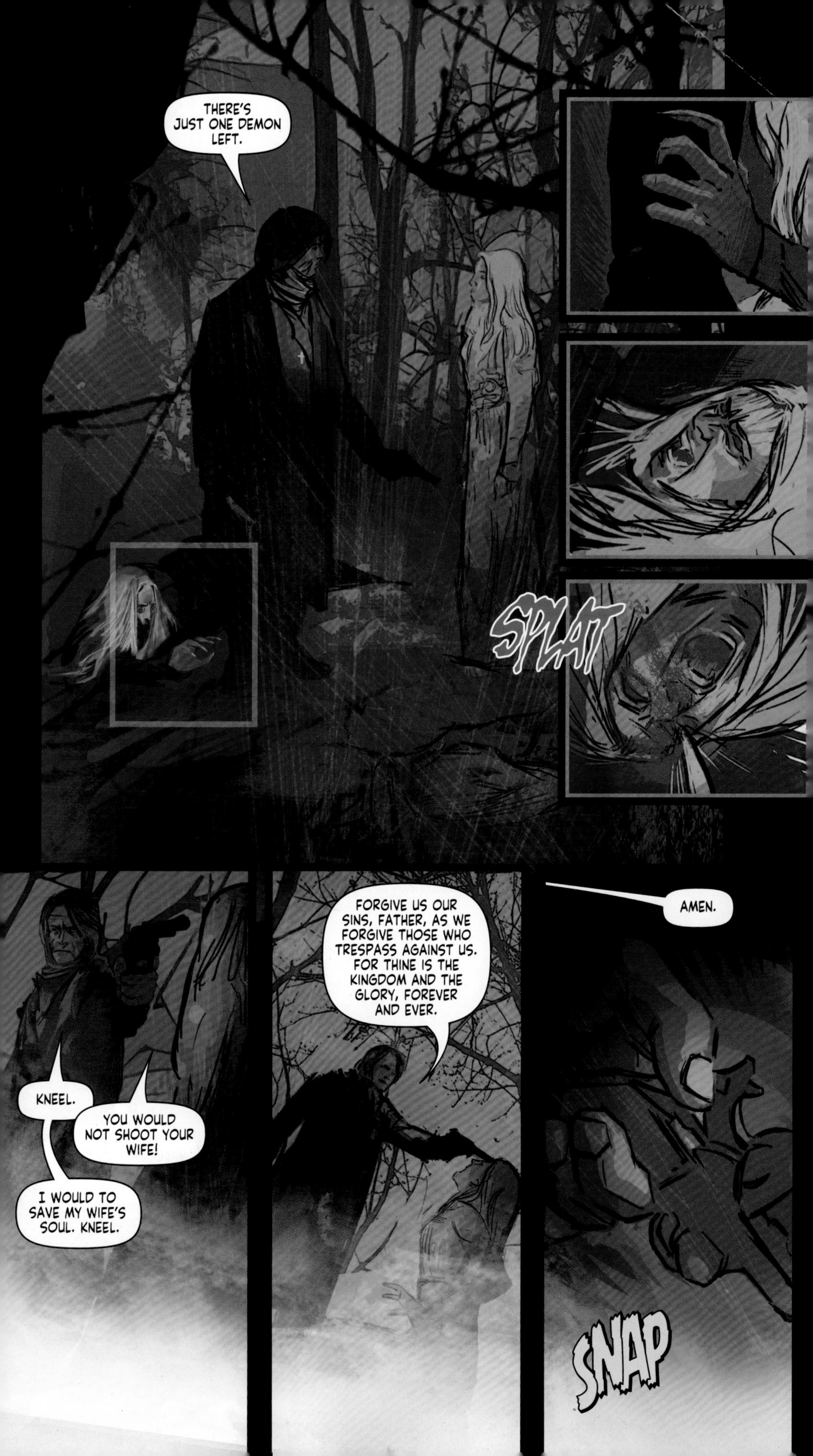
THERE'S JUST ONE DEMON LEFT.
SPLAT
KNEEL.
YOU WOULD NOT SHOOT YOUR WIFE!
I WOULD TO SAVE MY WIFE'S SOUL. KNEEL.
FORGIVE US OUR SINS, FATHER, AS WE FORGIVE THOSE WHO TRESPASS AGAINST US. FOR THINE IS THE KINGDOM AND THE GLORY, FOREVER AND EVER.
AMEN.
SNAP

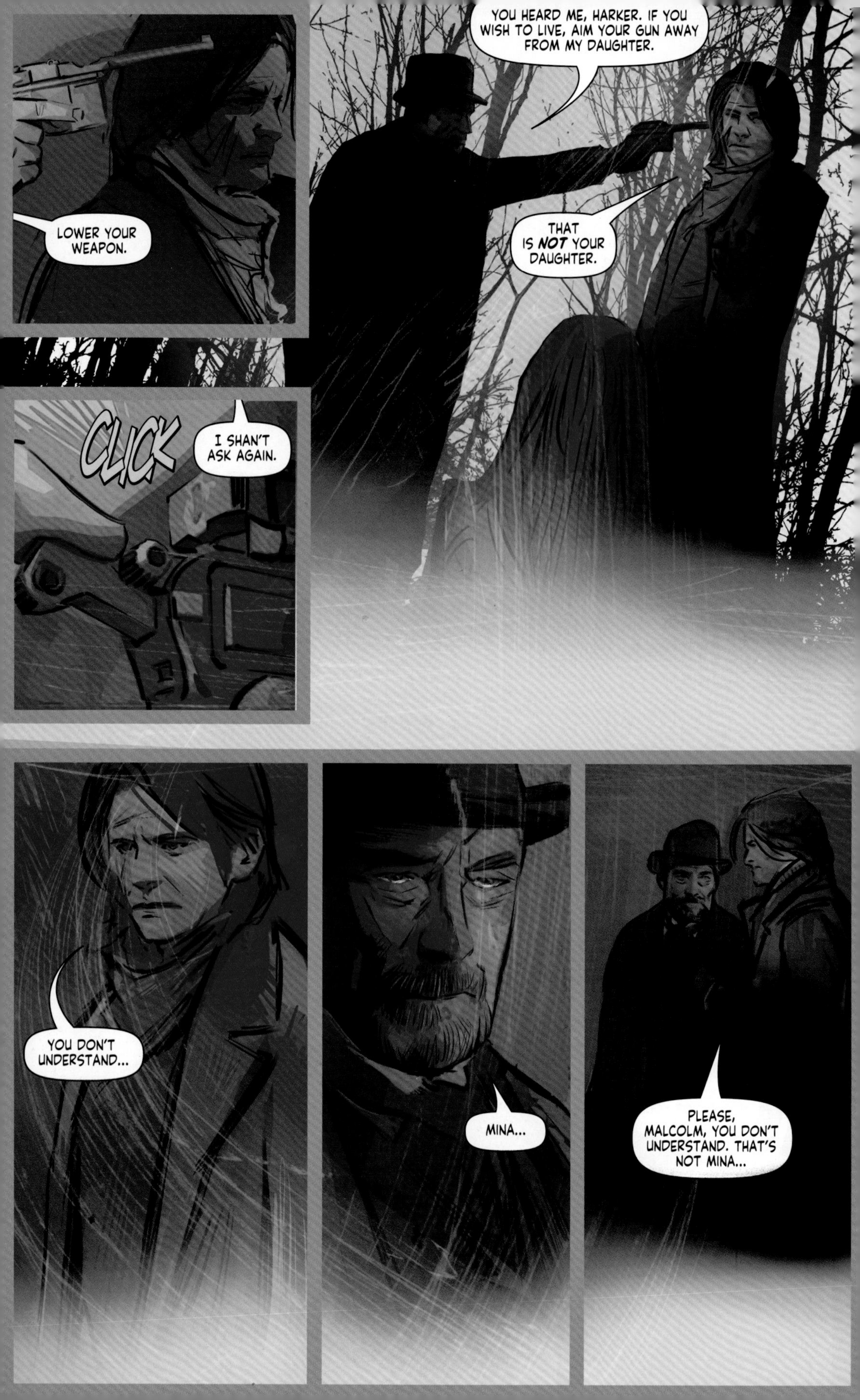
LOWER YOUR WEAPON.
YOU HEARD ME, HARKER. IF YOU WISH TO LIVE, AIM YOUR GUN AWAY FROM MY DAUGHTER.
THAT IS **NOT** YOUR DAUGHTER.
CLICK
I SHAN'T ASK AGAIN.
YOU DON'T UNDERSTAND...
MINA...
PLEASE, MALCOLM, YOU DON'T UNDERSTAND. THAT'S NOT MINA...

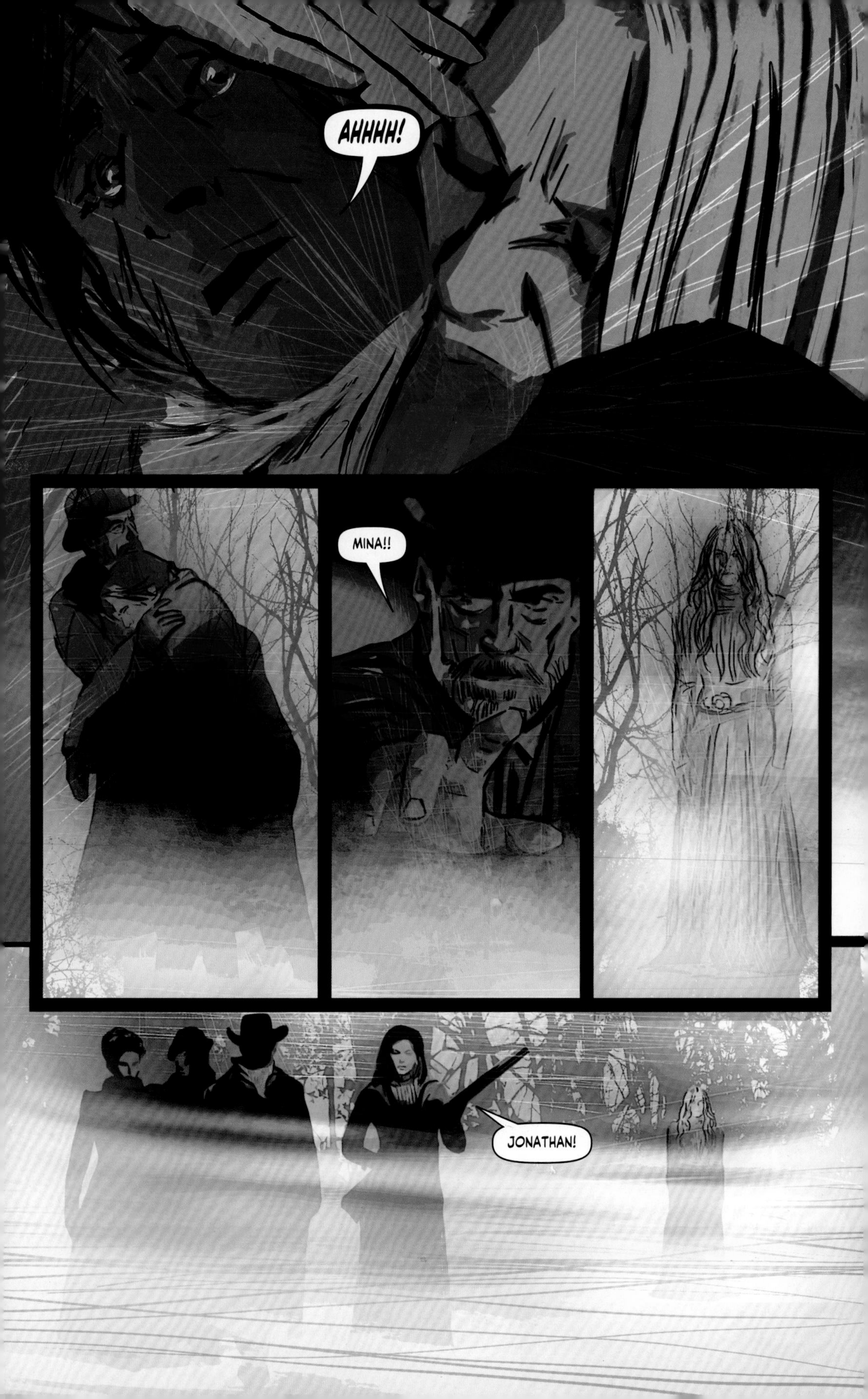
AHHHH!
MINA!!
JONATHAN!

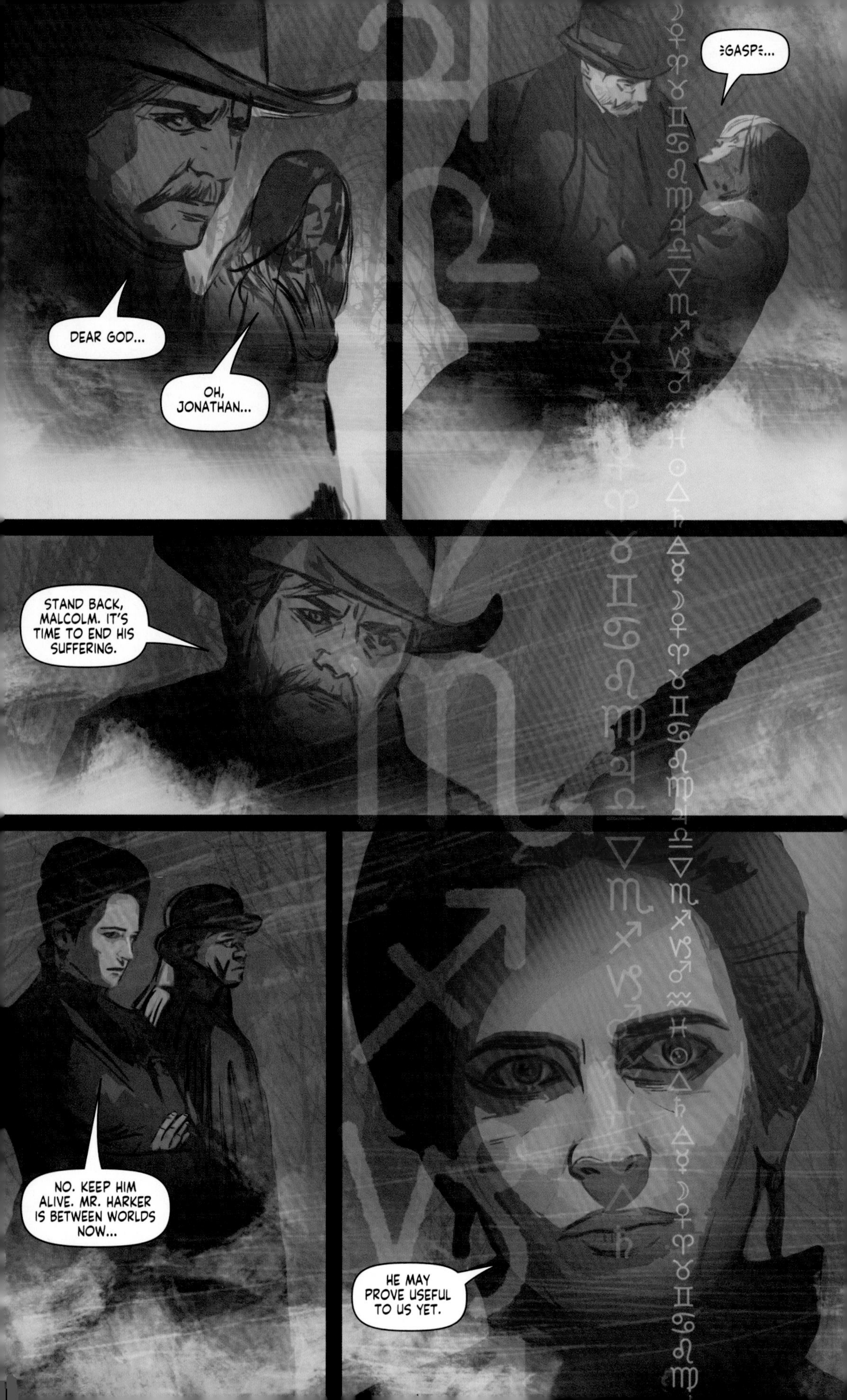
DEAR GOD...
OH, JONATHAN...
GASP...
STAND BACK, MALCOLM. IT'S TIME TO END HIS SUFFERING.
NO. KEEP HIM ALIVE. MR. HARKER IS BETWEEN WORLDS NOW...
HE MAY PROVE USEFUL TO US YET.

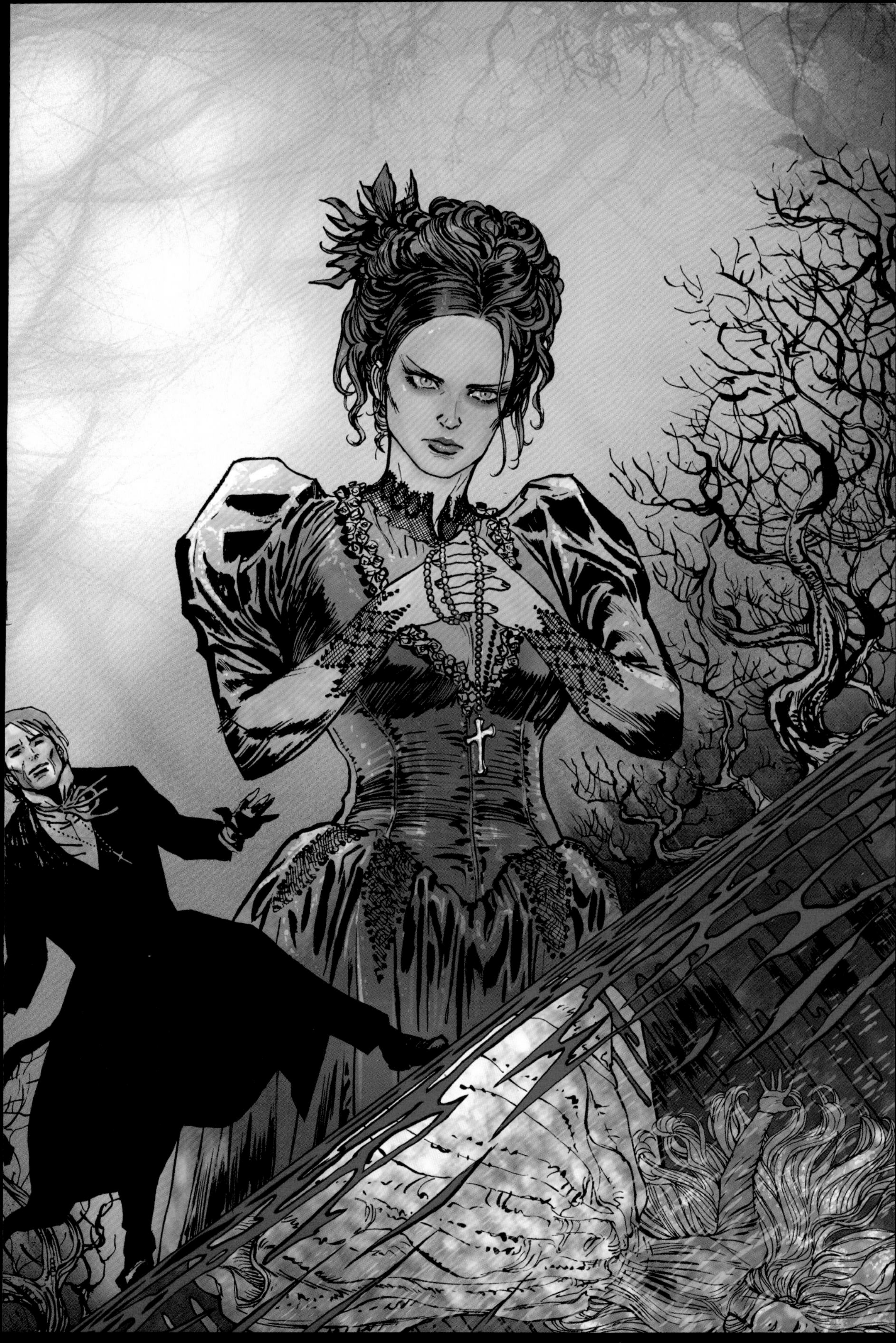

#5 COVER A - GUILLEM MARCH

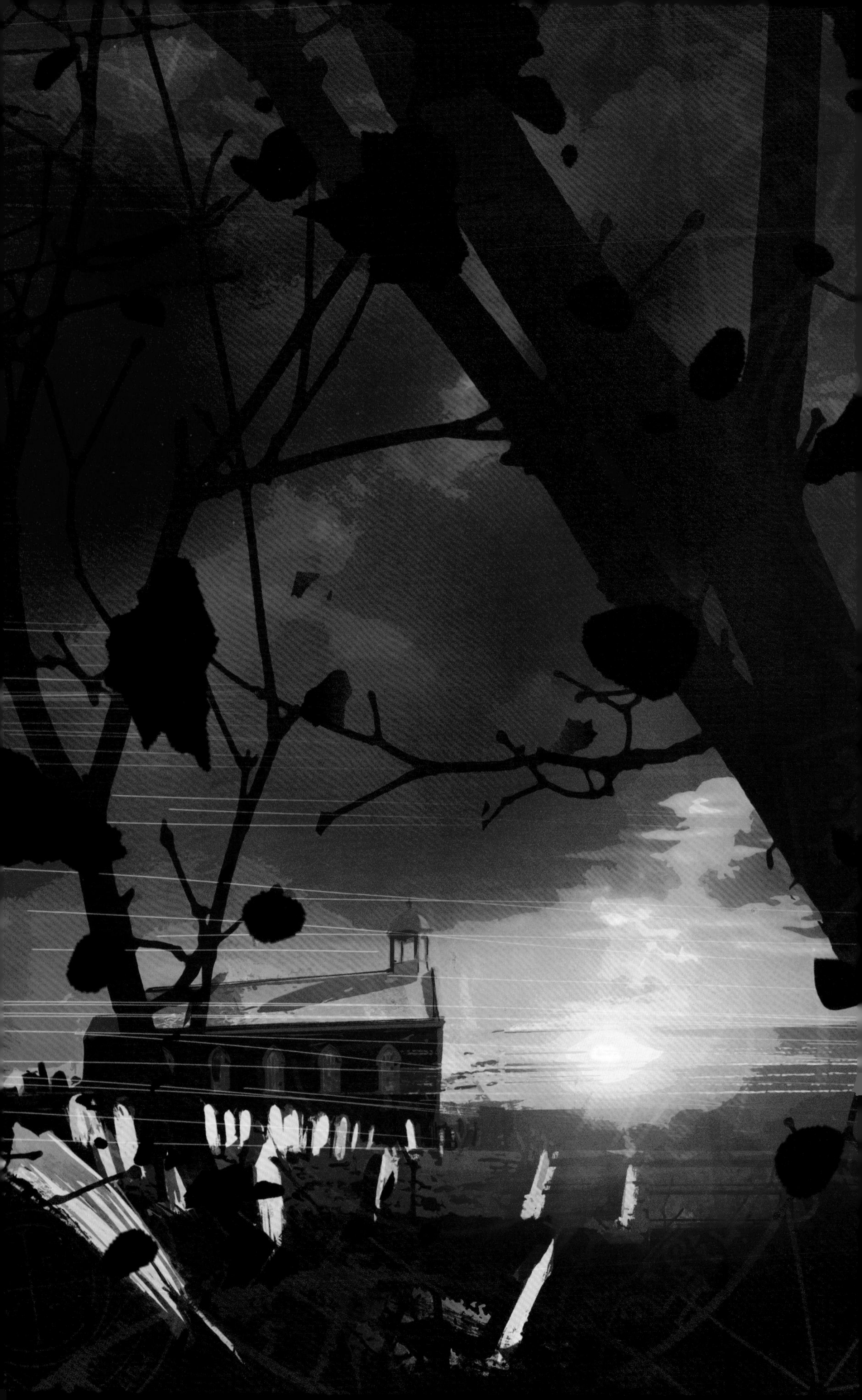

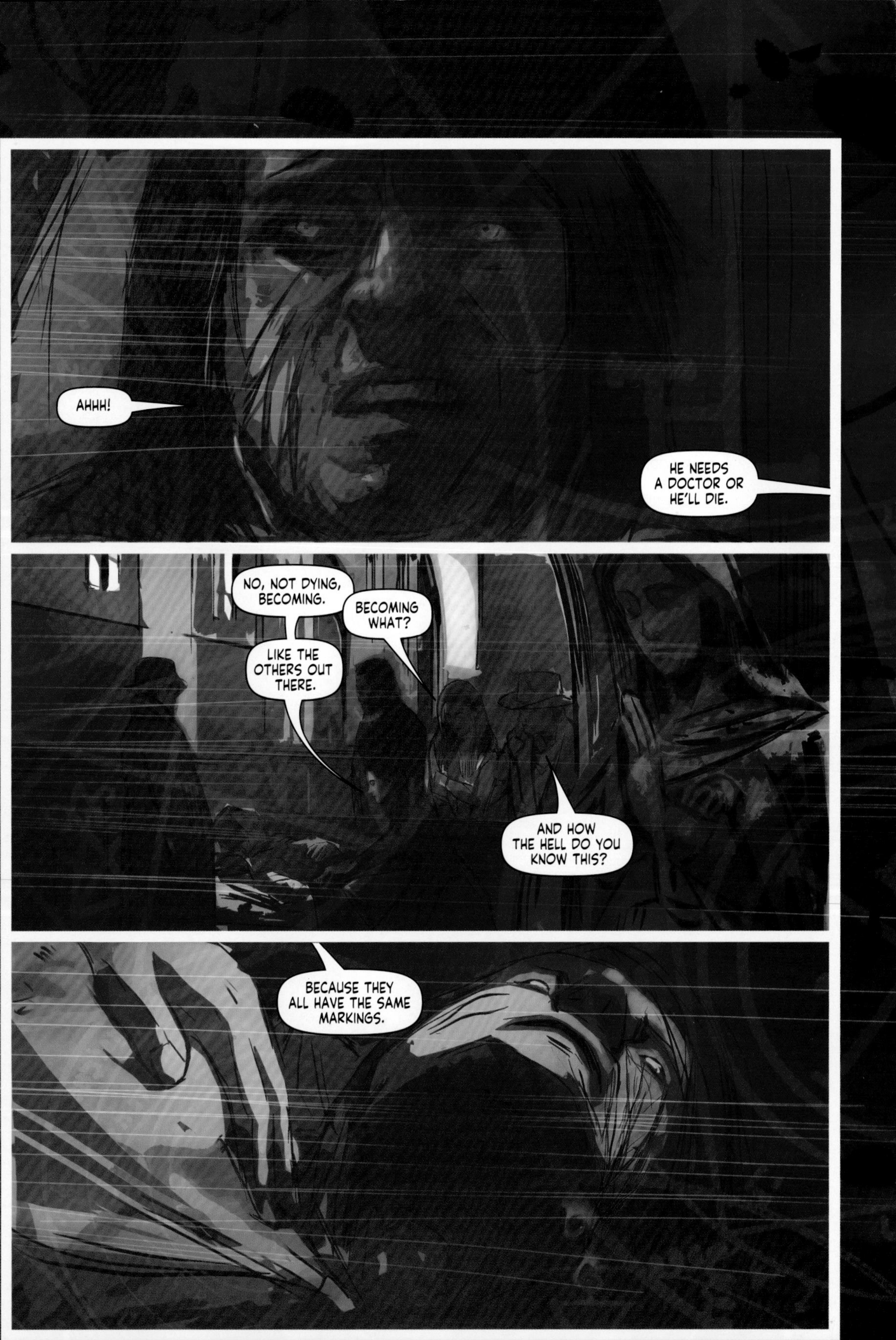
AHHH!
HE NEEDS A DOCTOR OR HE'LL DIE.
NO, NOT DYING, BECOMING.
BECOMING WHAT?
LIKE THE OTHERS OUT THERE.
AND HOW THE HELL DO YOU KNOW THIS?
BECAUSE THEY ALL HAVE THE SAME MARKINGS.

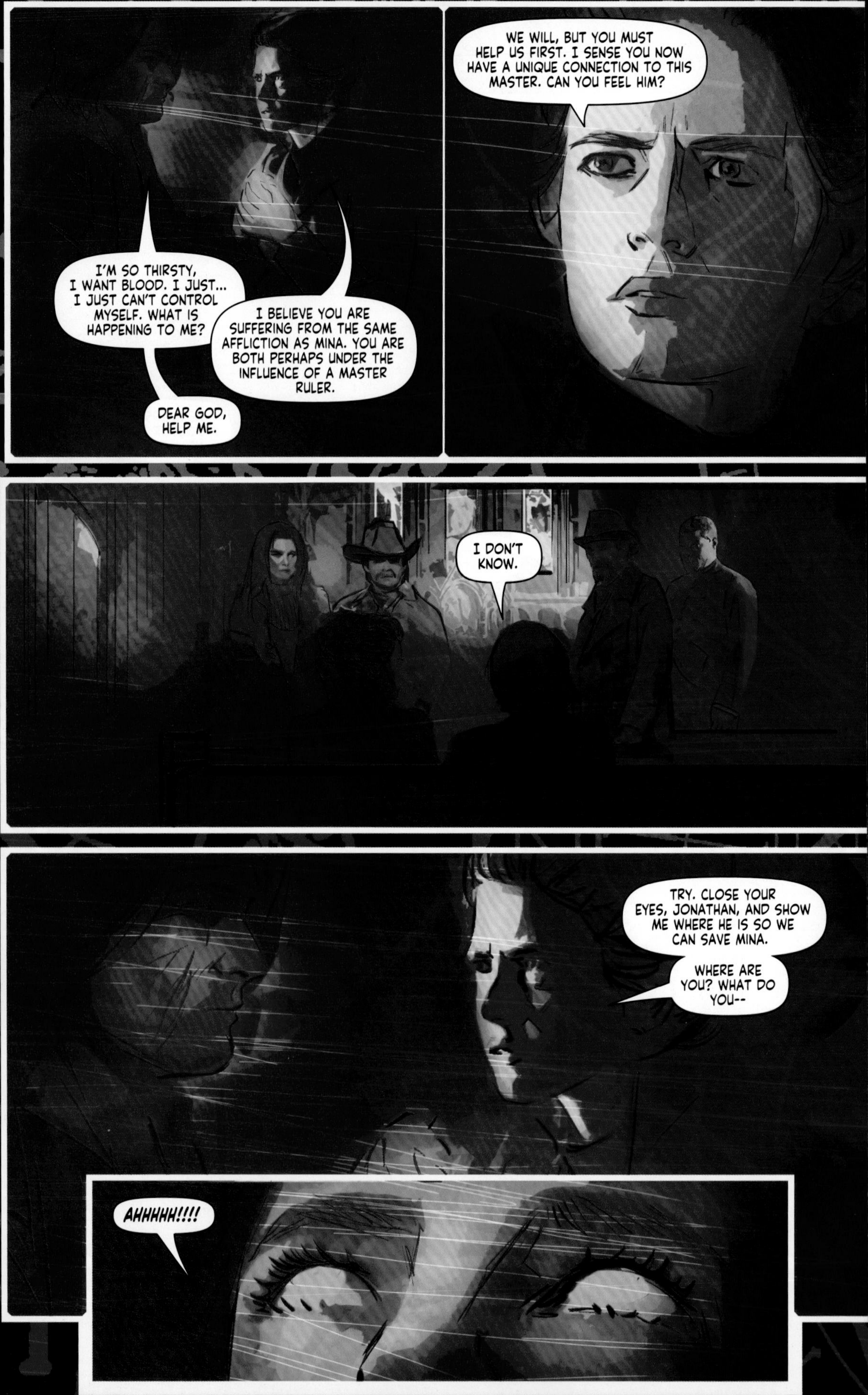
I'M SO THIRSTY, I WANT BLOOD. I JUST... I JUST CAN'T CONTROL MYSELF. WHAT IS HAPPENING TO ME?
I BELIEVE YOU ARE SUFFERING FROM THE SAME AFFLICTION AS MINA. YOU ARE BOTH PERHAPS UNDER THE INFLUENCE OF A MASTER RULER.
DEAR GOD, HELP ME.
WE WILL, BUT YOU MUST HELP US FIRST. I SENSE YOU NOW HAVE A UNIQUE CONNECTION TO THIS MASTER. CAN YOU FEEL HIM?
I DON'T KNOW.
TRY. CLOSE YOUR EYES, JONATHAN, AND SHOW ME WHERE HE IS SO WE CAN SAVE MINA.
WHERE ARE YOU? WHAT DO YOU--
AHHHHH!!!!

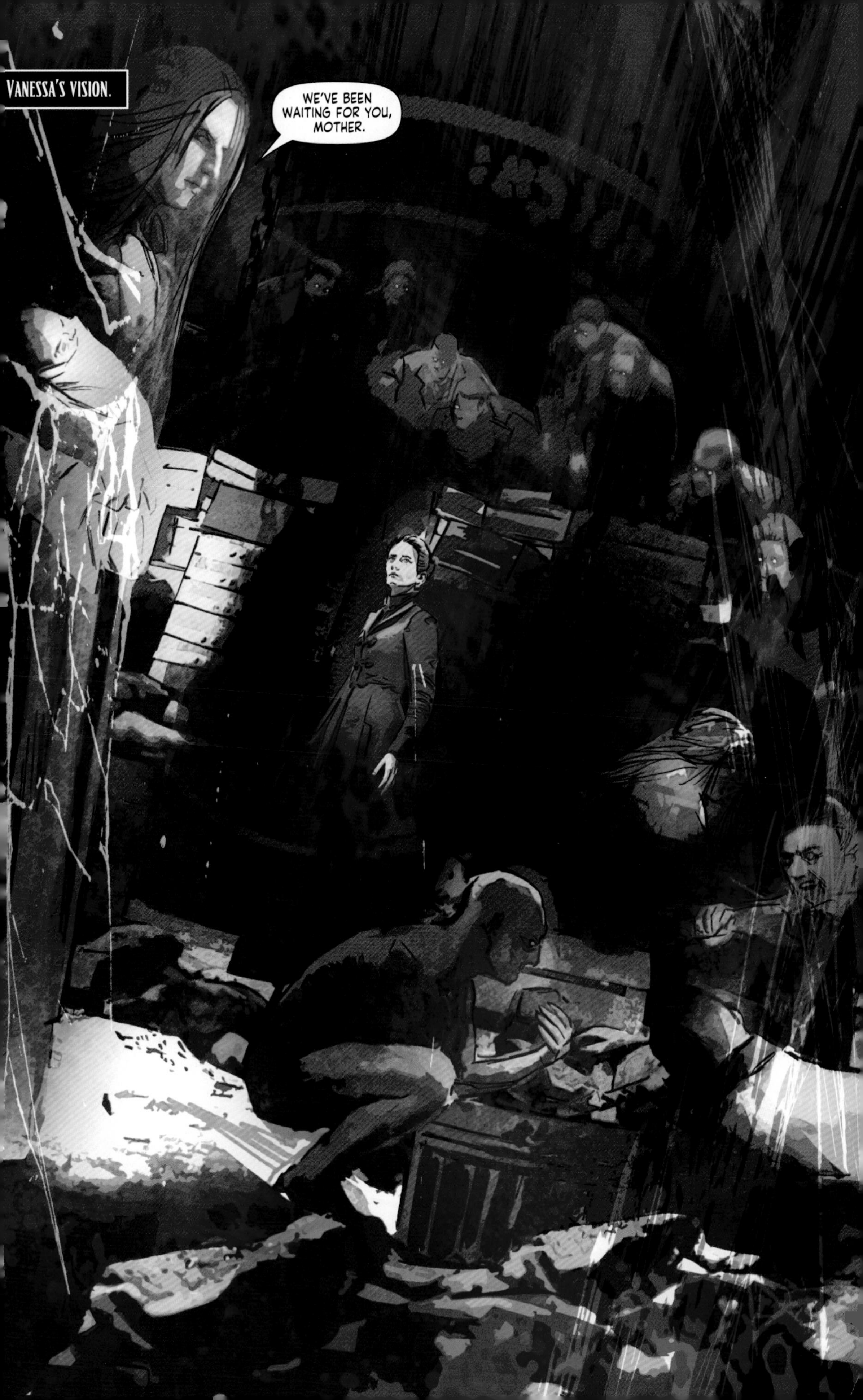
VANESSA'S VISION.
WE'VE BEEN WAITING FOR YOU, MOTHER.

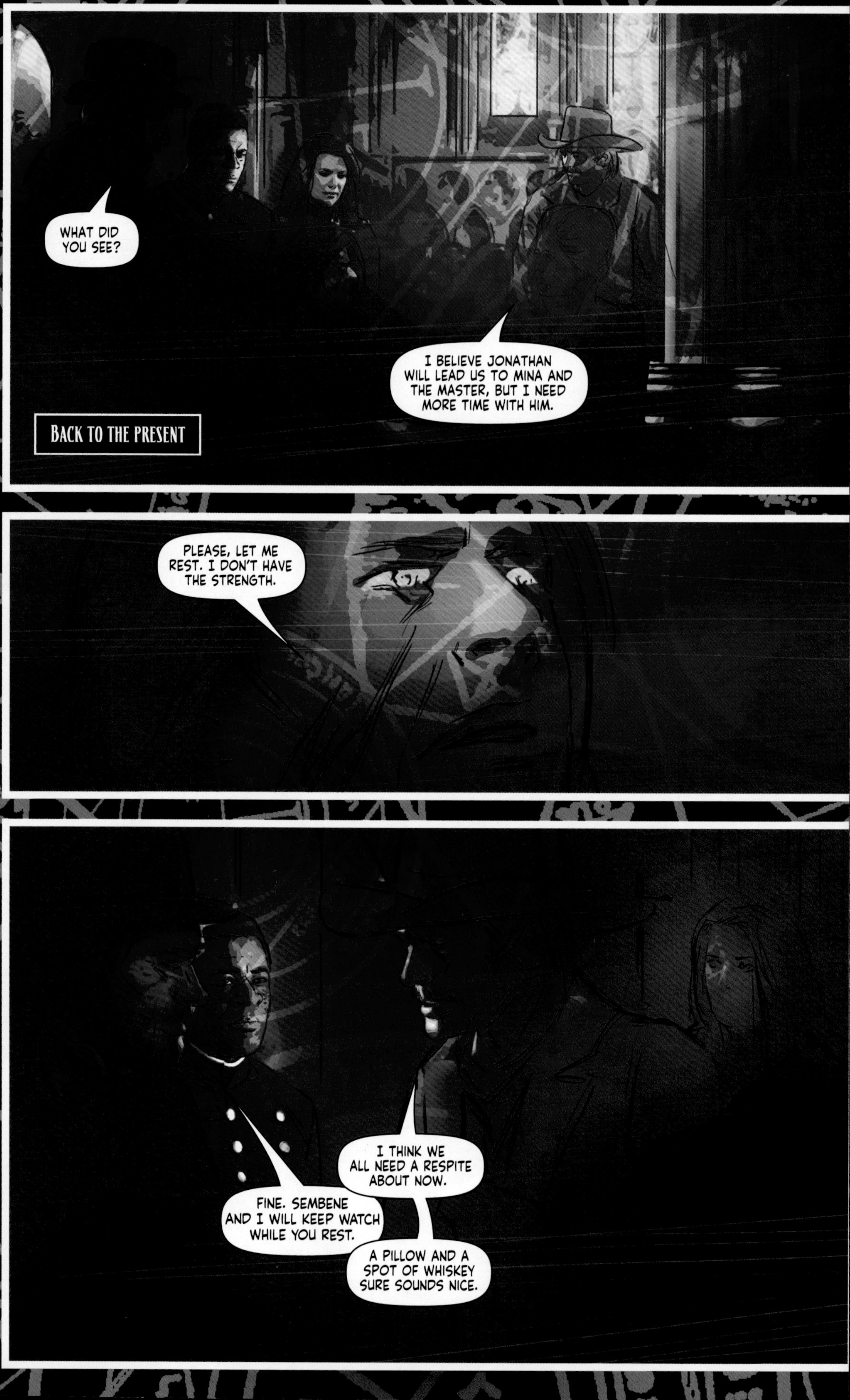
WHAT DID YOU SEE?
I BELIEVE JONATHAN WILL LEAD US TO MINA AND THE MASTER, BUT I NEED MORE TIME WITH HIM.
BACK TO THE PRESENT
PLEASE, LET ME REST. I DON'T HAVE THE STRENGTH.
I THINK WE ALL NEED A RESPITE ABOUT NOW.
FINE. SEMBENE AND I WILL KEEP WATCH WHILE YOU REST.
A PILLOW AND A SPOT OF WHISKEY SURE SOUNDS NICE.

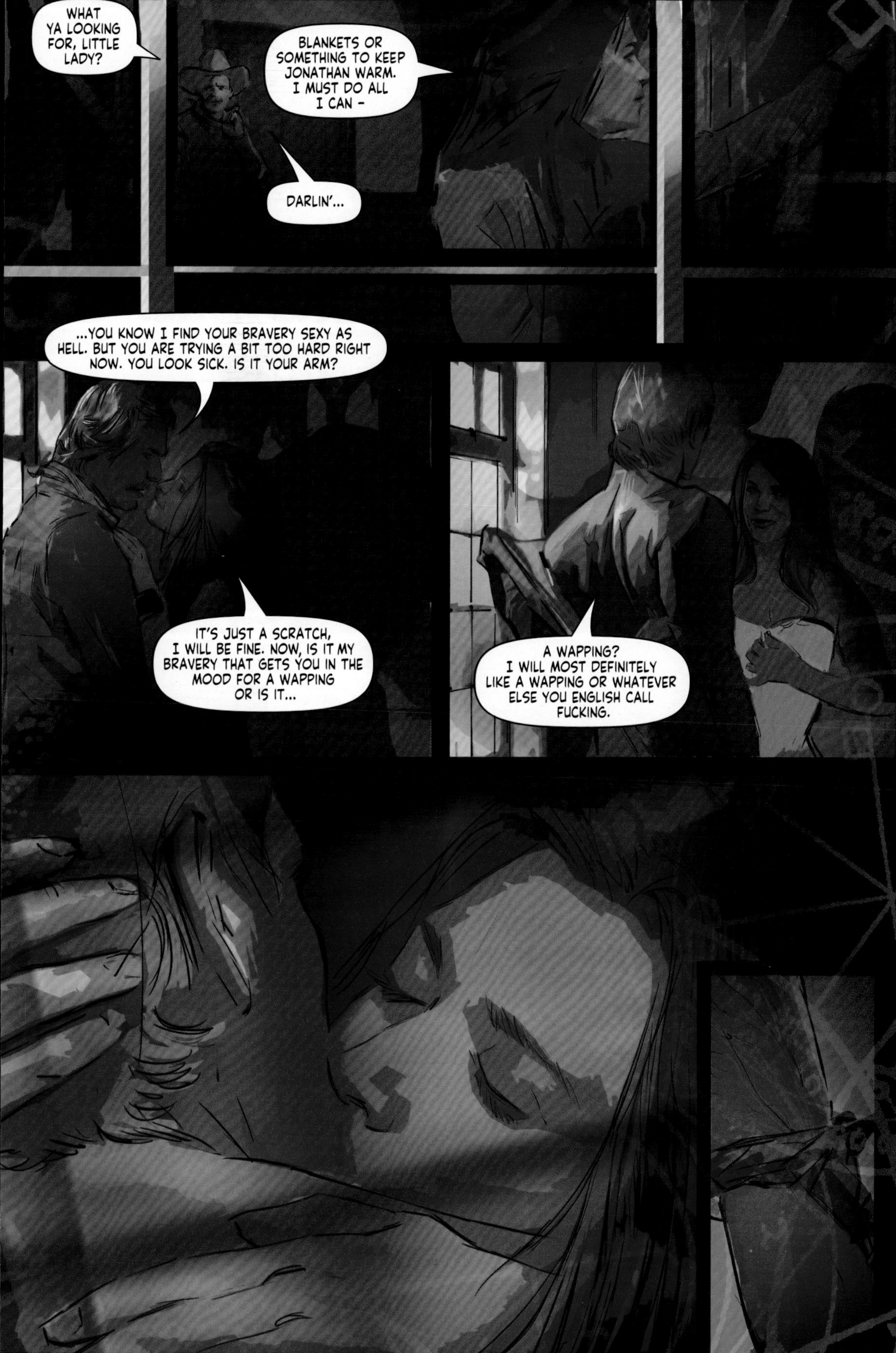
WHAT YA LOOKING FOR, LITTLE LADY?
BLANKETS OR SOMETHING TO KEEP JONATHAN WARM. I MUST DO ALL I CAN –
DARLIN'...
...YOU KNOW I FIND YOUR BRAVERY SEXY AS HELL. BUT YOU ARE TRYING A BIT TOO HARD RIGHT NOW. YOU LOOK SICK. IS IT YOUR ARM?
IT'S JUST A SCRATCH, I WILL BE FINE. NOW, IS IT MY BRAVERY THAT GETS YOU IN THE MOOD FOR A WAPPING OR IS IT...
A WAPPING? I WILL MOST DEFINITELY LIKE A WAPPING OR WHATEVER ELSE YOU ENGLISH CALL FUCKING.

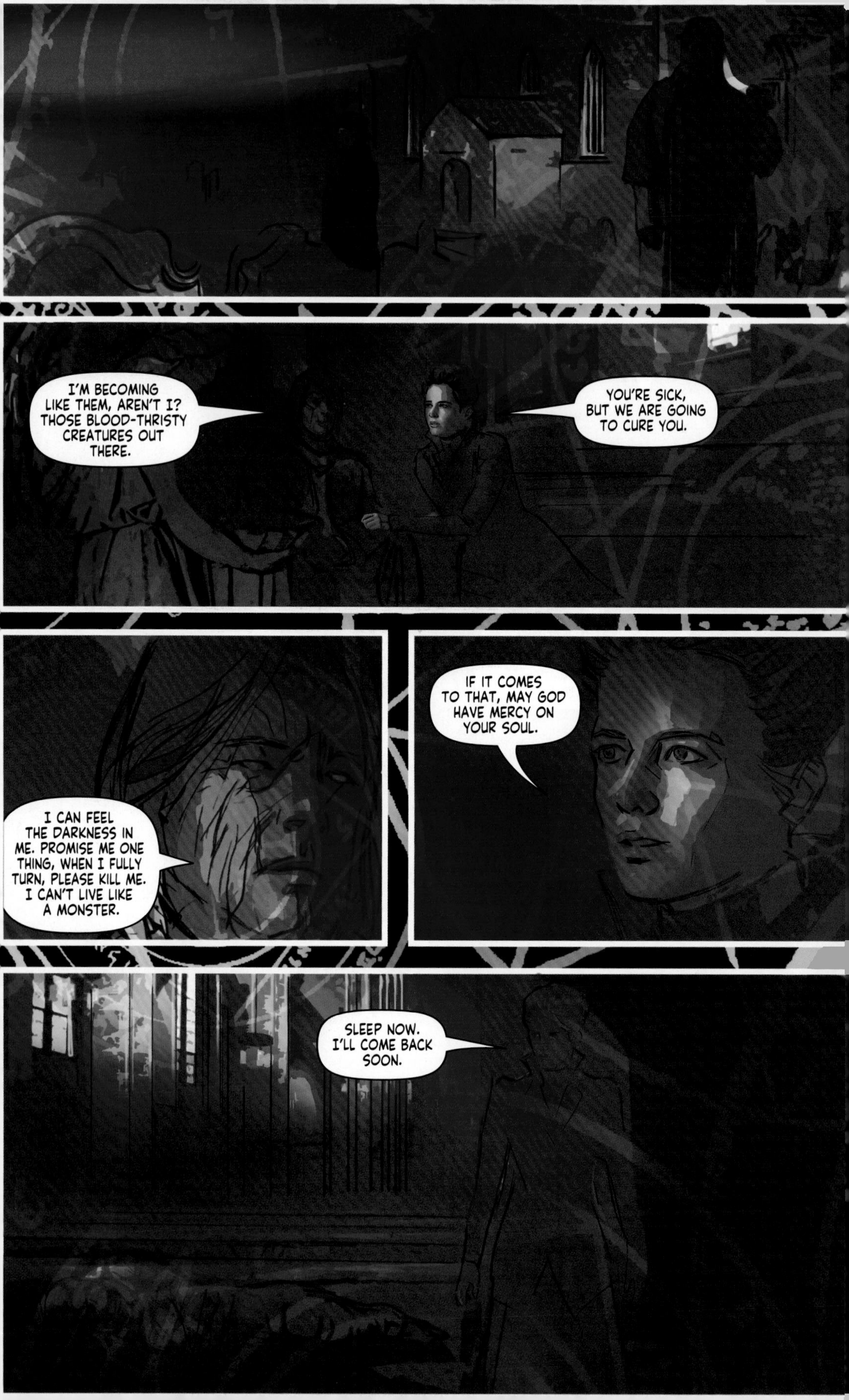
I'M BECOMING LIKE THEM, AREN'T I? THOSE BLOOD-THRISTY CREATURES OUT THERE.
YOU'RE SICK, BUT WE ARE GOING TO CURE YOU.
I CAN FEEL THE DARKNESS IN ME. PROMISE ME ONE THING, WHEN I FULLY TURN, PLEASE KILL ME. I CAN'T LIVE LIKE A MONSTER.
IF IT COMES TO THAT, MAY GOD HAVE MERCY ON YOUR SOUL.
SLEEP NOW. I'LL COME BACK SOON.

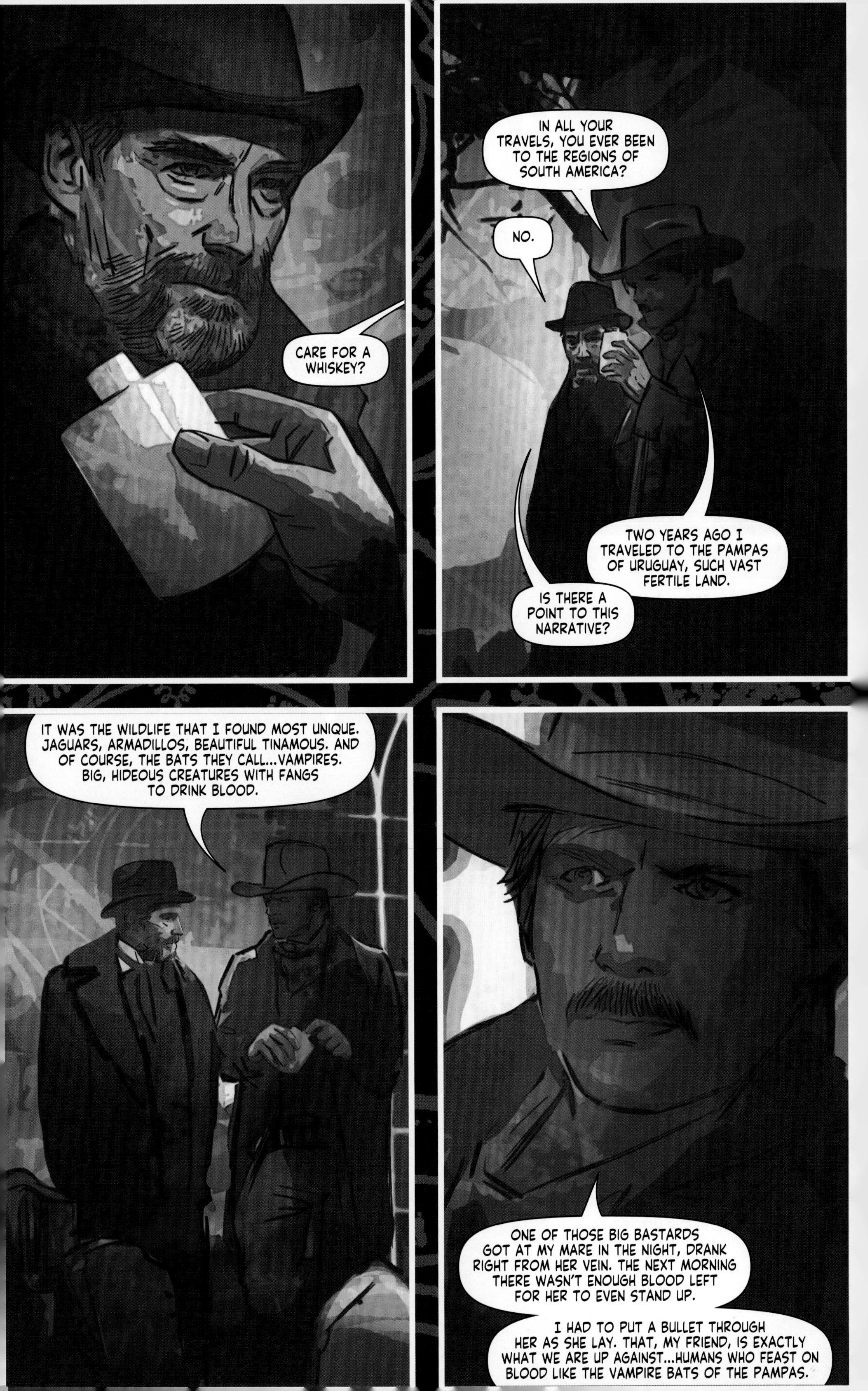
CARE FOR A WHISKEY?
IN ALL YOUR TRAVELS, YOU EVER BEEN TO THE REGIONS OF SOUTH AMERICA?
NO.
TWO YEARS AGO I TRAVELED TO THE PAMPAS OF URUGUAY, SUCH VAST FERTILE LAND.
IS THERE A POINT TO THIS NARRATIVE?
IT WAS THE WILDLIFE THAT I FOUND MOST UNIQUE. JAGUARS, ARMADILLOS, BEAUTIFUL TINAMOUS. AND OF COURSE, THE BATS THEY CALL...VAMPIRES. BIG, HIDEOUS CREATURES WITH FANGS TO DRINK BLOOD.
ONE OF THOSE BIG BASTARDS GOT AT MY MARE IN THE NIGHT, DRANK RIGHT FROM HER VEIN. THE NEXT MORNING THERE WASN'T ENOUGH BLOOD LEFT FOR HER TO EVEN STAND UP.
I HAD TO PUT A BULLET THROUGH HER AS SHE LAY. THAT, MY FRIEND, IS EXACTLY WHAT WE ARE UP AGAINST...HUMANS WHO FEAST ON BLOOD LIKE THE VAMPIRE BATS OF THE PAMPAS.

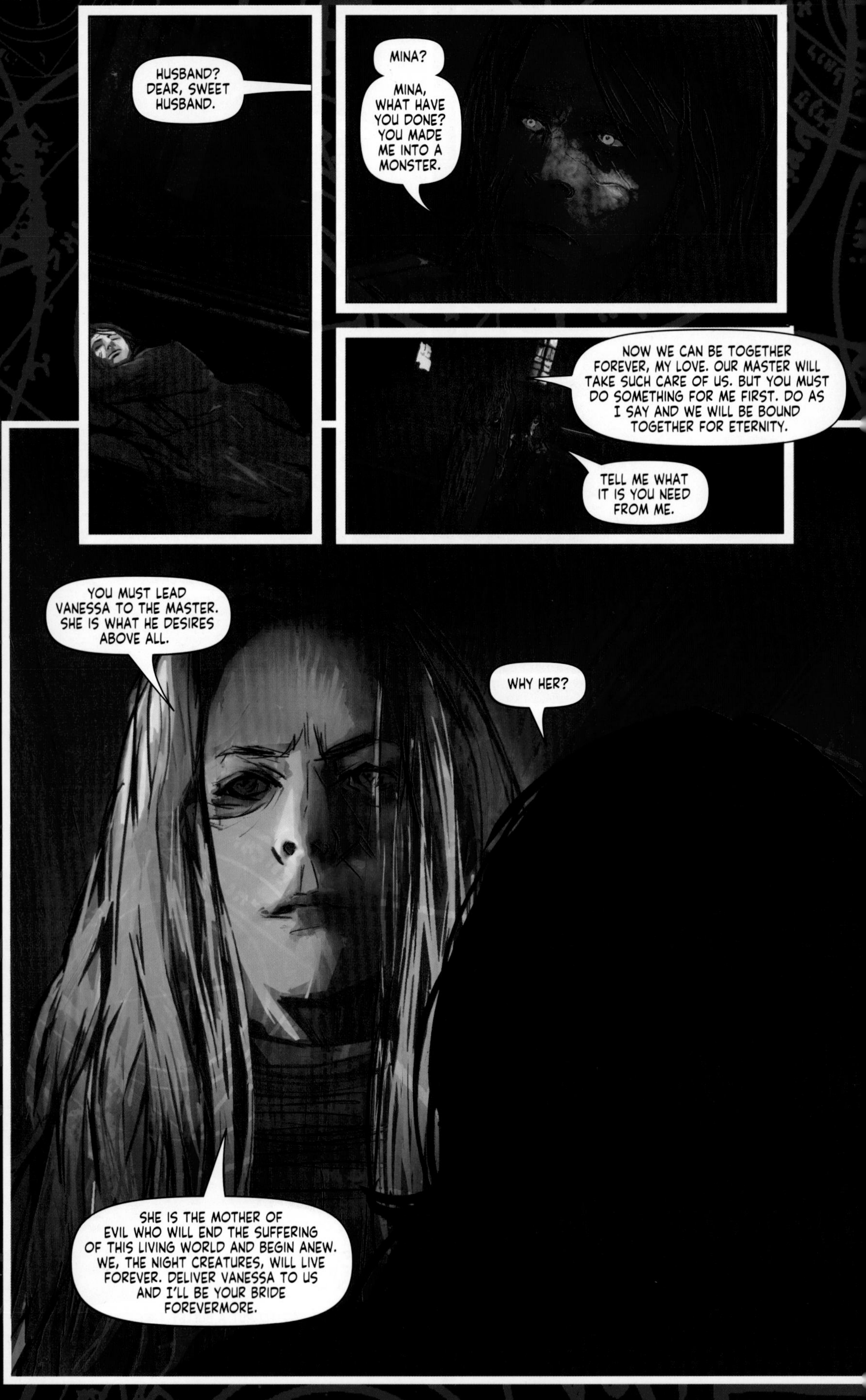
HUSBAND? DEAR, SWEET HUSBAND.
MINA?
MINA, WHAT HAVE YOU DONE? YOU MADE ME INTO A MONSTER.
NOW WE CAN BE TOGETHER FOREVER, MY LOVE. OUR MASTER WILL TAKE SUCH CARE OF US. BUT YOU MUST DO SOMETHING FOR ME FIRST. DO AS I SAY AND WE WILL BE BOUND TOGETHER FOR ETERNITY.
TELL ME WHAT IT IS YOU NEED FROM ME.
YOU MUST LEAD VANESSA TO THE MASTER. SHE IS WHAT HE DESIRES ABOVE ALL.
WHY HER?
SHE IS THE MOTHER OF EVIL WHO WILL END THE SUFFERING OF THIS LIVING WORLD AND BEGIN ANEW. WE, THE NIGHT CREATURES, WILL LIVE FOREVER. DELIVER VANESSA TO US AND I'LL BE YOUR BRIDE FOREVERMORE.

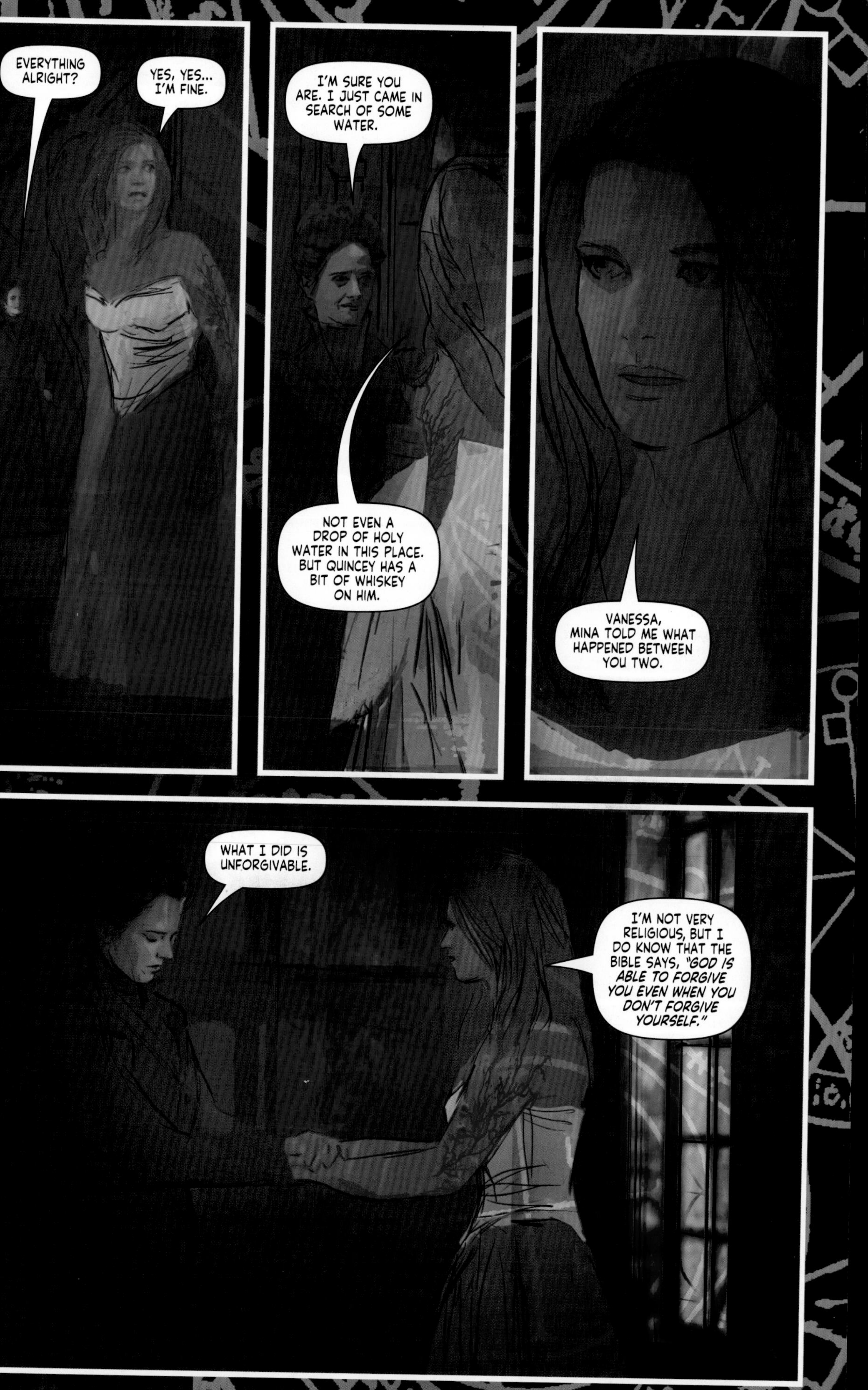
EVERYTHING ALRIGHT?
YES, YES... I'M FINE.
I'M SURE YOU ARE. I JUST CAME IN SEARCH OF SOME WATER.
NOT EVEN A DROP OF HOLY WATER IN THIS PLACE. BUT QUINCEY HAS A BIT OF WHISKEY ON HIM.
VANESSA, MINA TOLD ME WHAT HAPPENED BETWEEN YOU TWO.
WHAT I DID IS UNFORGIVABLE.
I'M NOT VERY RELIGIOUS, BUT I DO KNOW THAT THE BIBLE SAYS, "GOD IS ABLE TO FORGIVE YOU EVEN WHEN YOU DON'T FORGIVE YOURSELF."

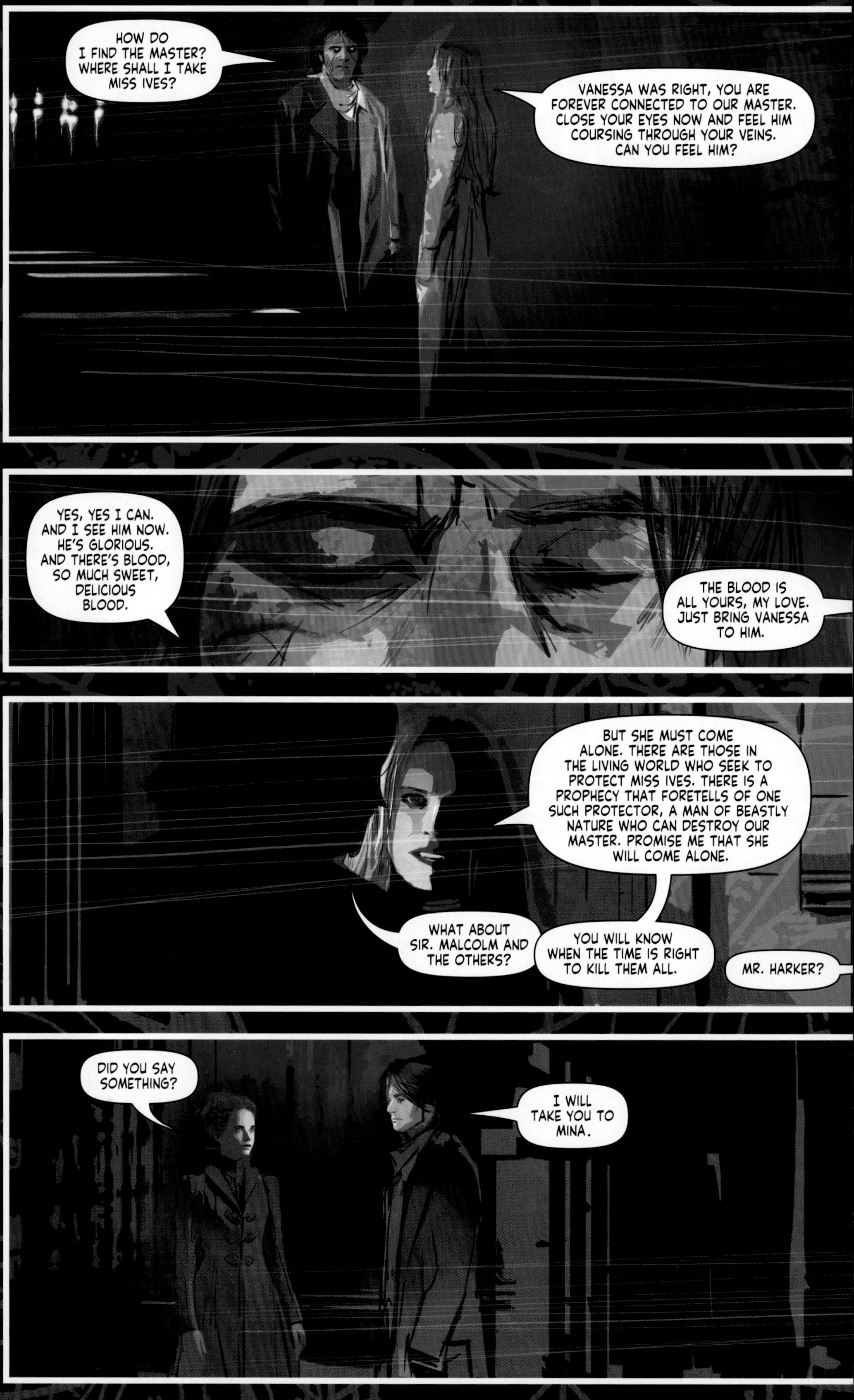
HOW DO I FIND THE MASTER? WHERE SHALL I TAKE MISS IVES?
VANESSA WAS RIGHT, YOU ARE FOREVER CONNECTED TO OUR MASTER. CLOSE YOUR EYES NOW AND FEEL HIM COURSING THROUGH YOUR VEINS. CAN YOU FEEL HIM?
YES, YES I CAN. AND I SEE HIM NOW. HE'S GLORIOUS. AND THERE'S BLOOD, SO MUCH SWEET, DELICIOUS BLOOD.
THE BLOOD IS ALL YOURS, MY LOVE. JUST BRING VANESSA TO HIM.
BUT SHE MUST COME ALONE. THERE ARE THOSE IN THE LIVING WORLD WHO SEEK TO PROTECT MISS IVES. THERE IS A PROPHECY THAT FORETELLS OF ONE SUCH PROTECTOR, A MAN OF BEASTLY NATURE WHO CAN DESTROY OUR MASTER. PROMISE ME THAT SHE WILL COME ALONE.
WHAT ABOUT SIR. MALCOLM AND THE OTHERS?
YOU WILL KNOW WHEN THE TIME IS RIGHT TO KILL THEM ALL.
MR. HARKER?
DID YOU SAY SOMETHING?
I WILL TAKE YOU TO MINA.

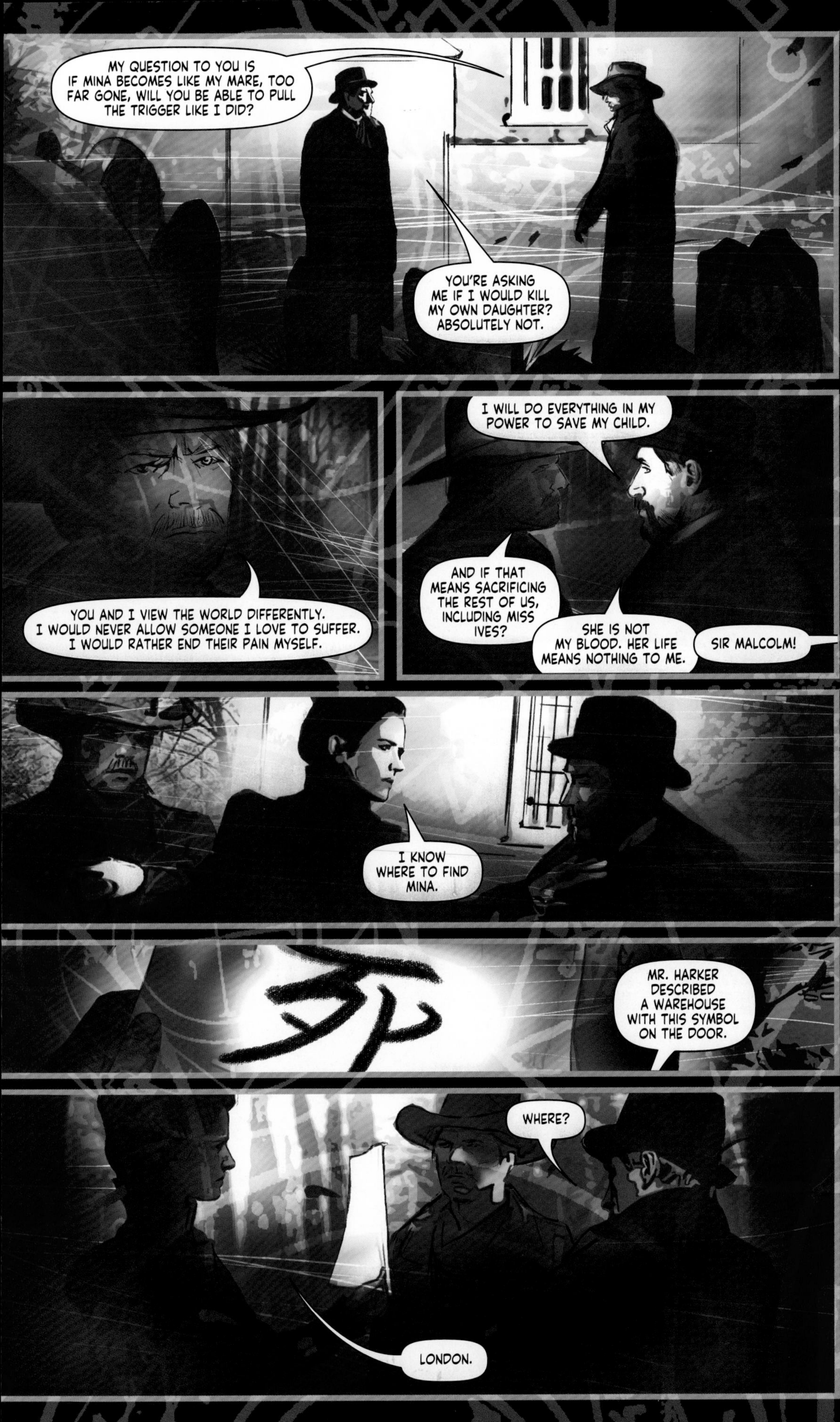
MY QUESTION TO YOU IS IF MINA BECOMES LIKE MY MARE, TOO FAR GONE, WILL YOU BE ABLE TO PULL THE TRIGGER LIKE I DID?
YOU'RE ASKING ME IF I WOULD KILL MY OWN DAUGHTER? ABSOLUTELY NOT.
YOU AND I VIEW THE WORLD DIFFERENTLY. I WOULD NEVER ALLOW SOMEONE I LOVE TO SUFFER. I WOULD RATHER END THEIR PAIN MYSELF.
I WILL DO EVERYTHING IN MY POWER TO SAVE MY CHILD.
AND IF THAT MEANS SACRIFICING THE REST OF US, INCLUDING MISS IVES?
SHE IS NOT MY BLOOD. HER LIFE MEANS NOTHING TO ME.
SIR MALCOLM!
I KNOW WHERE TO FIND MINA.
MR. HARKER DESCRIBED A WAREHOUSE WITH THIS SYMBOL ON THE DOOR.
WHERE?
LONDON.

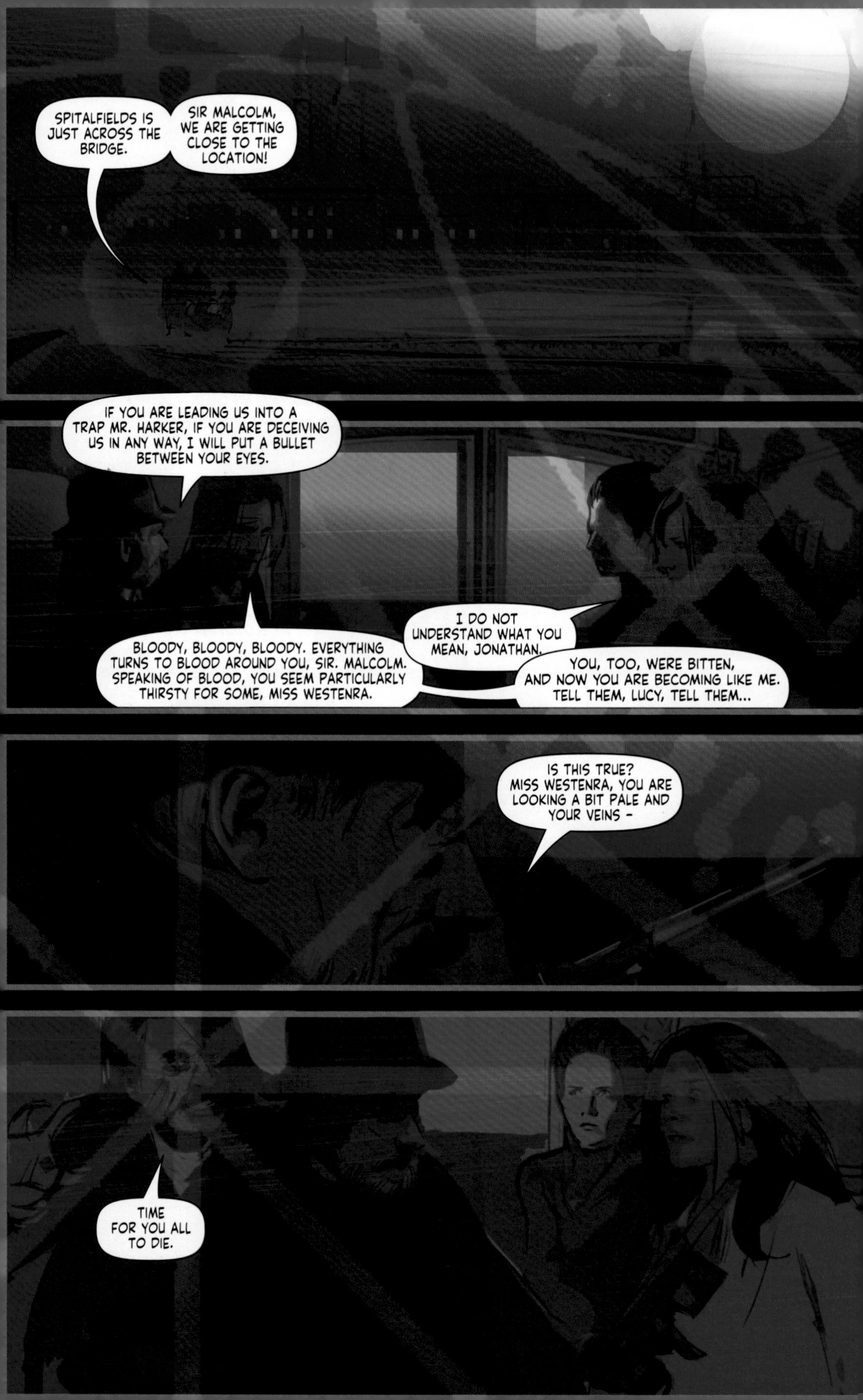
SPITALFIELDS IS JUST ACROSS THE BRIDGE.
SIR MALCOLM, WE ARE GETTING CLOSE TO THE LOCATION!
IF YOU ARE LEADING US INTO A TRAP MR. HARKER, IF YOU ARE DECEIVING US IN ANY WAY, I WILL PUT A BULLET BETWEEN YOUR EYES.
BLOODY, BLOODY, BLOODY. EVERYTHING TURNS TO BLOOD AROUND YOU, SIR. MALCOLM. SPEAKING OF BLOOD, YOU SEEM PARTICULARLY THIRSTY FOR SOME, MISS WESTENRA.
I DO NOT UNDERSTAND WHAT YOU MEAN, JONATHAN.
YOU, TOO, WERE BITTEN, AND NOW YOU ARE BECOMING LIKE ME. TELL THEM, LUCY, TELL THEM...
IS THIS TRUE? MISS WESTENRA, YOU ARE LOOKING A BIT PALE AND YOUR VEINS –
TIME FOR YOU ALL TO DIE.

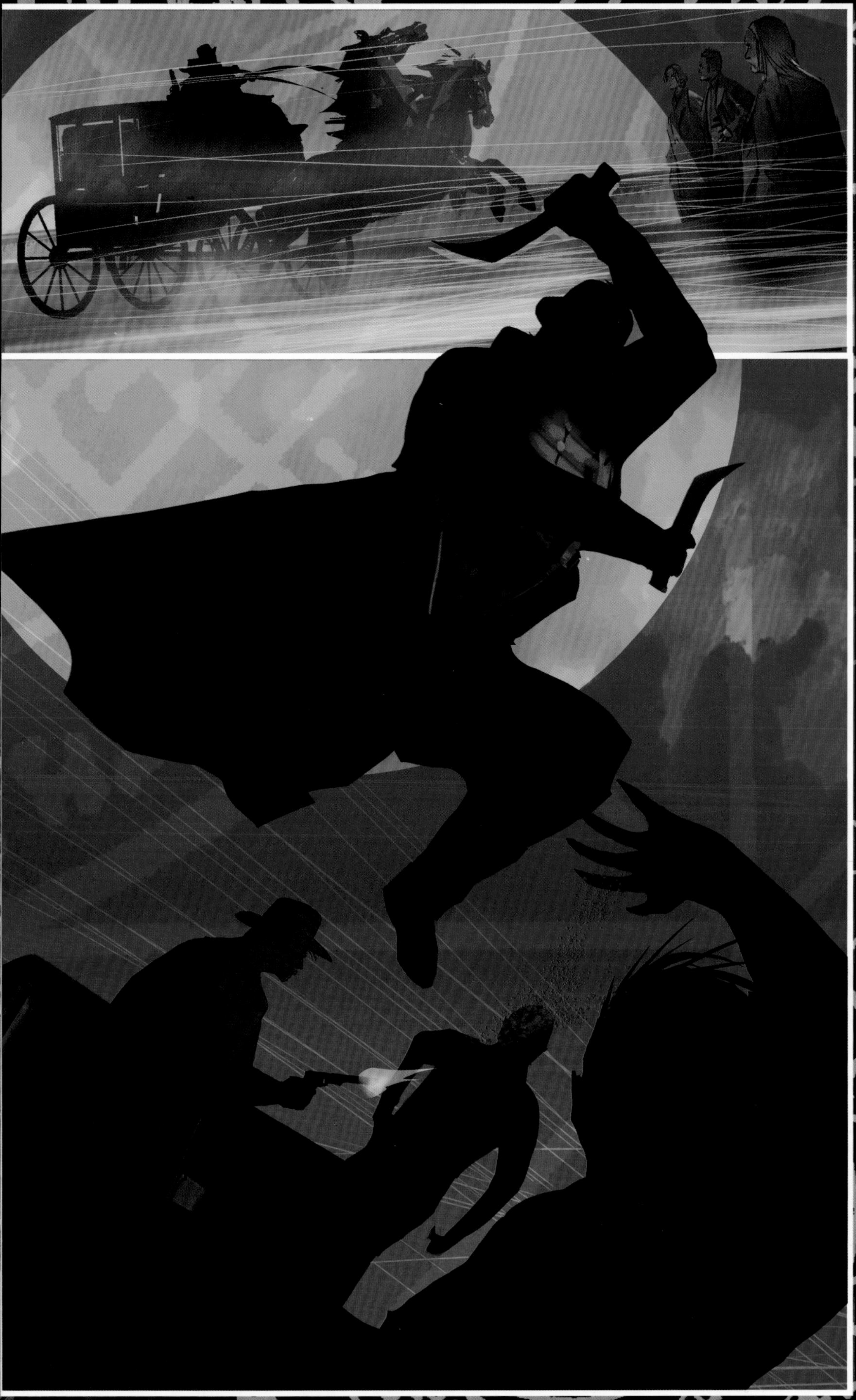

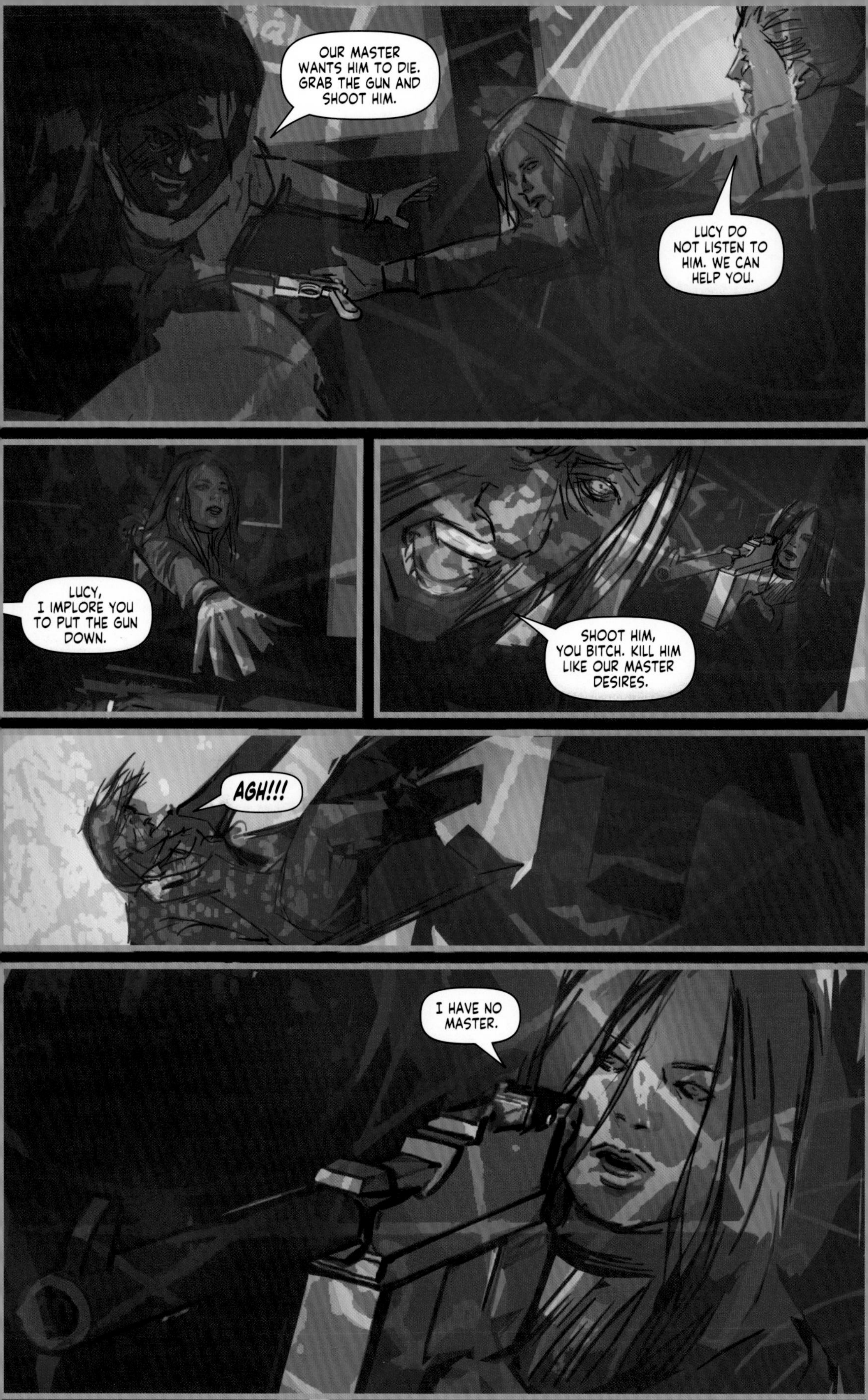
OUR MASTER WANTS HIM TO DIE. GRAB THE GUN AND SHOOT HIM.
LUCY DO NOT LISTEN TO HIM. WE CAN HELP YOU.
LUCY, I IMPLORE YOU TO PUT THE GUN DOWN.
SHOOT HIM, YOU BITCH. KILL HIM LIKE OUR MASTER DESIRES.
AGH!!!
I HAVE NO MASTER.

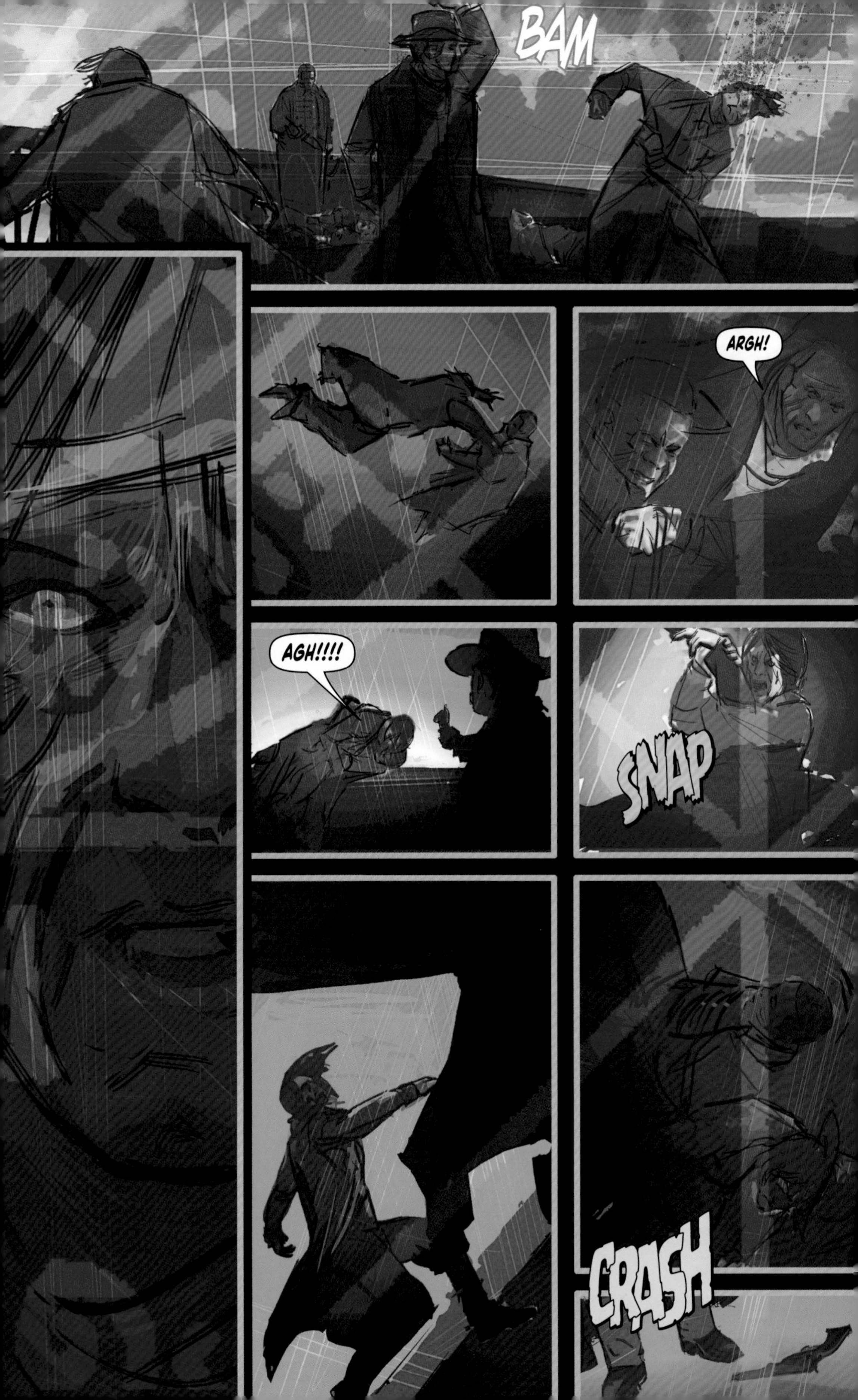
BAM
ARGH!
AGH!!!!
SNAP
CRASH

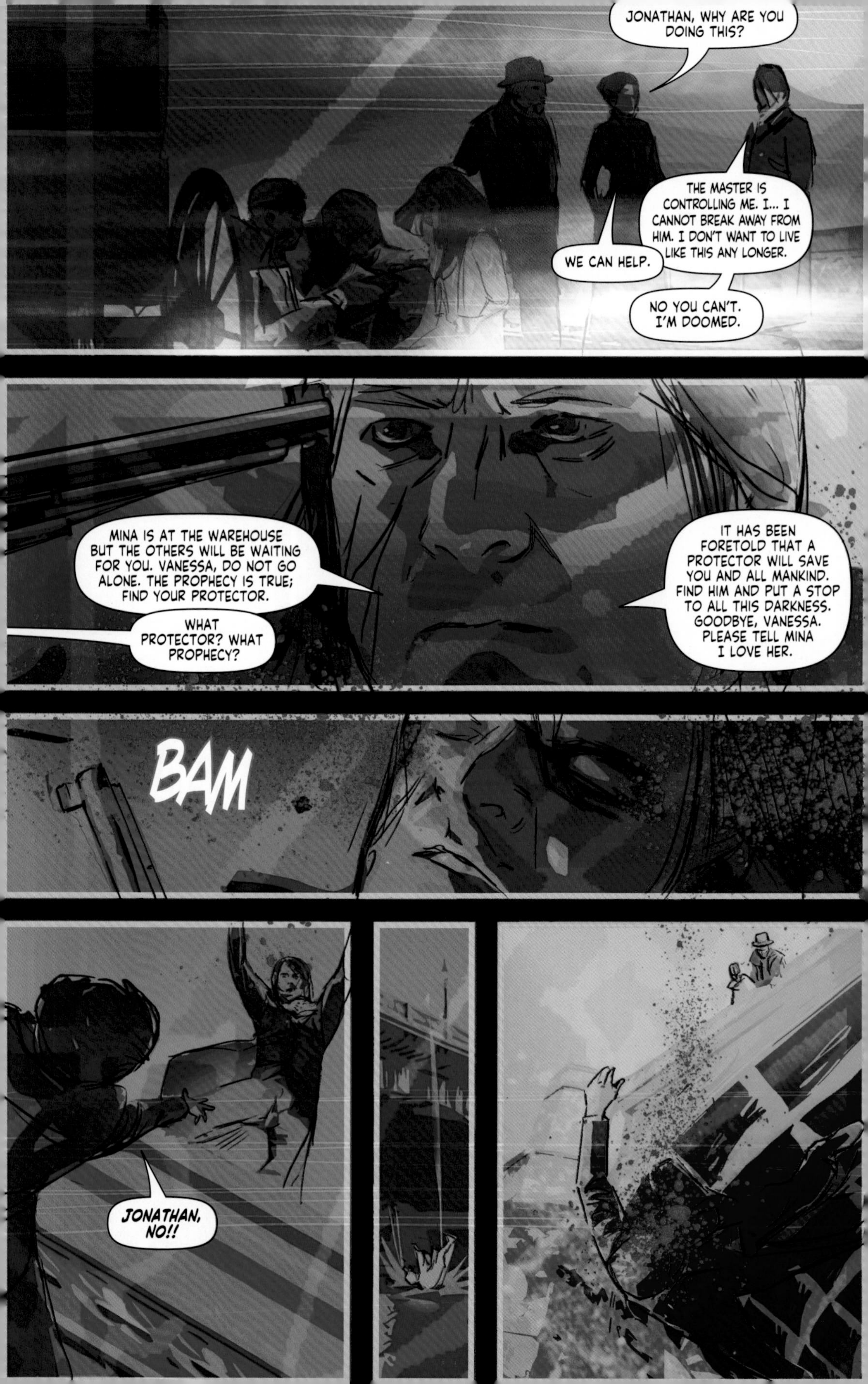
JONATHAN, WHY ARE YOU DOING THIS?
THE MASTER IS CONTROLLING ME. I... I CANNOT BREAK AWAY FROM HIM. I DON'T WANT TO LIVE LIKE THIS ANY LONGER.
WE CAN HELP.
NO YOU CAN'T. I'M DOOMED.
MINA IS AT THE WAREHOUSE BUT THE OTHERS WILL BE WAITING FOR YOU. VANESSA, DO NOT GO ALONE. THE PROPHECY IS TRUE; FIND YOUR PROTECTOR.
WHAT PROTECTOR? WHAT PROPHECY?
IT HAS BEEN FORETOLD THAT A PROTECTOR WILL SAVE YOU AND ALL MANKIND. FIND HIM AND PUT A STOP TO ALL THIS DARKNESS. GOODBYE, VANESSA. PLEASE TELL MINA I LOVE HER.
BAM
JONATHAN, NO!!

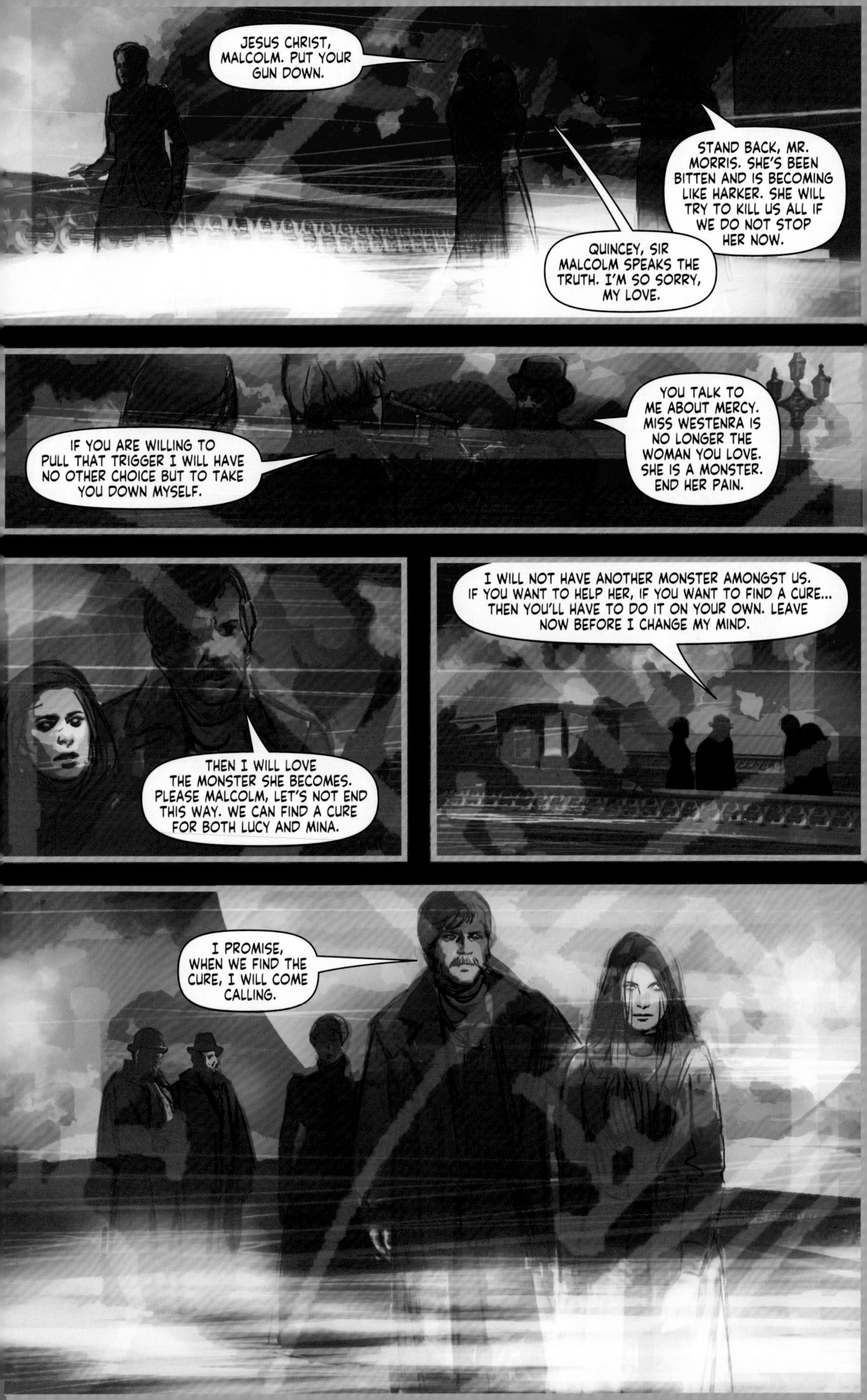
JESUS CHRIST, MALCOLM. PUT YOUR GUN DOWN.
STAND BACK, MR. MORRIS. SHE'S BEEN BITTEN AND IS BECOMING LIKE HARKER. SHE WILL TRY TO KILL US ALL IF WE DO NOT STOP HER NOW.
QUINCEY, SIR MALCOLM SPEAKS THE TRUTH. I'M SO SORRY, MY LOVE.
IF YOU ARE WILLING TO PULL THAT TRIGGER I WILL HAVE NO OTHER CHOICE BUT TO TAKE YOU DOWN MYSELF.
YOU TALK TO ME ABOUT MERCY. MISS WESTENRA IS NO LONGER THE WOMAN YOU LOVE. SHE IS A MONSTER. END HER PAIN.
THEN I WILL LOVE THE MONSTER SHE BECOMES. PLEASE MALCOLM, LET'S NOT END THIS WAY. WE CAN FIND A CURE FOR BOTH LUCY AND MINA.
I WILL NOT HAVE ANOTHER MONSTER AMONGST US. IF YOU WANT TO HELP HER, IF YOU WANT TO FIND A CURE... THEN YOU'LL HAVE TO DO IT ON YOUR OWN. LEAVE NOW BEFORE I CHANGE MY MIND.
I PROMISE, WHEN WE FIND THE CURE, I WILL COME CALLING.

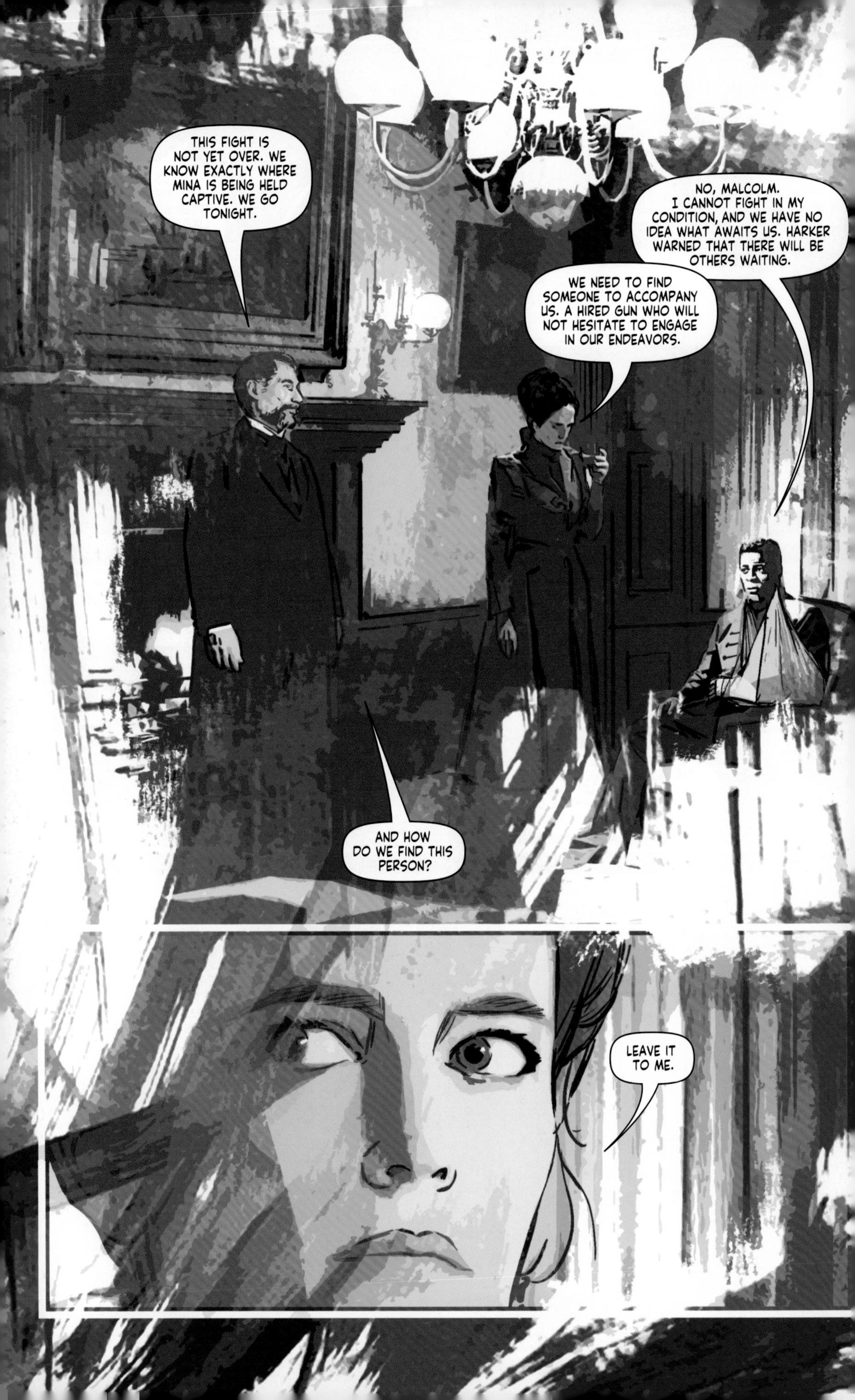
THIS FIGHT IS NOT YET OVER. WE KNOW EXACTLY WHERE MINA IS BEING HELD CAPTIVE. WE GO TONIGHT.
NO, MALCOLM. I CANNOT FIGHT IN MY CONDITION, AND WE HAVE NO IDEA WHAT AWAITS US. HARKER WARNED THAT THERE WILL BE OTHERS WAITING.
WE NEED TO FIND SOMEONE TO ACCOMPANY US. A HIRED GUN WHO WILL NOT HESITATE TO ENGAGE IN OUR ENDEAVORS.
AND HOW DO WE FIND THIS PERSON?
LEAVE IT TO ME.

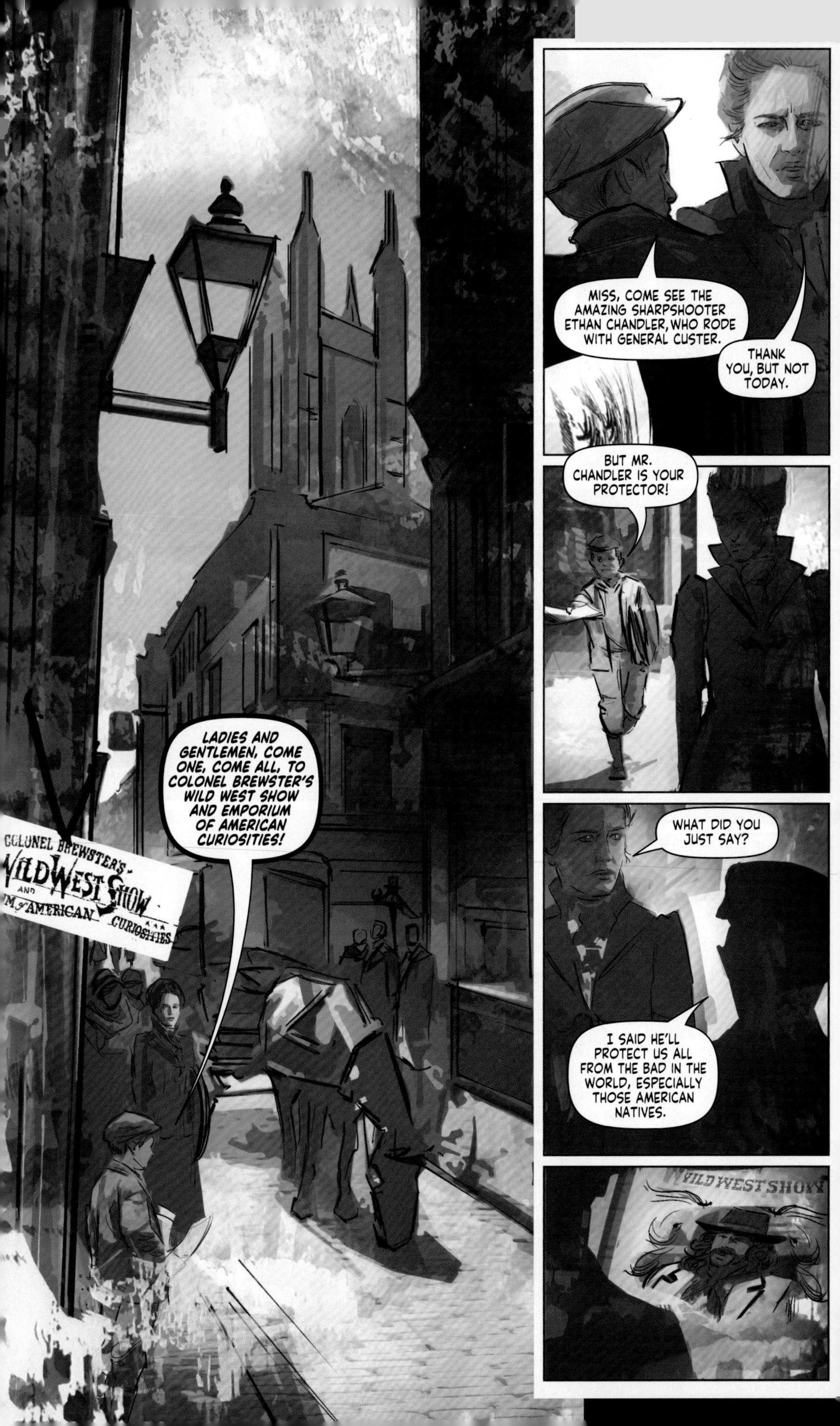
COLONEL BREWSTER'S WILD WEST SHOW AND ... AMERICAN CURIOSITIES
LADIES AND GENTLEMEN, COME ONE, COME ALL, TO COLONEL BREWSTER'S WILD WEST SHOW AND EMPORIUM OF AMERICAN CURIOSITIES!
MISS, COME SEE THE AMAZING SHARPSHOOTER ETHAN CHANDLER, WHO RODE WITH GENERAL CUSTER.
THANK YOU, BUT NOT TODAY.
BUT MR. CHANDLER IS YOUR PROTECTOR!
WHAT DID YOU JUST SAY?
I SAID HE'LL PROTECT US ALL FROM THE BAD IN THE WORLD, ESPECIALLY THOSE AMERICAN NATIVES.
WILD WEST SHOW

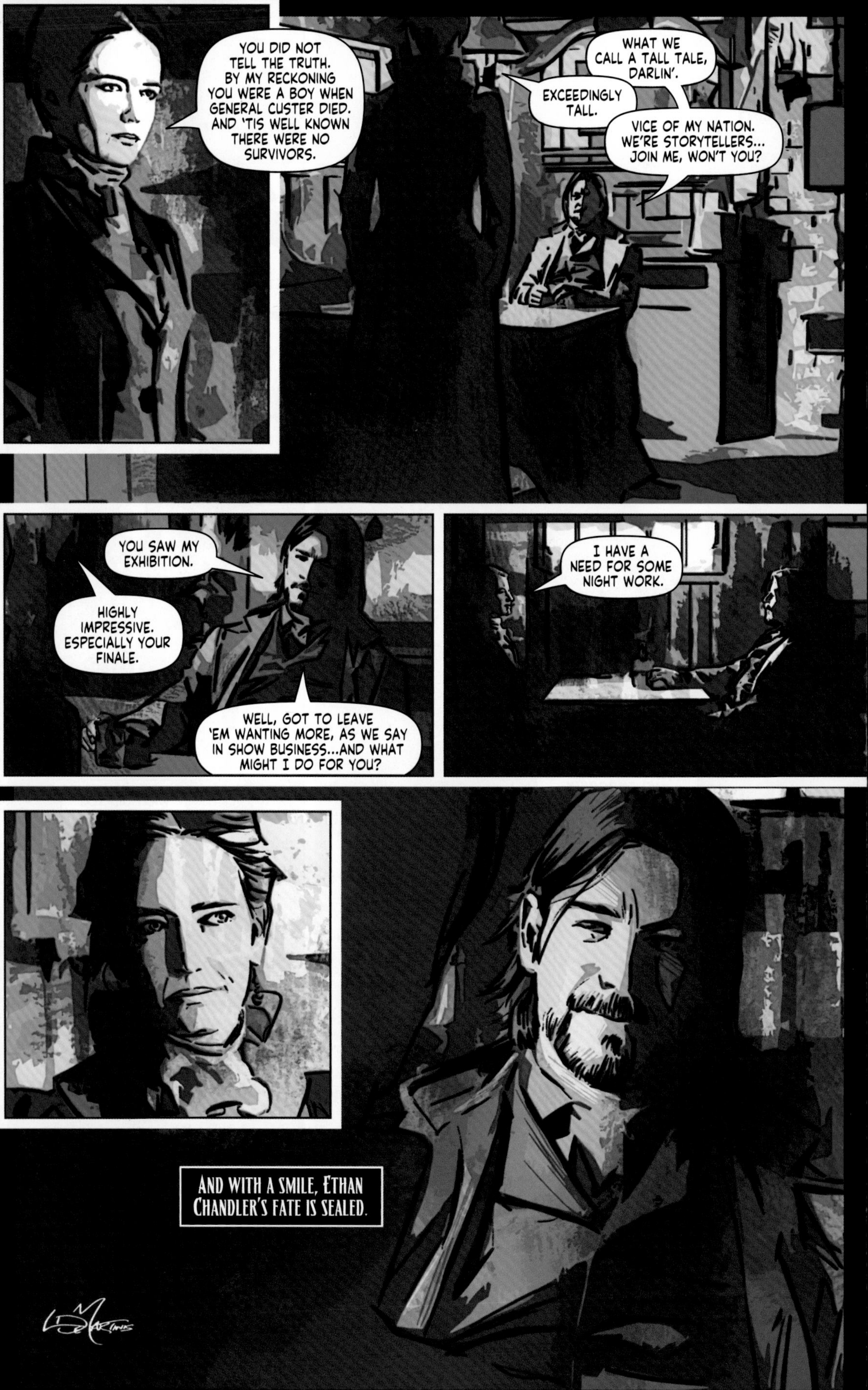

YOU DID NOT TELL THE TRUTH. BY MY RECKONING YOU WERE A BOY WHEN GENERAL CUSTER DIED. AND 'TIS WELL KNOWN THERE WERE NO SURVIVORS.
WHAT WE CALL A TALL TALE, DARLIN'.
EXCEEDINGLY TALL.
VICE OF MY NATION. WE'RE STORYTELLERS... JOIN ME, WON'T YOU?
YOU SAW MY EXHIBITION.
HIGHLY IMPRESSIVE. ESPECIALLY YOUR FINALE.
WELL, GOT TO LEAVE 'EM WANTING MORE, AS WE SAY IN SHOW BUSINESS...AND WHAT MIGHT I DO FOR YOU?
I HAVE A NEED FOR SOME NIGHT WORK.
AND WITH A SMILE, ETHAN CHANDLER'S FATE IS SEALED.

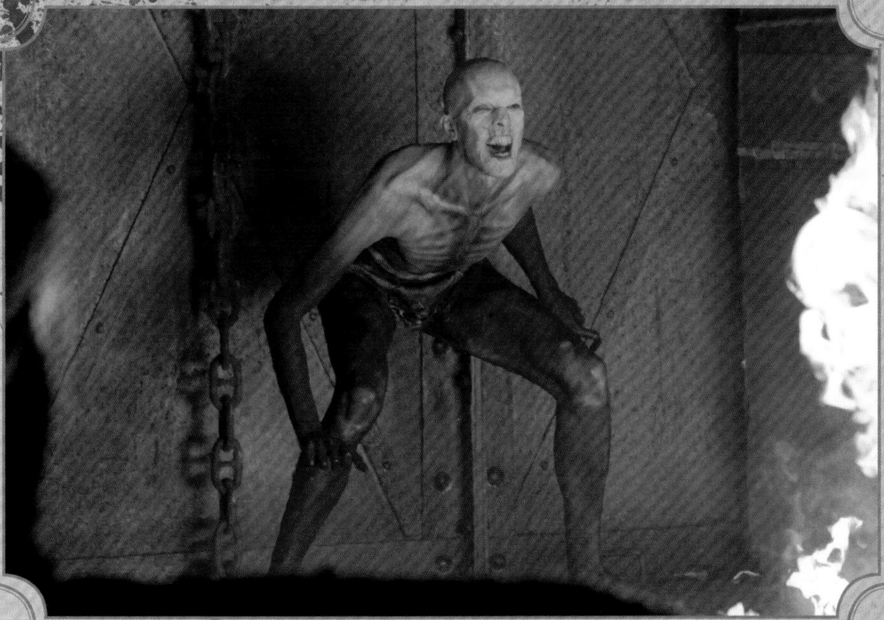

THE VAMPIRE

The problem with vampires is that everyone's seen them. They're everywhere – lurking in the murky shadows of graveyards; flapping in like bats through period windows; masquerading as good-looking teenagers who occasionally sparkle a bit; waiting menacingly in the icy darkness of long winters. Trying to do anything new within this familiar folklore trope is extremely difficult, a fact John Logan was acutely aware of when it came to designing the creatures for *Penny Dreadful*.

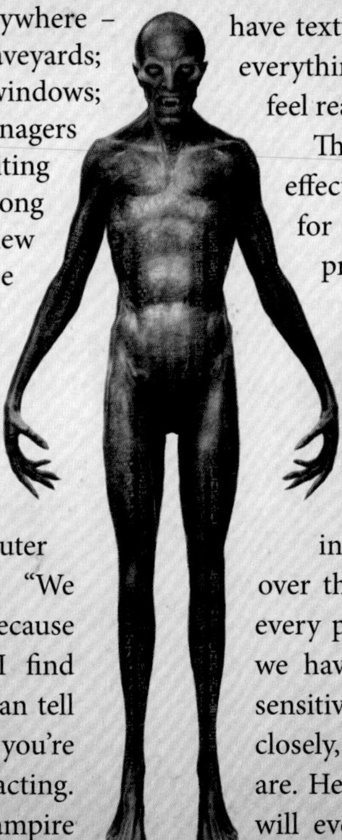

"The one thing we knew very early on was we didn't want computer generated monsters," says Logan. "We simply were not going to do that, because there is something about them I find inherently false. I think audiences can tell if you're watching an animation or if you're watching an actor, and I believe in acting. We knew we needed to *create* a vampire – an actor in old-fashioned makeup to fit with the ethos of what the show is. So it would have texture, so it would be grainy just like everything else in the show, and so it would feel real."

The production turned to special effects makeup maestro Nick Dudman for help. Dudman's experience in producing makeup effects for film and television stretches back decades, although in recent years much of his time has been taken up with the *Harry Potter* film franchise.

"Nick Dudman and his incredible group of artisans from all over the world created that vampire and every prosthetic effect and makeup effect we have," continues Logan. "Nick's very sensitive to text. He reads the script very closely, so he knows who the characters are. He lets them evolve in him before he will even suggest to me what he thinks they should look like, and there's a process

Nick Dudman commissioned artist and designer Howard Swindell to produce concept art of the vampire.

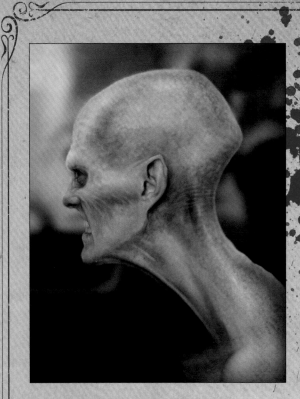

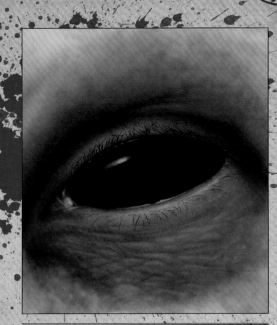

of refining and refining and refining. I had a particular idea for how the vampire moves, and what it feels like. Nick was able to fully embrace that, and then most importantly, he was able to make it."

"We decided that they were very skeletal and pale, and they just had to be *weird*," Dudman recalls. "The process that I've always used is I sketch out some ideas and think about what might work, and discuss whether the producers have a performer or a type of performer in mind so that I get a view of the kind of person that the character will be. I don't design makeups for the sake of prosthetics. I try to design characters. That meant first interrogating John to work out what was behind what he was saying – to get a flavor. Then I hired a concept artist, on this occasion a guy called Howard Swindell, who's done concepts for me a lot in the past. My son Jack did some as well. I got them to do a whole series of quick sketches. I also went on the internet and found pictures of every vampire ever produced and ran those by John and said, 'What do you like and why? What don't you like and why?' You end up producing concept art which hopefully then steers in a direction. You reach a point when John looks at something and goes, 'That's looking cool.' And so you go, 'Ahh, all right, OK, so whatever it is about that painting is what we pursue.' At this point I'm still not thinking about *how* this will be achieved. I just want to end up with a single piece of artwork where he and Bayona are going, 'Yep, that looks really cool.' So having done that, we arrived at a particular drawing and they loved the idea."

Nailing down the planned look of the vampire, however, was just the first step in the process. Before Dudman and his team could actually start finding a way of making their designs a reality, the producers had to cast an actor in the role, as the makeup needed to be cast, sculpted, molded, and painted to a particular body. They weren't going for a rubber mask monster – whoever ended up playing the vampire was going to become the creature, using full-body casts and other techniques that would take a considerable amount of time...

Casting the vampire turned out to be more challenging than anyone anticipated. Despite searching high and low, the producers just couldn't find an actor they felt would inhabit the part in the way they required. Time was a distinct factor. Everyone was getting anxious. Then in walked a young unknown called Robert Nairne. Rather than being put forward by a

ABOVE: *The large prosthetic chest piece at the sculpt stage and the vampire's fingers in the same state (right, top). The finished chest prosthetic, complete with paint (right, bottom).*

NEXT PAGE: *Makeup artist Sarita Allison puts the finishing touches to Robert Nairne's vampire on set.*

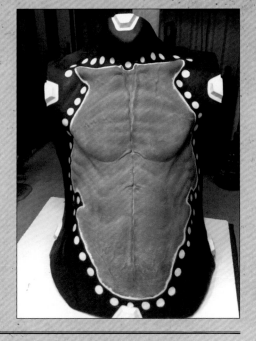

theatrical agent, Nairne had submitted himself as a possible for the part. Producers rarely cast outside the pool of actors represented by an agent, and for very good reason. Agented actors can be relied upon to have talent, discipline and experience – all qualities absolutely vital to the high pressure involved in making a television series. But in this case, with time running out, the production decided to give Nairne a chance.

"Casting Robert Nairne as our vampire was a very stressful situation," supervising producer Chris King recalls with a laugh. "John always had this vision of this very ectomorphic, tall, thin person to be the vampire. We had an idea of someone that we wanted to use, but unfortunately he wasn't available. So we did a search through London, trying to find actors who were tall and who could move right. Robert was the only actor who self-submitted. [Executive producer] Pippa Harris forwarded his picture and CV. I never quite trust those – you never know what you're going to get – but we looked at him and were like, 'OK, well, sure, we'll get him in.' So we did a casting. We hired a movement coach who would work with each actor prior to them putting themselves on tape and we rented a dance studio in London. Robert came in and the minute he started moving – and he was in normal clothes – instantly we knew, 'That's it!' He just had the right body type, the right face, and he could move. What Robert does is that he has this weird, insect style of movement. He actually brought it himself, too. The movement coach gave him some ideas, but Robert went with it. The minute he did it, there was no doubt in our minds that that was the vampire."

"Robert came over to Ireland and we basically studied him," Dudman continues. "I did a whole series of photos of him which I then returned to the concept artist and said, 'Adapt the artwork that we had originally done to suit this guy specifically.' We did concept work with different colored eyes and things like that and Howard did some beautiful production paintings of Robert with this particular look,

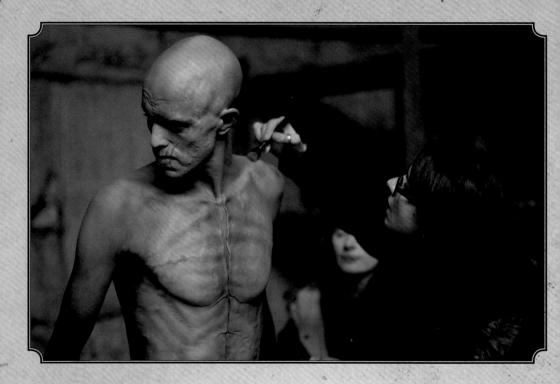

and that's how we ironed out the next phase."

Once the look had been refined to fit Nairne's physical features, work to create the makeup and required prosthetics could begin in earnest.

"The next step was to life-cast him, which is where you make a mold of his entire body," explains Dudman. "That enables us to produce a head and shoulders, a chest that we can sculpt on and legs that we can sculpt on. At that point you're still adapting the design. You photograph the sculpt, colorize it, and then we look at the original concept art and I get Howard to rework the concept art over the sculpt, so that we're still seeing whether something in the sculpt is better than was in the painting, or potentially it could be worse. At each stage, you're trying to preserve a nuance, a single flavor that was in a piece of artwork that of course isn't real, and you're trying to make it real. So at each stage, you're checking. He's covered from head to foot – he's got a completely fake chest. He's got prosthetics around his mouth, cheeks and forehead, he's got red contact lenses, he's got fangs, he's got

nails on his fingers, he's got silicone vampire feet. He's covered in paint and he's well and truly stitched up!"

Finally, the checks reached a stage that Dudman was happy with, which meant it was time to introduce *Penny Dreadful*'s new vampire to executive producer John Logan.

"My makeup department has a long corridor in it," says Dudman, "so I turned all the lights off in the corridor and turned the lights on in the rooms either side, and then sent Robert right down the far end. When John got there, I got him to come slowly towards us, being hit with shadow and light alternately as he came down the corridor, which was great. The way you know if something is going to work for whoever you're doing it for is that first five seconds: Have they bought it? Everything else after that is detail. And John bought it." ☩

*Excerpt from **The Art and Making of Penny Dreadful**, by Sharon Gosling, Titan Books, 2015, © SHOWTIME, reprinted with permission.*

VANESSA IVES

"I think… there are tremors around us. Like the vibrations of a note of music, hidden music. Some might be more attuned to them than others… What do those people do? Those who have been chosen, or have created the circumstances in which they must be chosen. To be alien. To be disenfranchised from those around you. Is that not a dreadful curse?"

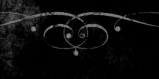

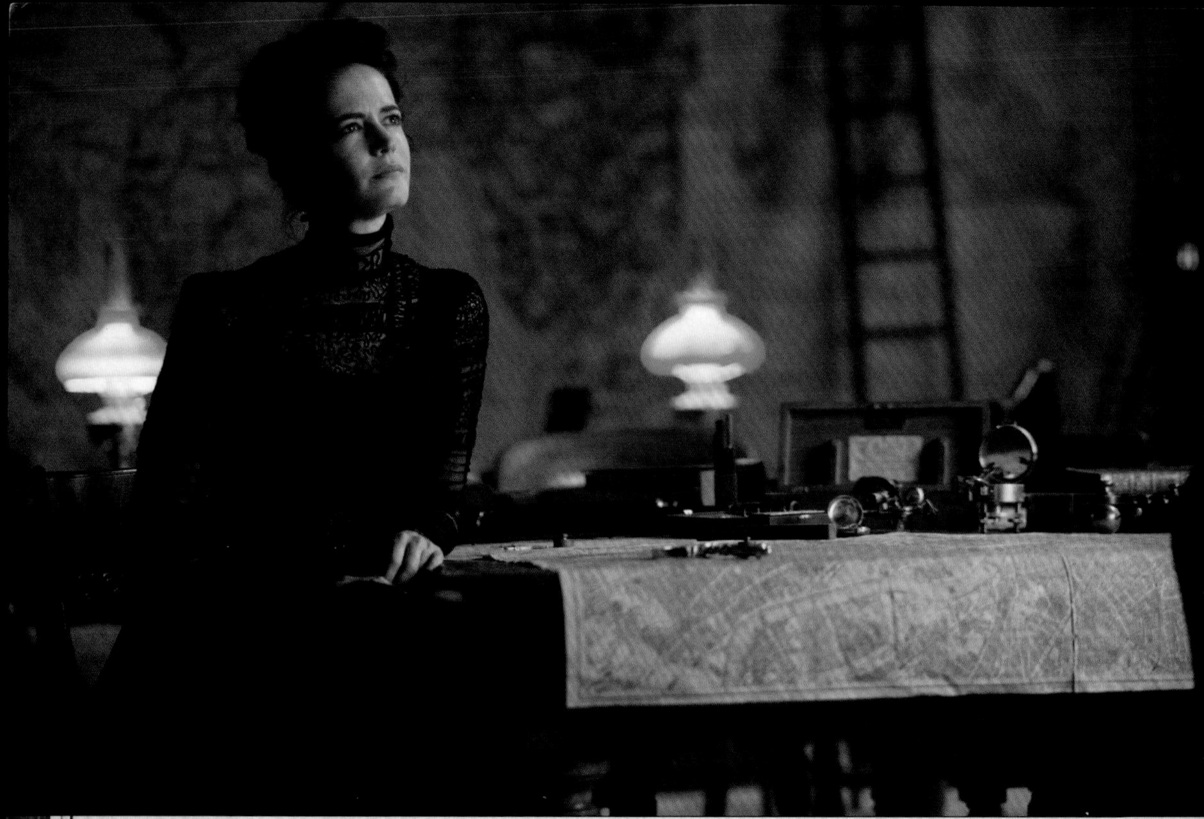

VANESSA IVES IS ONE OF THE CHARACTERS in *Penny Dreadful* that does not have a larger textual life as part of the literary cannon. And yet it is she who ties together the dramatis personae and events of the story's first season.

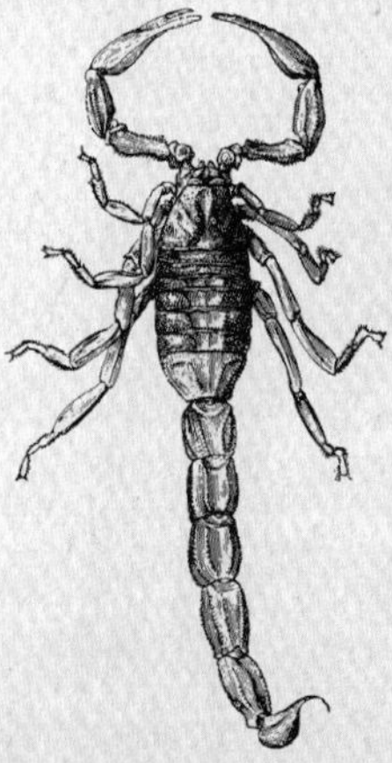

"I THOUGHT I JUST wanted to do a *Frankenstein* story, because that was the relationship that most intrigued me as a writer," says John Logan. "But then I began to realize there could be great joy in bringing other characters into that story, because I think all those stories are somewhat thematically linked, in terms of alienation, in terms of the need for love. I thought there would be a way to bring them all together. I knew I wanted to do Frankenstein and his Creature, I knew I wanted to do Dorian Gray and I knew I wanted to bring in elements of *Dracula* without dealing with Dracula himself. I thought, all right, what's the organizing principle? How do you bring all these disparate, exciting, joyous characters into one story?

"I decided to write about a female protagonist, because in 1891 London, women were quite literally corseted and constrained," Logan continues. "The societal, social, sexual conventions of the day kept women bound up. I thought creating a woman who had to live in that society and yet within her had these monstrous yearnings, or these yearnings for liberation, would make a very compelling central character. So I created Vanessa Ives, who to me most perfectly personifies what it is to be a 'monster.' Meaning, on one hand, she is tormented, she is cursed with something that tears her to pieces inside, but it is that very thing that also makes her strong, powerful and liberated in a time when women couldn't be. She most perfectly embodies both sides of that monstrous balancing act. So I built the show around her."

In some ways, Vanessa Ives is a microcosm

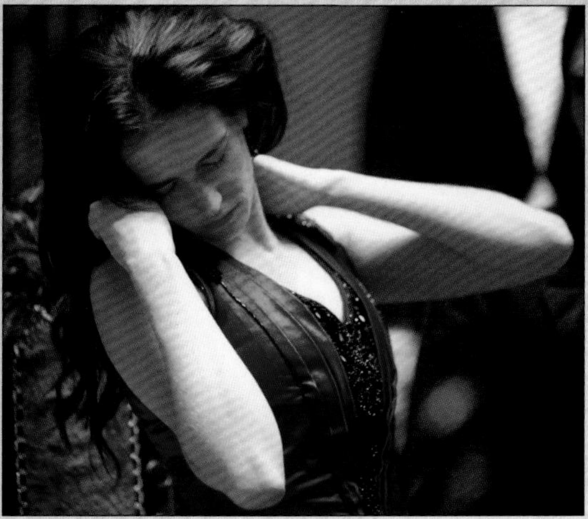

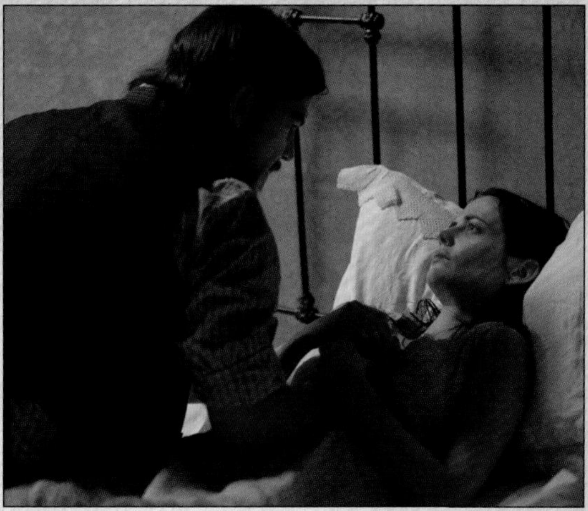

of the roles women found themselves contained within at the time. Vanessa is raised with no expectation other than that she will marry, and early on it is made clear that she is expected to marry Peter, whether or not she would choose him for herself. Her attempts at self-determination – of learning what life might be outside the male-circumscribed mores of the time – result in her ostracism and isolation. The treatment of her sickness is dictated by male ideas of 'female' sickness, and in order to help her friend Mina, she has to place herself in the house and under the care of Sir Malcolm. Yet for all that, there is something in her that is fiercely independent and always has been.

"Vanessa is a child given to boldness," Logan points out. "You see her in the first scene on the beach [in 'Closer Than Sisters'] and she wants to go deep into the ocean where her feet don't touch the ground. She's a bold, brave girl. That boldness, that braveness in Vanessa – both young Vanessa and the Vanessa we know that Eva Green plays – it's an admirable trait, but it also opens her up to being rebellious against societal norms, against the theological, social patterns of the day."

This willingness to push the boundaries is ultimately what brings her into contact with the demons that revel in her rebellious nature, in her interest in the darkness just beyond our consciousness and in the 'demimonde' of which Vanessa is so keenly aware.

"It was important to me not to create a victim, a central character who was victimized by the events around her," Logan explains. "So she has to be complicit in her own sin, in the wickedness that's a part of her. It was important for me to create a moment where the demon, speaking through Sir Malcolm, says to her, 'Vanessa, please. You've always had a choice. You allowed all this to happen. Hell, you sought it out and fucked it.' And *Penny Dreadful* always exists on that cusp of darkness and light, angel and demon. No one

BELOW: *Some of Gabriella Pescucci's early designs for Vanessa's wardrobe. Her favorite is the evening gown used for the séance scenes (above left).*

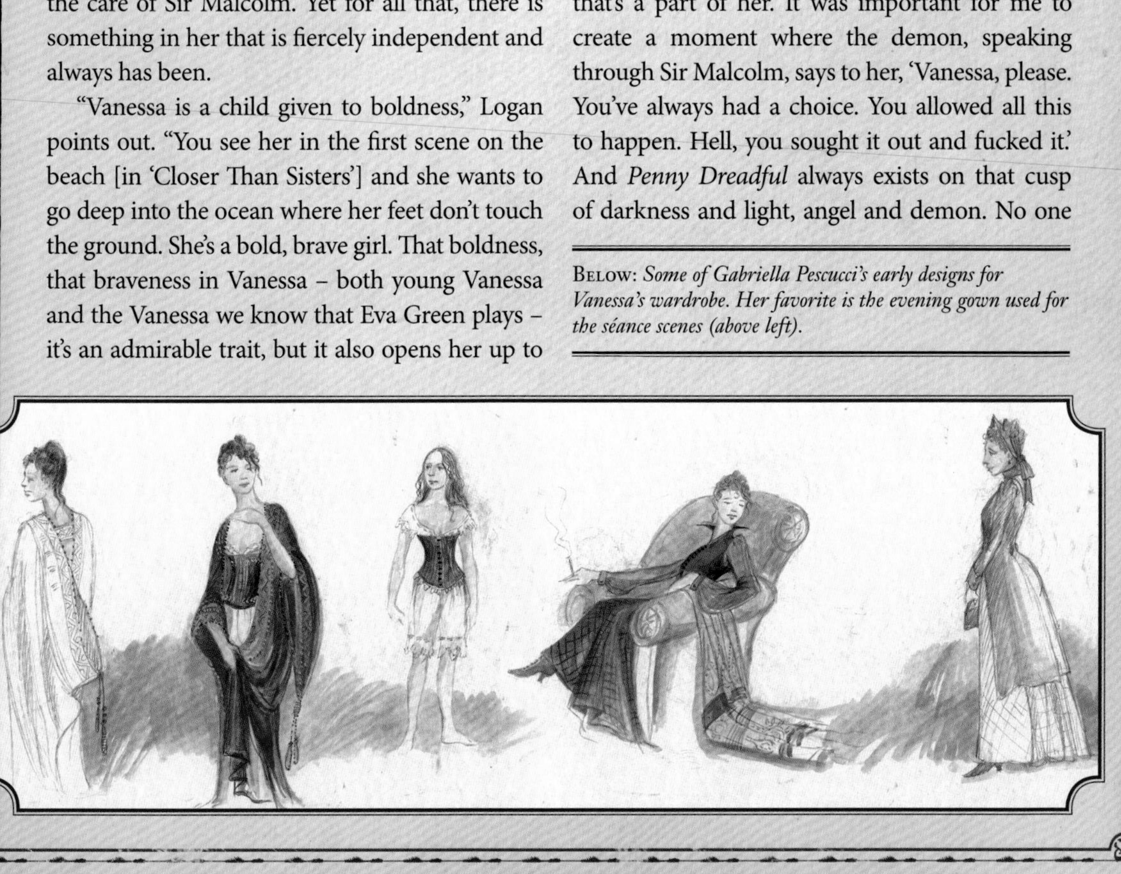

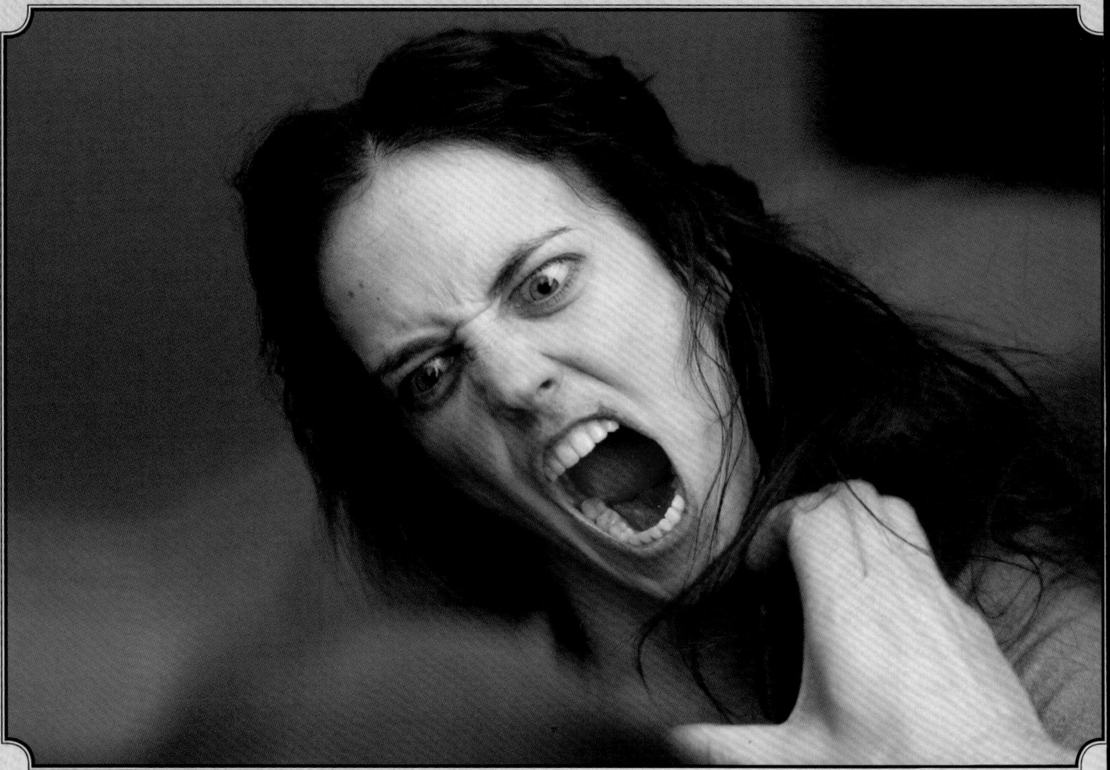

personifies that as much as Vanessa."

The extremes contained within the role of Vanessa Ives make for many explosive – and sometimes difficult to watch – moments on screen that would surely make an actress think twice about taking on such a role. For John Logan, there was only ever one choice of actress that he wanted to see in the part.

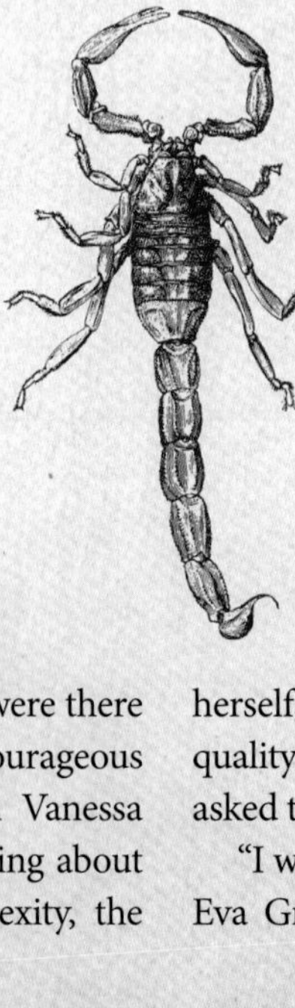

"I knew when I was building Vanessa's character I would need an actor of incredible range who could command the screen while doing practically nothing, because Vanessa Ives is very composed, so you need an actor who has fire, who can show where the demons were there always behind the eyes. You need a courageous actor, because in this season we run Vanessa from pillar to post, emotionally. Thinking about an actor who would have the complexity, the passion and frankly, the nerve to play this part, I fell in love with the idea of Eva Green and her playing Vanessa. She was initially resistant – she loved the writing, but was resistant. So I set about wooing her as much as I could. I sent her the scripts, we got on the phone, we talked, and gradually we built a shared vocabulary for how this character would emerge."

Green did, of course, agree to take the part, and it's hard to imagine anyone else in the role of Vanessa, as the actress inhabits the character so completely and commits herself so utterly to the full extent of her experiences. For Green, it was a chance to stretch herself, while being completely secure in the quality of the difficult material she was being asked to deliver.

"I was so lucky that John offered it to me," says Eva Green. "She's such a complex character. A

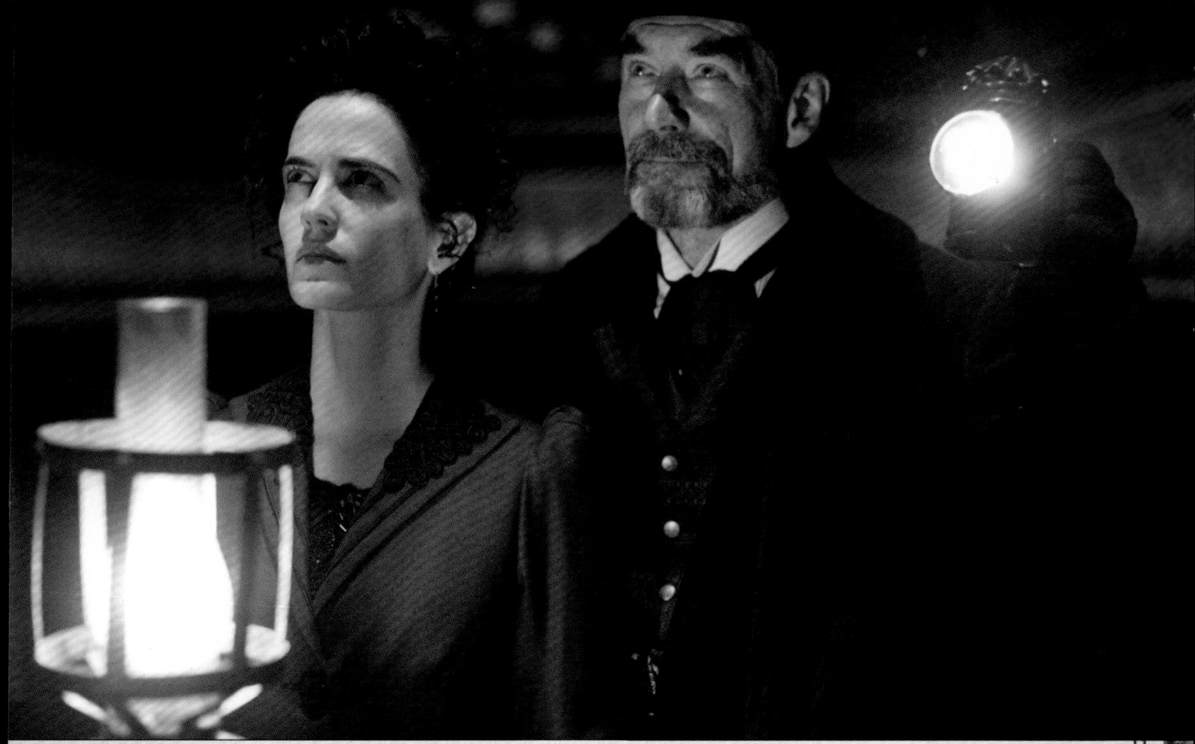

Right: *Vanessa with her mother, played by British actress Anna Chancellor.*

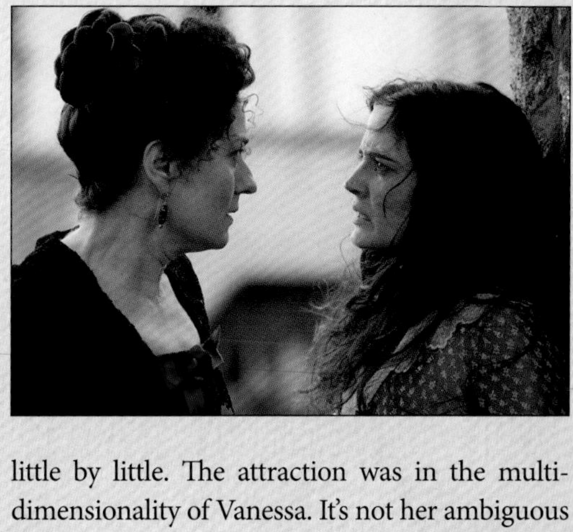

dream for an actor… a gift! It's a great opportunity to show many different facets of a character. I love playing extremes. It's rather exhilarating to be able to let it all out! John wrote such beautiful scenes; even some of Vanessa's possession scenes (with Sir Malcolm or Ethan as the Devil) are weirdly poetic, they're genius. Vanessa, like all the other characters in *Penny Dreadful*, is gifted and cursed with special powers, which make her unique but also alienate her. She is torn and tormented. She is possessed by some obscure force, but she has such an amazingly strong will that she is able to keep it dormant – except when temptation arises. Then it becomes a fight to see who will win: Vanessa and her iron will or the obscure force."

Despite the darkness in Vanessa's character, however, and the frequency with which her demons display themselves, for Green, the most interesting aspects of the character lie in other areas of her psyche.

"John sent me the first five episodes and I connected with the character straight away. I loved that she had such an amazing journey full of twists and turns. You discover her secrets little by little. The attraction was in the multi-dimensionality of Vanessa. It's not her ambiguous powers that make her interesting, but rather her all-too-human vulnerabilities," the actress points out. "She is a very tormented and torn human being and she is at war with herself constantly. She seems very smooth and in control, but underneath is all of this fire and all of these demons. She seems very cold sometimes and then she has these mad moments."

"The challenge with Vanessa Ives was always going to be, you're the fulcrum of the series, you're the manifestation of what it is to be a monster," say Logan. "What's sensational about Eva is that she embraces the challenge." ♱

*Excerpt from **The Art and Making of Penny Dreadful**, by Sharon Gosling, Titan Books, 2015,*

PENNY DREADFUL

*The masterpieces you see before you are
the Chosen Ones: three of the Grandeur Prize victors of
The Art of the Dreadful Gallery Fan Art Contest.*

This contest summoned all of the talented Dreadfuls in
the Demimonde to conjure up their most masterful *Penny
Dreadful*-inspired artwork, in the lead-up to the Season 3
Premiere. Hundreds of beautiful (and grotesque) pieces were
submitted and put on display in The Dreadful Gallery
on the *Penny Dreadful* Tumblr page.

Three Grand Prize winners were chosen to receive an
authentic, one-of-a-kind prop from the set of *Penny Dreadful*,
as well as official merchandise to display in their own galleries.
Five Master Dreadfuls were named as the Grandeur Prize
winners – winning $1,000.00 each. Two of the Master Dreadfuls
were commissioned to transform their creations into official
merchandise, while the remaining three were asked to submit
their artwork for a feature in the *Penny Dreadful* comic book series,
as seen in the following pages.

View all of the glorious horrors now at:
pennydreadful.tumblr.com
and a special thank you to all Dreadfuls who participated!

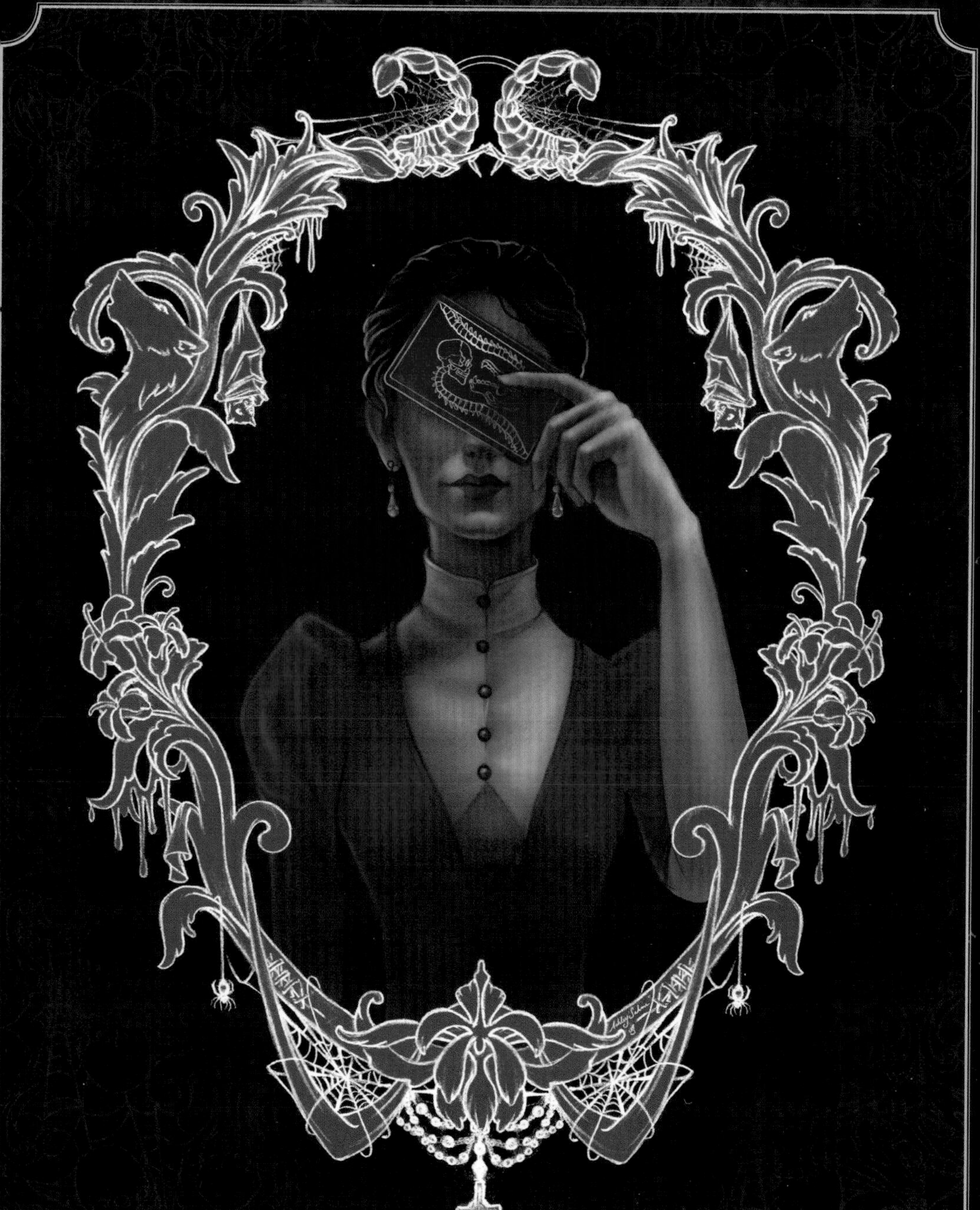

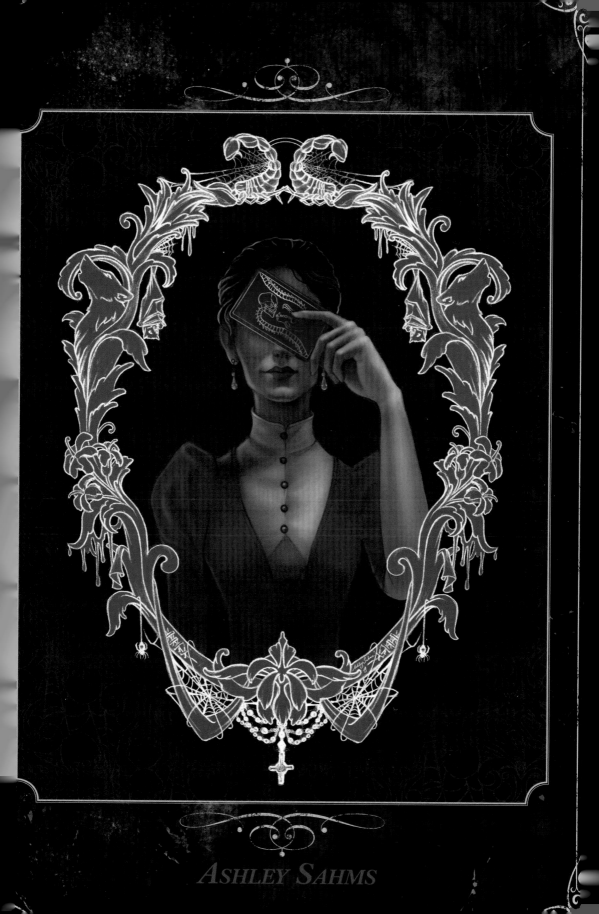

ASHLEY SAHMS

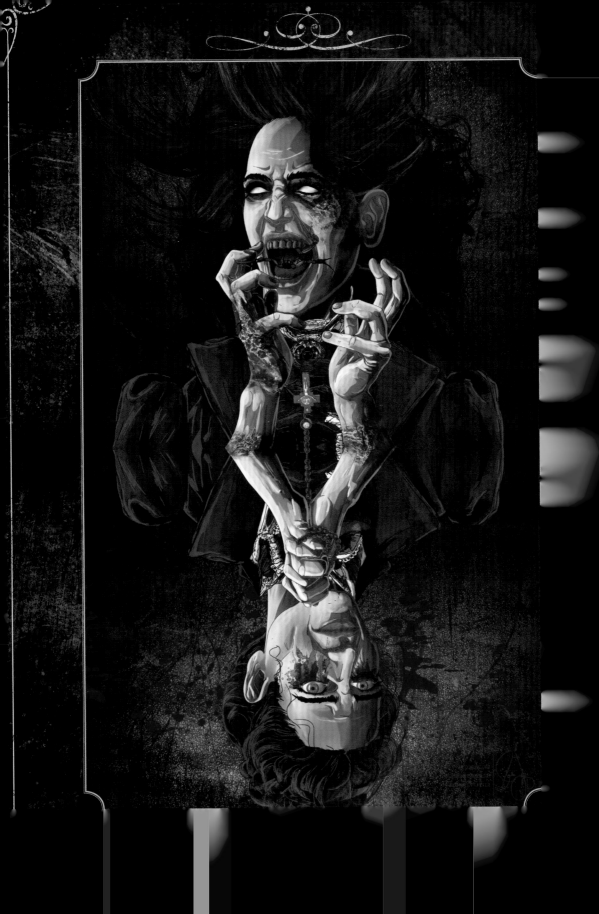

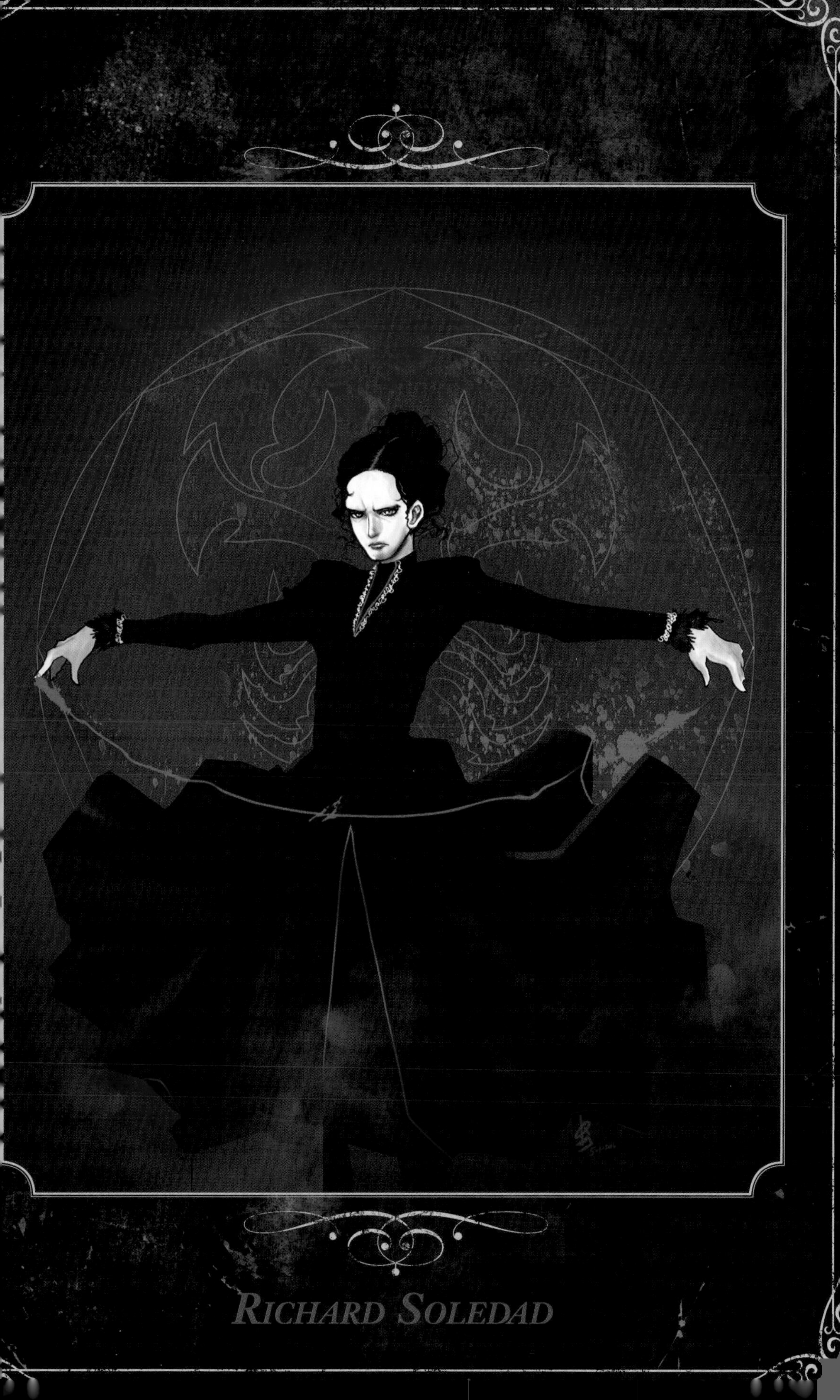
RICHARD SOLEDAD

COVERS GALLERY

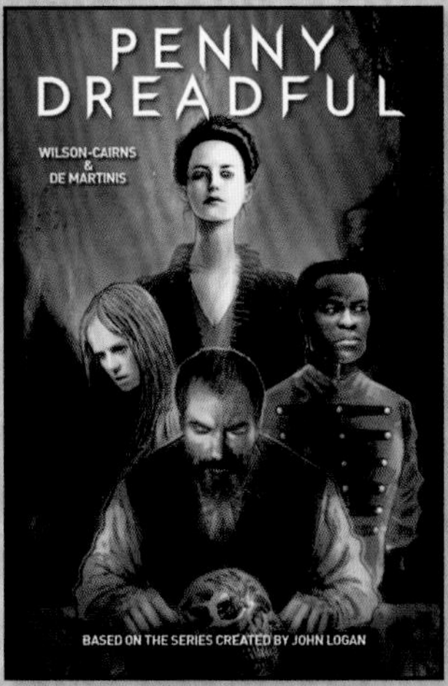
PENNY
DREADFUL
WILSON-CAIRNS
&
DE MARTINIS
BASED ON THE SERIES CREATED BY JOHN LOGAN

#1 COVER A
BEN TEMPLESMITH

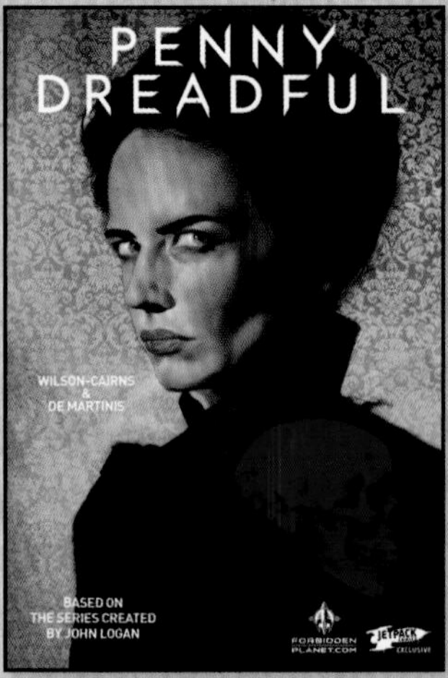
PENNY
DREADFUL
WILSON-CAIRNS
&
DE MARTINIS
BASED ON
THE SERIES CREATED
BY JOHN LOGAN

#1 FORBIDDEN PLANET COVER
BEN OLIVER

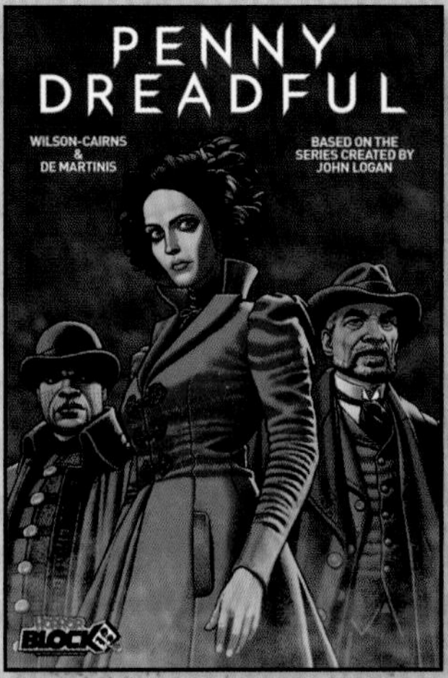
PENNY
DREADFUL
WILSON-CAIRNS
&
DE MARTINIS
BASED ON THE
SERIES CREATED BY
JOHN LOGAN

#1 NERDBLOCK COVER
PAUL MCCAFFERY

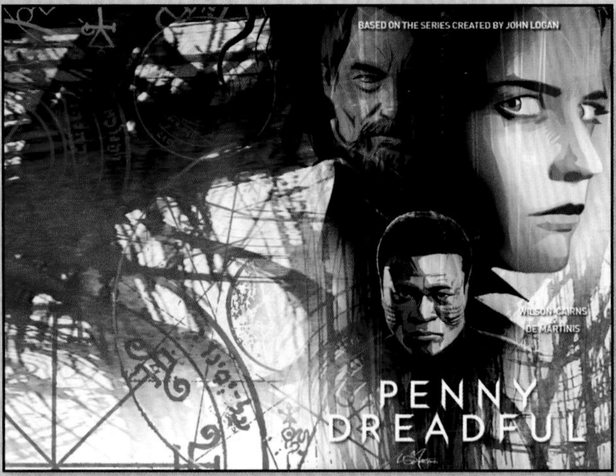
BASED ON THE SERIES CREATED BY JOHN LOGAN
WILSON-CAIRNS
&
DE MARTINIS
PENNY
DREADFUL

#1 COVER C
LOUIE DE MARTINIS

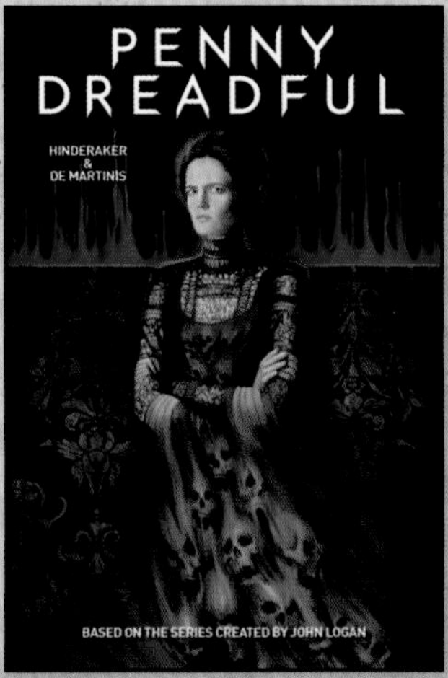
PENNY
DREADFUL
HINDERAKER
&
DE MARTINIS
BASED ON THE SERIES CREATED BY JOHN LOGAN

#2 SHOWTIME COVER
SHANE PIERCE

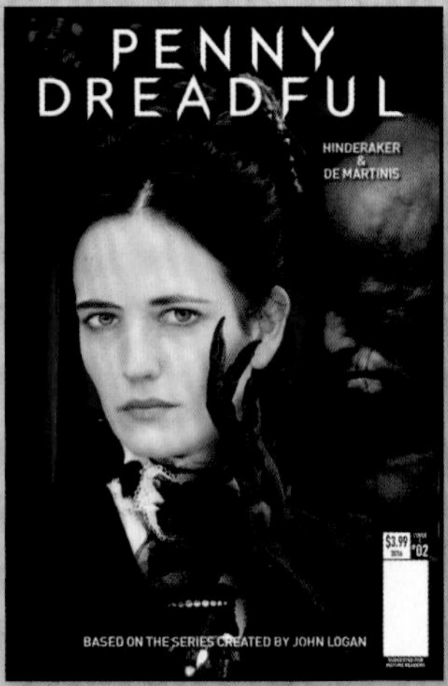
PENNY
DREADFUL
HINDERAKER
&
DE MARTINIS
BASED ON THE SERIES CREATED BY JOHN LOGAN

#2 COVER C
RUSSELL SEAL

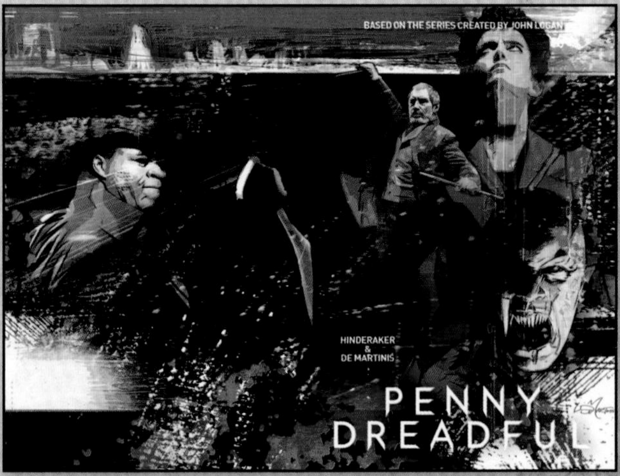
BASED ON THE SERIES CREATED BY JOHN LOGAN
HINDERAKER
&
DE MARTINIS
PENNY
DREADFUL

#2 WRAPAROUND COVER B
LOUIE DE MARTINIS

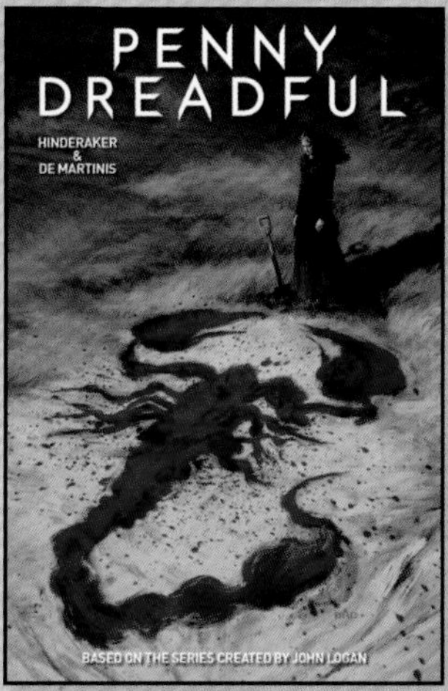
PENNY
DREADFUL
HINDERAKER
&
DE MARTINIS
BASED ON THE SERIES CREATED BY JOHN LOGAN

#3 SHOWTIME COVER
SHANE PIERCE

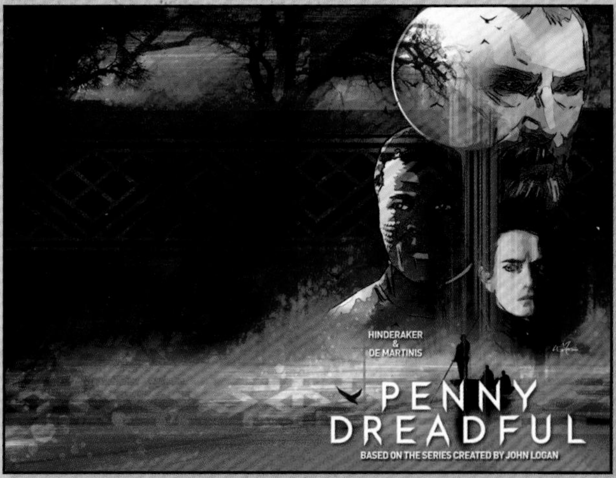
HINDERAKER
&
DE MARTINIS
PENNY
DREADFUL
BASED ON THE SERIES CREATED BY JOHN LOGAN

#3 SAN DIEGO WRAPAROUND COVER B
LOUIE DE MARTINIS

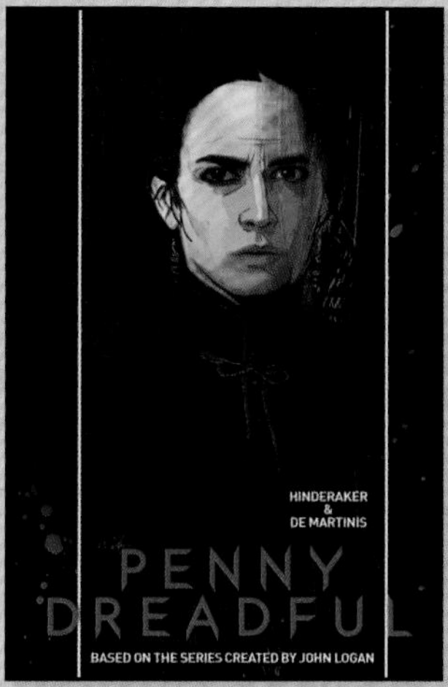
HINDERAKER
&
DE MARTINIS
PENNY
DREADFUL
BASED ON THE SERIES CREATED BY JOHN LOGAN

#3 SHOWTIME SDCC PROMO COVER
LOUIE DE MARTINIS

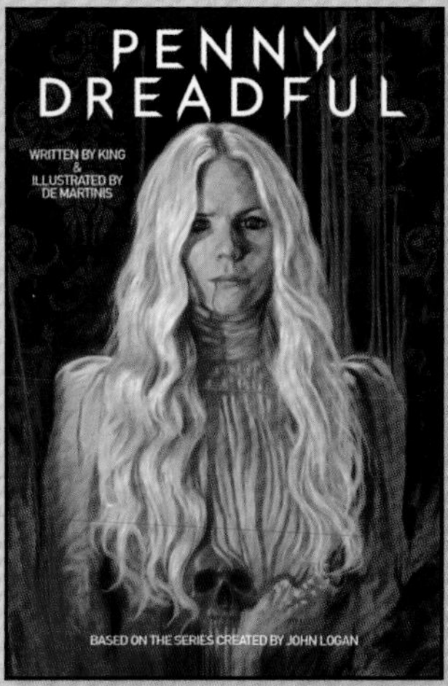
PENNY
DREADFUL
WRITTEN BY KING
&
ILLUSTRATED BY
DE MARTINIS
BASED ON THE SERIES CREATED BY JOHN LOGAN

#4 SHOWTIME COVER
SHANE PIERCE

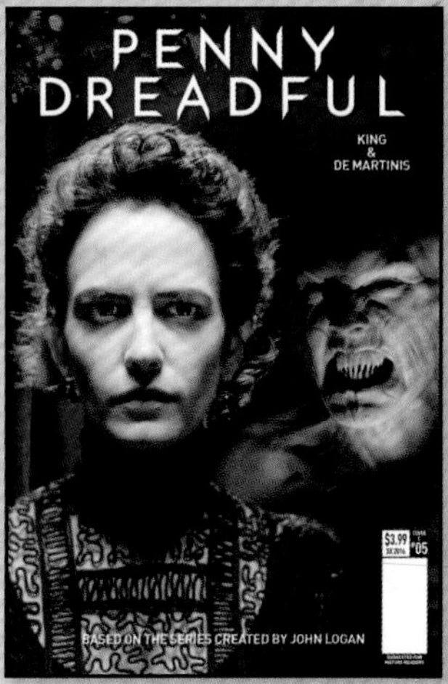
PENNY
DREADFUL
KING
&
DE MARTINIS
BASED ON THE SERIES CREATED BY JOHN LOGAN

#5 COVER C
RUSSELL SEAL

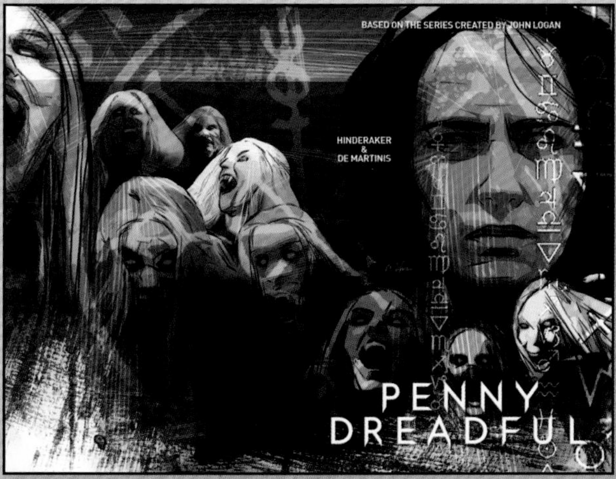
BASED ON THE SERIES CREATED BY JOHN LOGAN
HINDERAKER
&
DE MARTINIS
PENNY
DREADFUL

#4 WRAPAROUND COVER B
LOUIE DE MARTINIS

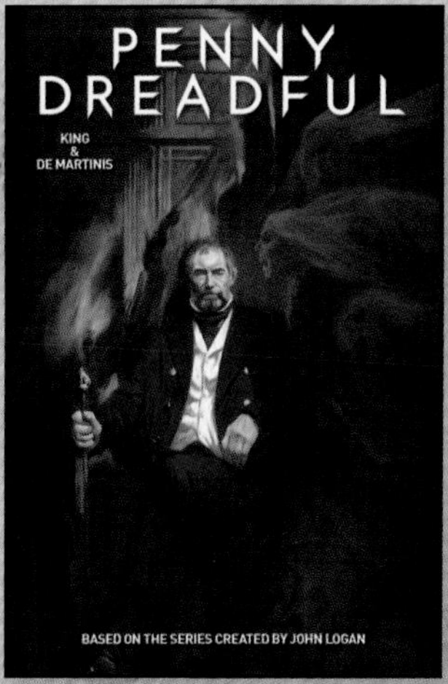
PENNY
DREADFUL
KING
&
DE MARTINIS
BASED ON THE SERIES CREATED BY JOHN LOGAN

#5 SHOWTIME COVER
SHANE PIERCE

CREATOR BIOGRAPHIES

KRYSTY WILSON-CAIRNS is a Glaswegian screenwriter, famous for her work on *Penny Dreadful*, and the short film *All Men's Dead*. She is an alumna of the Royal Scottish Academy, and is the recipient of several prestigious awards, including 'Screen Star of Tomorrow' and the Dewar Arts Award.

ANDREW HINDERAKER is a Resident Playwright of Chicago Dramatists, an ensemble member of the Gift Theatre in Chicago, and a three-time Jeff Award Nominee. *Penny Dreadful* has been one of his first forays into television writing

CHRIS KING is the co-executive producer of *Penny Dreadful*, with many more Hollywood credits to his name, both from producing and as an actor. He is perhaps best known for his work on the acclaimed documentaries *Foo Fighters: Back and Forth* and *Comics Superheroes Unmasked*.

LOUIE DE MARTINIS is a Canadian artist who has worked on *Tron: Ghost in the Machine*, *Female Force: Anne Rice* and *Grimm Fairy Tales*.

SIMON BOWLAND is an accomplished comics letterer, who has brought his talents to such titles as *2000AD*, *Numbercruncher*, *Happy!*, *Cry Havoc*, *Mycroft Holmes*, and many more.

ROB STEEN is a veteran letterer, having worked for Marvel, DC and on titles like *The Troop*, *Dark Souls*, *Astro City* and *X-Men*.